ABSTRACTS

of

CRAVEN COUNTY NORTH CAROLINA DEEDS

- 1761-1766 -

(Volume #4)

Compiled by:
Dr. A.B. Pruitt

Southern Historical Press, Inc.
Greenville, South Carolina

This volume was reproduced
from a personal copy located in
the Publishers private library

Please direct all correspondence and book orders to:
www.southernhistoricalpress.com
or
SOUTHERN HISTORICAL PRESS, Inc.
1071 Park West Blvd.
Greenville, SC   29611

Southernhistoricalpress@gmail.com

Originally Copyright: Albert Bruce Pruitt, 2006
Copyright Transferred 2026 to:
    Southern Historical Press, Inc.
ISBN #978-1-63914-731-1
Printed in the United Sattes of America

Introduction

This book contains abstracts of deeds in Craven County, NC, in books 11, 12, & 13.   All these books are in the Register of Deeds' office in New Bern and on roll C 028.40004 in the North Carolina archives.   Book 6 has deeds recorded from 1761 to 1764 and on in 1756.   Books 12 & 13 are in 2 parts with no indication where one ends and the other begins and have deeds recorded from 1764 to 1766.

Craven County was formed from Craven Precinct which was formed in 1705 from Bath County and in 1712 by name change from Archdale Precinct.   The following counties were formed from Craven: Carteret in 1722, New Hanover in 1729, Johnston in 1746, part of Dobbs in 1764, Jones in 1778, part of Pitt in 1787, Pamlico in 1872.   Part of Craven County was moved to the following: Lenoir in 1798, 1804, & 1819, Greene in 1801, and Pamlico in 1875; part of Beaufort was moved to Craven in 1801.   Published material for Craven County includes: court minutes 1712-1715, 1730-1741, 1742-1748, 1749-1756, & 1757-1763 by Mrs. Weynette P Haun [1716-1729 are missing]; deed books 1 & 5 (1707-1775) by Mrs. Weynette P Haun; deeds, wills, & inventories 1737-1766 and 1742-1801 by Stephen E Bradley jr; wills (1801-1812) by Stephen E Bradley jr; records (deeds etc) by Elizabeth Moore; estates 1745-1945 by North Carolina Archives; census 1850 by Zae M Gwynn; Christ Episcopal Church Register by Gertrude S Carraway; NC Gazette (newspaper) 1788-1798 (2 vol.) by Raymond P Fouts; and deed books 2-4 and 6-10 by A B Pruitt.

Please note: deed for maintenance of a wife is in item 3328; problem with a sheriff's sale is in item 3403; deposition about a survey is in 3407; inventories & sales of estates and some wills are in 3425-3486, 3536, and 3874-3881; apprentice bonds are in 3537-3546; statement about a ship is in 3548; a resurvey is in 3558; lease of land is in 3573; a deed proved in 1756 is in 3684; an infant as grantee is in 3751; division of a lease is in 3765; a deposition is in 3868; wills are in 3869 and 3871-3873; a long title chain is in 3968; a marriage agreement for Chief Justice James Hasell to widow Ann Nan Bade Durlace Baron Nome Rosentaine is in 3979; and some livestock marks are recorded at random.

Following is the format of the abstracts in this book:
1. A number is assigned to each deed.   This number is used in the index of this book.   Following this number and in parenthesis is the number of the deed which appears in the deed book.
2. Following these numbers is the date, when mentioned in the deed.
3. Next is the name (or names) of the grantor (seller) followed by his county of residence, when indicated.   The county in is North Carolina unless noted otherwise.
4. Following the word "to" is the name (or names) of grantee (or buyer) followed by his county of residence, when indicated <u>and</u> when it differs

from the residence of the grantor.   The word "same" indicates the grantee's residence is the same as the grantor's.

5. Following a semicolon and the work "for" is the amount of the "consideration" in dollars, pounds, Spanish dollars, English pounds sterling, etc.   Deeds of gift don't mention the exchange of money; for these deeds after "for" are words such as "love and affection".

6. Following the word "sold" or "mortgaged" is the amount of land.   For deeds of gift "gave" replaces "sold".   When the amount of land isn't indicated in the deed, "omitted" appears in the abstract unless the land area could be simply calculated from the metes and bounds.

7. The water course--creek, river, fork, branch, etc--is mentioned next.   In the deeds "on" the creek usually means the land actually abuts the creek. But "on the waters" of the creek may indicate the land is near but not on the creek.   All the land is in Craven County unless noted otherwise.

8. Following a semicolon and the word "border" are the names of adjoining land holders, buildings, or unusual natural features mentioned in the metes and bounds.   Also mentioned are such things as improvements, barns, mills, etc, when they are mentioned in the deed.

9. Next is the title chain, when given, beginning with the grant and continuing (when possible) to the grantor of the deed.

10. Following "(signed)" is the spelling or mark made by the grantor(s). Unusual marks are added by hand.   Please note the "signature" in the deed book is really a copy (made by a clerk) of the original signature on the original deed.   Also note: an "X" written at an angle may look like a "+" in the book; so these two marks may be the same mark.

11. Following "witness" are the names of the witnesses to the sale.   The word "jurat" follows the witness who proved the deed in court; "acknowledged" indicates the grantor proved the deed in court, & "recorded" indicates the clerk didn't indicate who proved the deed.

The map which follows this introduction is included to help the reader locate the waterways mentioned most frequently in the index.   The creek locations are not meant to be exact.   More complete and accurate maps of the counties can b obtained from the North Carolina Department of Transportation (highway maps), Department of Water Resources (maps grouped by major river basins), a book of county maps (from Puetz place, Lyndon Station, WI), or a book of county maps (from DeLorme, Box 298-6900, Freeport, ME 04032).

The plat for the town of New Bern (in 3 parts) is from MC 195 N534 1819 p. 2 in the North Carolina archives.   Also included is a plat from NC Supreme Court cast 1419 courtesy of Mrs. Grace Turner.

This book is dedicated to the late John H Oden III who for many years assisted genealogists in the Beaufort County area with their work. Some of the fun and enjoyment of genealogical work departed with Mr. Oden.   The author also thanks Lillie R Belllingrath (known to most people for 70 years as Mrs. W H Pruitt) for the loan of the family magnifying glass which was a big help in reading the film.

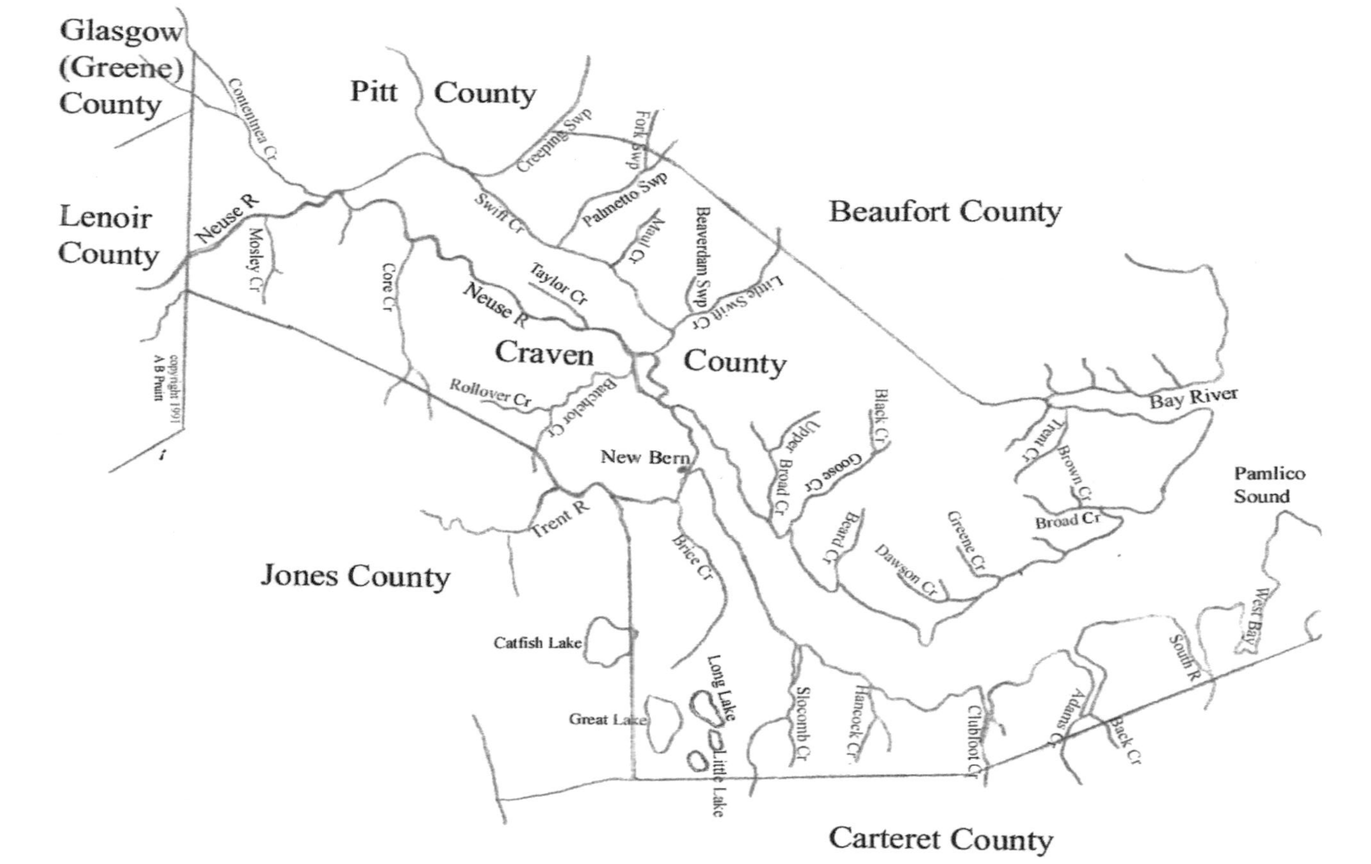

Glasgow (Greene) County
Pitt County
Contentnea Cr
Creeping Swp
Fork Swp
Beaufort County
Lenoir County
Neuse R
Mosley Cr
Swift Cr
Palmetto Swp
Maul Cr
Beaverdam Swp
Little Swift Cr
Core Cr
Taylor Cr
Neuse R
Craven
County
copyright 1991
A B Pruitt
Rollover Cr
Batchelor Cr
Black Cr
Bay River
New Bern
Upper Broad Cr
Goose Cr
Trent Cr
Brown Cr
Pamlico Sound
Trent R
Brice Cr
Beard Cr
Greene Cr
Broad Cr
Jones County
Dawson Cr
Catfish Lake
Long Lake
West Bay
Great Lake
Little Lake
Slocomb Cr
Hancock Cr
Clubfoot Cr
Adams Cr
South R
Back Cr
Carteret County

Craven County, NC Deed Books 11-13

Craven Co book 11

3322. Oct. 7, 1761 [or 17S1] Richard Cogdill, high sheriff (Craven Co) to John Physick (same); for £0.31 sold 30 ac on S side of Nuse R & W side of Hancock Cr; border: begins at a stake "set up in the march" of a small creek side, joins Obadiah Yarborough, Slocumb, Jones, & mouth of a small creek that parts the premises from "Weellifs Lane"; granted Apr. 14, 1761 by Gov. Arthur Dobbs to Gregg "Yarboaroug", doctor of physick deceased (late of Craven Co); at time of his death, Yarboarough owed "several" persons £12.12.5 proclamation money for fees payable to clerk of Newbern "Supreme" Court; writ of fieri facias issued ordering sheriff to sell the land due to act of Parliament of Great Britain & General Assembly of North Carolina. (signed) R Cogdill, sher; (witness) George "Hais" & David Gorden; Oct. 1762 acknowledged; [Peter Conway in clerk of court]; book 11 p. 1

3323. Aug. 31, 1762 [2nd year of reign of George III] Thomas Sitgreaves (Craven Co) to Marth. Worsly (Newbern, Craven Co); for £150 proclamation money sold 0.5 ac in lot #303 in Newbern; border: begins at corner of New Street & Craven Street; lot is 13 by 6 poles; sold Feb. 13, 1749 by the town commissioners to Mathew Arthur who sold Feb. 23, 1754 to John Williams who sold Oct. 12, 1754 to Samuel Lawson who sold Oct. 29, 1755 to James Parkinson who sold [blank] 16, [blank] to John Isler "but not registered" &, by "consent" of John Isler, Parkinson sold to William Sitgreaves recorded in Craven Co Register's office who sold May 22, 1758 to said Thos Sitgreaves. (signed) Thos Sitgreaves; (witness) Richd "Blacklige" jr & John Moor; wit. oath Oct. 1762 by Richd Blacklege; book 11 p. 2.

3324. Sept. 11, 1762 Martin Worsley (Newbern, Craven Co) to William Sitgreaves, merchant (Philadelphia, Pennsylvania; for £156 proclamation money sold 2 tracts: (a) 0.5 ac in lot #276 in Newbern; border: begins at corner of Craven Street & New Street; lot is 6 by 13 poles; & (b) 0.5 ac in lot #303 in Newbern; border: begins at corner of New Street & Craven Street; lot is 13 by 6 poles; sale void if Worsley pays Sitgreaves £156 proclamation & interest by Dec. 25, 1763 due by bond for £312. (signed) Martin "Worsly"; (witness) Thomas Sitgreaves & Richd Fenner; [note at end indicates W Sitgreaves paid Worsley £156 on Sept. 11, 1762]; wit. oath Oct. 1762 by Richd Fenner esq; book 11 p. 4.

3325. Jun. 22, 1762 John Granade, planter (Craven Co) to Earnest Granade, gun smith (same); for £50 proclamation money sold 200 ac on S side of Trent R & head of Island Cr; border: begins at Hardy Jones' corner hickory; granted May 25, 1757 to John Hinsey. (signed) John Granade [or Dranade]; (witness) John Pearce & Ann Granade; wit. oath Oct. 1762 by John "Pierce"; book 11 p. 7.

3326. Mar. 1, 1756 Samuel Collins (Craven Co) to James Smith (same); for £13.13.4 proclamation money sold 80 ac; border: begins at mouth of "Owyens" Br, joins "the" head line, & Sandy Run; formerly owned by John Simon Caloras as by patent; Smith to pay yearly quit rent of £0.0.6 per 100 ac to the king. (signed)

Samuel Collins; (witness) "Jacob Joshua" Taylor; wit. oath Oct. 1762 by Jacob Taylor; book 11 p. 8.

3327. [blank], 1762 James Carraway (Craven Co) to Elizabeth West; for note for £5 proclamation money, dated Jul. 1 past, sold 500 ac on N side of Nuse R; border: begins at a creek & joins Charles Hopton (or Hoptor) on E; granted in 1729 to Elizabeth West & sold Oct. 1, 1762 Elizabeth West, wife of John West (late of Craven Co) to said Carraway, for a note for £5 proclamation money dated Jul. 1 past, after a "report was made" that John West was dead; Carraway agrees to return the land to Elizabeth when she gives him the note for £5. (signed) Jas Carraway; (witness) James Jones & John Carney's mark "D" (sic); wit. oath Oct. [blank] by James Jones; book 11 p. 9.

3328. Aug. 3, 1762 Samuel Warner to John Kerney; I empower you to take my Negro man, all my cattle, hogs, household goods, store goods, & merchandise, & all other goods & chattels in Craven Co to be used for maintenance of my wife Pheby Warner; property to be taken from your hands only by "Phebe" or her friends; also take deeds & papers of my land, notes of hand, & accounts that I intend to sell for same purpose. (signed) (signed) Samuel Warner; (witness) Richd Cogdil & Philip Ambrose; wit. oath Oct. 1762 by Richard Cogdil esq; book 11 p. 10.

3329. Feb. 8, 1761 Steven Glair, planter (Craven Co) to Peter Glair, planter (same); for £5 proclamation money sold 10 ac on S side of Trent R; border: begins at a pine in said Steven Glair's line & joins a peach tree; part of land where Steven Glair lives. (signed) Steven Glair's mark "X"; (witness) John Granade & John Granade (sic); wit. oath Oct. 1762 by John Granade; book 11 p. 11.

3330. Jul. 31, 1762 John Kinsey, planter (Craven Co) to James Smith, planter (same); for £10 proclamation money sold 150 ac on W side of head of Island Cr; border: begins at an "iron oak" on side of Jumping Run & joins a mapole at the creek swamp; part of 520 ac granted May 25, 1757 to said John Kinsey. (signed) John "Kensey's" mark "IK"; (witness) John Granade & Samuel Granade; wit. oath Oct. 1762 by John Granade; book 11 p. 12.

3331. Aug. 22, 1761 Samuel Box (Dobbs Co, NC) to James Newport; for £15 sold 85 ac on S side of Nuse R; border: begins at a pine in Neal [or Neale] Watson's line, joins Juniper Swamp, & Jonathan "Markparson". (signed) Samuel Box; (witness) William Eaker "L——-" & Henry Heith; wit. oath Oct. 1762 by Henry Heith; book 11 p. 13.

3332. Oct. 13, 1761 James Smith, planter to Richard Blacklege; for £35 proclamation money sold my share or a third of land and Negroes willed by my father William Smith deceased to me; Negro wench Rachel & her increase delivered until the division is made. (signed) James Smith; (witness) Benjamin Keith, John Allin, & Joseph Allin; wit. oath Oct. 1762 by John Allin; book 11 p.

15.

3333. Nov. 21, 1755 Thomas Pollock, gentleman (Craven Co) to Christopher Shilling & Michael Brewer, planters; for yearly rent sold for 60 years 214 ac on E side of Mill Cr; border: begins at a hickory on side of the creek, joins a swamp, & easternmost branch of Mill Cr; part of "a large" tract on N & S side of Trent R; yearly rent is £0.15 sterling per 100 acres; lease expires in 1815. (signed) Thos Pollock; (witness) Henry Scibbow & John Granade; [note at end] Dec. 22, 1756 land divided so that Christopher Shilling has lower part & Michael "Bener" has upper part (signed) John Granade Dec. 23, 1756 (sic); Dec. 23, 1761 Mr. Shilling to have 6 acres more that specified (signed) Thomas Pollock; wit. oath Oct. 1762 by John Granade; book 11 p. 15.

3334. Apr. 25, 1762 Joseph Risenover, planter (Craven Co) to John Granade; for £20 proclamation money sold 50 ac on E side of Mill Cr; border: begins at a cypress on the creek side & joins a line of marked trees [no more description]; Joseph is eldest son & heir of his father Jacob Risenover "late" deceased who owned 150 ac by grant dated Oct. 14, 1749; border: begins at a hickory near Paradise Br, crosses the branch, crosses Mill Cr, & joins John Granade; the 50 ac is part of the 150 ac tract. (signed) Joseph Risenhover; (witness) Earnest Granade & Jhn. Pearce; wit. oath Oct. 1762 by Earnest Granade; book 11 p. 17.

3335. Jan. 31, 1762 Joseph Davis, planter (Craven Co) to Patterson Gillit, planter (same); for £20 proclamation money sold on Vine Swamp; border: begins at an ash on Deep Br in Thomas "Fookes" line. (signed) Joseph Davis; (witness) Benjamin Davis' mark "C" & Thomas Fookes; wit. oath Oct. 1762 by Thomas Fookes; book 11 p. 19.

3336. May 10, 1762 [2nd year of reign of King George III] William Carrathers, planter (Beaufort Co, NC) to John Carrathers, planter (Craven Co); for £345 proclamation money sold 4 Negroes: Dick, Subina, Flowra, & "Fransua", a mare "cold" Fancy, 3 feather beds & the covering belonging to them, 3 iron pots, 2 tables, all my pewter, chairs, & other household goods. (signed) W Carrathers; (witness) Thomas Delamare & Elizabeth Carrathers; wit. oath Oct. 1762 by Thomas Delamare; book 11 p. 20.

3337. Jul. 13, 1762 Farnifold Green, planter (Smiths Creek) to John Carrathers, planter (Craven Co); for £10 proclamation money sold 90 ac on N side of Nuse R & E side of Tarkill Cr; border: begins at beginning pine of said patent on "Tarrkil" Cr & joins "the" back line; part of 295 ac granted Oct. 23, 1761 to said Farnifold Green. [not signed & no witness mentioned]; wit. oath Oct. 1762 by John Bryan; book 11 p. 21.

3338. Aug. 6, 1762 William Stringer, planter (Craven Co) to Robert Reynolds (same); for £30 proclamation money sold 70 ac on E side of "Gumb" Swamp; border: begins at a white oak at mouth of Poplar bee tree Br, joins "the" third line,

& land George Stringer sr bought of Col. Francis Stringer; part of grant Oct. 8, 1747 to Francis Stringer. (signed) William Stringer; (witness) Fredric Beckton & William "Islar"; wit. oath Oct. 1762 by William Isler; book 11 p. 22.

3339. Jun. 16, 1762 William Sitgreaves, merchant (Philadelphia, Pennsylvania) & acting partner of partnership "lately subsisting" between Clitheral & Sitgreaves in Newbern and partner in partnership now between William & Thomas Sitgreaves, to my trusty & loving friend Richard "Blacklidge", merchant (Craven Co); power of attorney to recover money & goods owed to me by anyone in North Carolina due to partnership of Clitheral & Sitgreaves or partnership of William & Thomas Sitgreaves or in my own name and to dissolve the 2 partnerships. (signed) William Sitgreaves; (witness) Paul Isaac "Voto" & Fredric Isler; wit. oath Oct. 1862 by Fredric Isler; book 11 p. 23.

3340. Sept. 1, 1762 Frances Blount, planter (Craven Co) to George Malard, planter (same); for £30 proclamation money sold 100 ac; border: begins at a red oak in Hudson's line & joins Parsons. (signed) Frances "Blunt's" mark "B"; (witness) Robert Myser & John Malard; Oct. 1862 acknowledged by "Francis" Blunt; book 11 p. 24.

3341. (no date) dower renounced by "Mirnd", wife of "within" Willis Simmons, before James Davis; book 11 p. 26.

3342. Jan. 24, 1761 John Taneyhill, planter (Craven Co) to James Jones, planter (same); for £40 proclamation money sold 100 ac on S side of Nuse R & W side of "Gorbaeon" Cr; border: begins at a small gut above Gum thickett Point, joins a branch of the gut, Nelson's head line, a branch of the main creek, & land formerly owned by Lipper. (signed) John Taneyhill; (witness) William "Buchlid", Thomas Baker, & Richard Lovett; [note at end indicates Jones paid Taneyhill £40 Jan. 24, 1760 (sic)]; wit. oath Oct. 1762 by Richard Lovitt; book 11 p. 26.

3343. Dec. 17, 1761 Solomon Smith (Craven Co) to Owin Daughity; for £16 sold 17 ac on S side of Nuse R; border: begins at a gum in "the" swamp being corner between Solomon Smith, Owin Daughity, & Richard "Blackled", joins an old line, a branch, & crosses a meadow. (signed) Solomon Smith's mark "S"; (witness) Jonathan Meckferson & "James Carmack jr"; wit. oath Oct. 1762 by James Cormack; book 11 p. 27.

3344. Jan. 6, 1762 Patterson Gillett [or Gillat] (Craven Co) to Joseph Daws, on account of Benjamin Davis "Barth planters" (Craven Co); for £20 NC money sold [omitted] ac on NW ridge of Trent R & E side of Wilsons Cr; border: begins at a red oak [land is 10 by 200 poles]. (signed) Patterson Gillett; (witness) Joseph Davis, John Hutson, & Thomas Fookes jr; wit. oath Oct. 1862 by Thomas Fookes (sic); book 11 p. 28.

3345. Apr. 7, 1763 recorded for Mary Reele, daughter of Peter Reele (Craven Co), "a proper" mark "Vix" and under "squear" in right "year" by slit in left [ear]. (signed) Pet. Conway, CJC; book 11 p. 30.

3346. Oct. 4, 1762 Frederick Becton, planter (Craven Co) to George Becton, planter (same); John "Bection" deceased (late of Craven Co) signed his will Mar. 22, 1753 & died "soon after" and gave his son Edmond Becton, now deceased, 122 ac known as Jacob Wills which was granted Feb. 15, 1737 to Robert Jones, now deceased, and sold by John Jones to said John Becton; at his death Edmond Becton also owned 200 ac, joining above 122 ac, which was granted to said Robert Jones and sold by John Jones, now deceased, to Edmond Becton; Frederick Becton is heir of both tracts; SO for £25 proclamation money sold [his share of] both above tracts; George to pay all quit rents due to King George. (signed) Frederick Becton; (witness) William Isler jr & William Stringer; wit. oath "Oct." by William Isler (sic); book 11 p. 30.

3347. Feb. 4, 1762 Owin Daughity (Craven Co) to John Cormack (same); for £15 sold on S side of Nuse R; border: begins at a pine on "the" meadow side on N side of said John Cormack's "plantation", joins "said" Solomon Cormack, "the" back line formerly Levi Trunohitt's, & Neal Watson. (signed) Owin Daughity; (witness) Jonathan Mekforson, James Cormack, & Edward Cox; Oct. 1762 acknowledged; book 11 p. 31.

3348. Oct. 1, 1762 Abraham Bailey, planter ("Onslo" Co, NC) to Alexander Ranol sr ("Edgecomb" Co, NC); for £86 proclamation money sold 100 ac on S side of Trent R & S side of Tuckho [Cr], on "Bayings Nest Polscat" Br, & Poles cat Swamp; granted Sept. 1, 1753 to [omitted]. (signed) Abraham Bailey; (witness) John Bryan, William Randal jurat, & John Fillyan; wit. oath Oct. 1762 by William "Randall"; book 11 p. 33.

3349. [blank], 1761 Nathan Ward (Craven Co) to Henry Roberts, planter (same); for £20 proclamation money sold 130 ac on E side of South West Cr; border: begins at a hickory on Hays Br below Taylor's "plantation", joins Henry Roberts' corner on South West Cr, & mouth of a branch; granted in 1759 to John Taylor. (signed) Nathan Ward; (witness) John White, Samuel White, & John Loften; Oct. 1762 acknowledged; book 11 p. 34.

3350. [blank] 1759 David Smith, planter (Craven Co) to John Tutte, planter (same); for £50 sold 100 ac on S side of Swift Cr; border: begins at a white oak near Gum Swamp & joins a branch of Broad Br; granted Mar. 5, 146 by Gov. Johnston to my father Henry Smith. (signed) David Smith; (witness) Henry Cannon jurat & David Kermedy; wit. oath Oct. 1762 by Henry Cannon; book 11 p. 36.

3351. Feb. 29, 1761 (sic) Benjamin Cooper, planter (Craven Co) to Owin Daughity, planter (same); for £17 proclamation money sold 250 ac on S side of Nuse R; border: begins at a red oak on upper side of Moselys Cr & joins Colonel

Lovick; part of grant in Nov. 1744 to "said" Levi Truewhitt. (signed) Benj Cooper; (witness) "Jonathon" Meckfarson & John Cormack; wit. oath Oct. 1762 by John Cormack; book 11 p. 37.

3352. Sept. 2, 1762 William Perdue, planter (NC) to James Willis, planter (same); for £30 proclamation money sold 125 ac on Mill Br; border: begins at a pine beside a small pond, joins head of Mill Br, near Willis, & joins or near James Perdue's [or Perdere] head line; granted Dec. 5, 1757 to William Perdue. (signed) William Perdue; (witness) George Fisher, Edward Gattin, & Zebulon Rilas; Oct. 1762 acknowledged; book 11 p. 38.

3353. [no date] William Easterling (Craven Co) to Thomas Box (Dobbs Co, NC); for £6 proclamation money sold 100 ac on S side of Nuce R; border: begins at a pine & joins "the" back line. (signed) William Easterling; (witness) Samuel Box jurat & William Arandall; wit. oath Oct. 1762 by Samuel Box; book 11 p. 40.

3354. Nov. 5, 1761 Richard Cogdell, high sheriff (Craven Co) to Christopher Dawson esq (same); for £10.16 proclamation money sold 0.5 ac in lot #274 & house in New Bern; border: begins at Jude Hall's upper corner on New Street; lot is 13 by 6.5 (sic) poles; sold Nov. 1, 1757 by James Durham to Samuel Lawson; sold due to 2 writs of fieri facias from New Bern Dist Superior Court of Pleas & Grand Sessions May 11 first year of reign of King George III & returnable to court Nov. 2 "instant" ordering sheriff to sell land of Samuel Lawson, inn keeper deceased (late of New Bern, Craven Co) in hands of Margaret Lipscomb, surviving executor of Samuel Lawson's will, (a) due to suit by Andrew Scott for £25.19 and (b) due to suit by "Prip Van Darn" & Isaac Van Darn for £38.1.10; & sold due to act of Parliament of Great Britain passes in 5th year of reign of King George II concerning recovery of debts in America. (signed) R "Cogdell"; (witness) Phill Ambrose & Richard Fenner jurat; wit. oath Oct. 1762 by Richard Fenner; [note at end indicates Dawson paid Cogdell £10.16 Nov. 5, 1761]; book 11 p. 41.

3355. Jul. 19, 1762 Thomas Franklin ("Run" River, Craven Co) to Benjamin Williams ("Nuce" [R], Craven Co); for £4.5.6 proclamation money sold 50 ac on N side of Nuce R [no more description]; part of "survey" run Sept. 6, 1753 for John Franklin. (signed) Thomas Franklin; (witness) Joseph Wright, James Edmondson, & Prudel Franklin; Oct. 1762 acknowledged; book 11 p. 43.

3356. Mar. 15, 1760 John Willcocks, mill wright (Craven Co) to Thomas Willcocks, mill wright (same); for £15 proclamation money sold 480 ac on S side of Trent R; border: begins at John Willcocks' upper corner pine "of" Crooked Run, joins George Mallard, a branch, & T Taylor. (signed) John Willcocks; (witness) James Rogers & Stephen Willcocks jurat; wit. oath Oct. 1762 by Stephen Willcocks; book 11 p. 44.

3357. Aug. 16, 1762 John Heath sr to my well beloved son John Heath jr; for natural love & affection gave 90 ac on E side of Nuce R; border: begins at a red oak near Hancock Cr; includes "plantation" where I live. (signed) John Heath sr; (witness) Henry Heath & Thos Heath jurat; wit. oath Oct. 1762 by Thomas Heath; book 11 p. 46.

3358. Sept. 2, 1762 Edward Gatlin, planter (Craven Co) to William Perdue, planter (same); for £47.10 proclamation money sold 120 ac on N side of Nuce R on a point above Francis Linkfield's upper line; border: begins at a red oak on the river pocoson & joins a marsh; granted Apr. 20, 1745 to John Arthur. (signed) Edward Gatlin sr; (witness) James Willis, Zebulon "Ribe", & James Pearce; wit. oath Oct. 1762 by James Willis; book 11 p. 47.

3359. May 10, 1762 "Elisabeth Carrathers", widow (Craven Co) to John Carrathers (same); for £200 proclamation money sold all my real & personal estate: my Negroes & servants, all my household goods, all my cattle, all my hogs, & sheep. (signed) Elizabeth Carruthers' mark "X"; (witness) W Carruthers, Thomas Delamare jurat, & Sarah Delamare; wit. oath Oct. 1762 by Thomas Delamare; book 11 p. 48.

3360. Aug. 6, 1762 John West, cooper (NC) to Wm Brice Fonville (Craven Co); for £10 proclamation money sold 100 ac on S side of Nuce R, S side of a branch of Bachelder Cr, & on a place called Limbo; border: begins at a red oak by "the" branch. (signed) John West; (witness) John Fonville jurat, Francis Fonville, & Frederick Fonville; wit. oath Oct. 1762 by John Fonville; book 11 p. 49.

3361. Feb. 12, 1761 William Palmer, heir at law (Newbern, Craven Co) to John Pender jr, mariner (same); for £50 proclamation money sold 240 ac on S side of Nuce R; border: begins at a small gum on the river side, joined on W by Jacob Slobuck, & on E by George Lovick. (signed) William Palmer; (witness) John Smith jurat & Ripa Dam; wit. oath Oct. 1762 by John Smith; [note at end indicates Pender paid Palmer £50]; book 11 p. 50.

3362. Jul. 12, 1762 Benjamin Williams & wife Mary Williams, "wife relinct" of John Franklin deceased, to John Carney (Craven Co); for £65 sold our right & dower to land of John Franklin deceased. (signed) Benjm Williams & Mary's mark "m"; (witness) Chrisr. Neal, Joseph Chrispen, & Abner Neal; [note at end indicates John paid Benjamin & Mary £65 Jun. 12, 1762]; wit. oath Oct. 1762 by Abner Neal; book 11 p. 52.

3363. Aug. 12, 1762 Richard Cogdell, sheriff (Craven Co) to John Kerney (of Adams Cr, Craven Co); for £100 proclamation money, secured to be paid to Phillip Ambrose, sold a desk and "several" goods & chattels as per attached schedule; sold for maintenance of Phebe Warner & child (of New York) wife of Samuel Warner, and due to warrant signed by Samuel Warner to me to sell his goods & chattels as per attached schedule dated 7th "instant". (signed) Richd Cogdell, sher; (witness) John Oliver & Richd Fenner; wit. oath Oct. 1762 by

Richd "Femer"; book 11 p. 53;

Aug. 12, 1762 I acknowledge within bill of sale and am satisfied with it. (signed) Samuel Warner; (witness) John Oliver & Richd Fenner jurat; wit. oath Oct. 1762 by Richard Fenner;

Aug. 7, 1762 I authorize you to sell goods & chattels and land mentioned in underneath schedule for 6 months credit or for ready money as you judge most advisable (signed) Samuel Warner; (witness) Richd Davis jurat & Perrigan Cox; wit. oath Oct. 1762 by Richd Davis; book 11 p. 54;

schedule referred to above: a desk & sundry things in it, a table & carpet, 2 pillows & a polster, a Ozenbrigs tick with straw, a server & 4 brass candle sticks, a tool chest & pair of tongs, a candle stick & sniffers, a china pint mug, 11 plates & 2 glass salts, 4 dram glasses, 7 tea cups & 6 saucers, 3 delf tea sausers, an old tub, a tumbler, 2 smoothing irons, a tea table, 2 old table cloths, 17 "sinnon" hankfs., 24 knives & forks, 10 caggs butr., a pair garters & parcel of [blank], 3 thimbles, 8 combs, parcel of needles, 4 "all blady", 6 pair cards, 2 pair scales with some weights, a shot in a gab, 6 chairs, a quilt, 2 sheets, a shaddar, a suit of curtains, a brass copper pot, 24 silver spoons, 8 earthen plates, a china milk pot, a white milk pot, a glass milk pot, 3 delf bowls, 2 white dishes, a decanter, a tea shille, a bed stead & cord, 2 cakes of bees wax, 11 new plates, 6 old plates, 5 tin funnels, 28 sticks mohair, 5 peggin auls, a quire paper, a tin pot, a tin quart pot, small quantity of nails,

(continued) 2 twists of silk, a box & little brimstone, a cask with about 130 lbs "shegr", 2 barrels of coffee, pair hand irons, an ole sail, 2 pcs. sole leather, 2 small dishes, a plate, 2 basons, a small stone mug, a small skillet, pair bellows, old sauce pan, a ladle, a bason, brass clock, saddle & 2 cradles, hand mill, 2 cows & calves, "a few" pipes in a "runlet", a cask about 50 lbs oakum, a plate, small keg with vinegar, crate with earthen ware, frying pan, coffee mill, 2 pot trammels, an old leather, 7 case knives, 10 forks, 3 small razors, a flesh fork, a large pot, 2 old pots & pot hooks, large pair steelyards, part of Hnd. of thums, a small basson, a tin callender, 30 hogs, 8 young cattle, 2 horses,

(continued) a small mare, an old putty auger, some corn growing, 2 old guns, a plow & furniture, 1,000 staves, "some" old casks, Negro man Harry, a barrel turpintine, pair gold sleeve buttons, 300 ac in Craven Co on S side of Neuse R between Adams Cr & the river, 275 ac at Mattimuskut [in] Hyde Co, "sundry" other things if they can be found, 18 pewter tea pots, about 15 barrels corn, a bag of feathers, 2 axes, a grubbing hoe, a gun, a canoe "ore", a bolt ozenbrigs, 2 china bowls, a case of bottles, 2 weeding hoes, a hilling hoe, a raccoon trap at John Passon's, crowder peas & potatoes now growing on land Samuel Warner rents from John & Joseph "Palman" with liberty to carry away the crops. (signed) Samuel Warner; book 11 p. 55.

3364. (continued) sundries belonging to estate of Edward Cummings deceased sold May 10, 1762: (buyers are William Nelson (£5 for a bed, most expensive item), William "Thookson", John Mallard, William Cookson sr, John Colvit, Daniel Mallard, Martin "Iriarh", Wm Cookson jr, Frances Blount, Thomas Wharton, John Cummins, Peter "Oanyett", Nathan Parsons, Martin Fuch, Thomas

Wood, John Parker, John "Mallad", John Yates, Robert Messer, George Mallad, Peter Mallad, Humphry Wilks, Isaac Mackey, Stephen Willcocks; [total of sale is £40]; separate total for William Cookson £11.19 (includes £4 for 2 beds). (signed) Rd Cogdell, shff; book 11 p. 56.

3365. Oct. 12, 1762 John Turner (Craven Co) to Thomas Dyas, planter (same); for £15 proclamation money sold 150 ac on head of Core Cr; border: begins at a pine on S side of the creek, joins a run of the creek, Samuel Pope, & "head line" of said land; part of 310 ac granted Oct. 23, 1756 to John Turner. (signed) John Turner; (witness) Solomon Busley & Samuel Heath; wit. oath Oct. 1764 (sic) by Solomon Busley; book 11 p. 58.

3366. Jan. 28, 1763 William Barren, carpenter (Craven Co) to John Moore, cooper (same); for £36 proclamation money sold 100 ac on Batchelors Cr; border: begins at a pine near said creek "bridge"; sold by Rev. John Lappierre to Benjamin Fordham & wife Martha who sold to William Sitgraves who sold to William Barren. (signed) William "Barran"; (witness) Farnifold Green & John Nun; wit. oath Oct. 1762 by Farnifold Green; book 11 p. 59.

3367. Feb. 7, 1763 John Stanaland, planter (Craven Co) to Christopher Reynolds (Isle "White" Co, Virginia); for £200 proclamation money sold 300 ac on N side of Trent R & N side of Beaver Cr; border: begins at a maple; Reynolds to pay the king quit rent of £0.4 proclamation money per 100 acres. (signed) John Stanaland; (witness) William Isler, Fredr. Harget, & Thomas Wharton; [note at end indicates "Ronolds" paid Stanaland £200 on Apr. 6, 1763]; Apr. 1763 acknowledged; book 11 p. 61.

3368. Dec. 13, 1762 Mary Crawford, executrix, & John Starkey, executor of Joseph Carruthers, to William Wickliffe, gentleman (Craven Co); on Sept. 19, 1754 Joseph Carruthers deceased signed a bond to his brother John Carruthers deceased to sell front of lots #29 & 30 in New Bern; on Feb. 27, 1761 John Carruthers sold front of said lots to William Wickliffe for £9 proclamation money as written on back of the bond; executors of Joseph Carruthers' will were his wife Mary Carruthers & John Starkey, who were directed to sell the land to pay debts; since then, Mary married Charles Crawford (of Craven Co); but deed to Wickliffe hasn't been made until now; SO for £0.5 proclamation money sold front of lots #29 & 30 in New Bern. (signed) Mary Crawford & John Starkey; (witness) Jon. Rice jurat & James Mansfield; wit. oath Oct. 1762 by John Rice; book 11 p. 62.

3369. Nov. 12, 1762 Elizabeth Martin, widow (Craven Co) to my loving grand child Slocum Ferguson, planter (same); for love & good will gave 130 ac on S side of Nuce R & W side of South R; border: begins at a stone wall near the river, joins a "breck" wall, a "gum field fined" agreeable to Samuel Masters' line, back of the land, "courses" of a deed by Wm Dufres to Isaac Gold; part of land Thomas Martin purchased Aug. 12, 1720 of Isaac Gold. (signed) Elizabeth Martin's mark "E"; (witness) Jno Jones, Adam Fergerson, & Lydia Latemore; wit. oath Oct.

1762 by John Jones; book 11 p. 64.

3370. Apr. 2, 1763 Lewis Bryan (Craven Co) to his son William Bryan (same); for £50 proclamation money sold 200 ac on N side of Nuce R; called Beasleys Island; border: begins at a pine on the river side, joins a swamp, & the pecoson; "held by" deed from William Charlton "from" Oxford Beasley's grant dated Apr. 20, 1745. (signed) Lewis Bryan; (witness) Thomas Moore & Benjamin "Beeckman"; Apr. 1763 acknowledged; book 11 p. 66.

3371. Nov. 22, 1762 Mary Simmons, widow (Craven Co) to Jacob Lewis, planter (same); for £13.4 proclamation money sold 50 ac on S side of Bay R & W side of Trent Cr; border: begins at a post in the marsh by said Simmons Landing, joins line that divides said Lewis & Simmons, & Simmons' back line. (signed) Mary Simmons; (witness) John Carruthers, Thomas Delamore, & Joseph Brooks; wit. oath Apr. 1763 by John Carruthers; book 11 p. 67.

3372. Mar. 4, 1763 William Baston Whitford, planter (Craven Co) to John Stanaland, planter (same); for £100 proclamation money sold 300 ac on N side of Trent R; border: begins at R Jones' corner hickory, joins a branch, & a pocoson; part of grant to Robert Jones. (signed) W B Whitford; (witness) William Knox & Thomas Stanaland; [note at end indicates Stanaland paid Whitford £200 on Mar. 23, 1763 (sic)]; Apr. 1763 acknowledged; book 11 p. 68.

3373. Apr. 2, 1763 John Martin (Craven Co) to James Odond [or Odande] (same); for £13 proclamation money sold 50 ac on N side of Nuce R & N side of Lower Broad Cr; in fork of the creeks making out of said Broad Cr: one called Martins Cr & other called Grums [Cr]; border: begins at a pine in the fork of a gut that makes out of Martins Cr, joins a branch, crosses a neck, & joins head of a gut that makes out of Grums Cr. (signed) John Martin; (witness) John Carruthers & Thomas "Dallmore"; wit. oath Apr. 1763 by John Carruthers; book 11 p. 70.

3374. Mar. 15, 1763 John Carruthers, planter (Craven Co) to Stephen York, sadler (Newbern, Craven Co); for £0.5 proclamation money sold 0.5 ac in lot #72 in Newbern; sold due to writ of fieri facias for £9.10.0½ proclamation money May 11, first year of reign of King George III returnable to court Nov. 2 next directing Craven Co sheriff to sell land of Abiah Boggs deceased (late of Craven Co), in hands of William "Caruthers" executor of Boggs' will, due to suit by "Obediah" Boggs against John Hill which action abated by plaintiff's death and A Boggs owned above land; and sold due to act of Parliament of Great Britain in fifth year of reign of King George II concerning collection of debts in America; land was sold Oct. 24, 1761 by Sheriff Richard Cogdell to John Carruthers for £29 proclamation money and Carruthers now assigns to York whose money was used to buy the lot. (signed) John Carruthers; (witness) James Green & Charles Dundre; Apr. 1763 acknowledged; book 11 p. 71.

3375. Feb. 7, 1763 Benjamin Peters (Craven Co) to Charles Fallinsworth (same);

for £8 proclamation money sold 100 ac on N side of Nuce R; border: begins at a pine in "his" line, near a road, & joins William Peters. (signed) Benjamin Peters' mark "X"; (witness) John Collins & William Duderly; wit. oath Apr. 1763 by William Duderly; book 11 p. 73.

3376. Jan. 27, 1763 William "Keeth", planter (Prince Frederick Parish, Carolina province [SC}) to James Keith, planter (Prince Frederick Parish, SC); for £40 proclamation money sold 170 ac on N side of Nuce R; border: begins at a white oak. (signed) William Keeth; (witness) Benjm. Buck & James Smith; wit. oath Apr. 176[blank] by Benjm. Buck; book 11 p. 74.

3377. "Ant" 10, 1761 estate of John Franklin by Benjn & Mary Williams, admrs: DR: paid for letters administration £1.6, paid Peter Conway fees for sundry services as per rents £2.7.8, paid James Conway balance account £3.15.4, paid Wm Herritage for retain fee & advice on estate's "affaird" £0.13.4, paid Michael Hyman £0.12, paid Thomas Franklin £0.12.4, paid John Dillahanta for leveys for 1759 £3.15.5, paid John Physic £0.12, paid William Ewin £32.2.8, paid David Smith £14.3.10, paid Luke Flanagan £2.8.8, paid John Stamey exr of Jos Carruthers for fees on sales of part of estate £3.15.6, paid Richard Cogdell for do £9.14, 6 gallons rum expended at funeral £12.5, paid for offin £0.10, 2.5 gallons run at vendue £0.18, gallon rum to Jos Crispin formerly bond £0.8, paid Michael Hyman for riding after horses £0.8, paid Richd Fenner for extra fee in cause against admr Nathan Buner £0.15, to commrs. £542.14.8 pet. £54.4.4 [total ?] £143.10.9;
  CR: 34 barrels ricc sold Mr. Euin & David Smith £86.0.2, 24 gallons rum remaining at time of Mr. Franklin [death ?] £9.12, 115 lbs rice sold Capt. Crispin 13/4 £0.15.4, proc. left by Mr. Franklin's death £3.3.4, sundry accounts recd £5.0.6, judgment recovered against admrs. of Nathan Barn £12, by amount of accounts sold of estate £542.14.8 [total] £659.6; balance remaining inhands of administrators £515.15.3; [total ?] £659.6; £515.15.3 being "neat" estate divided between widow & children or £171.18.5 to widow as her third and £38.4.1 to each child; "errors excepted". (signed) Apr. 8, 1762 "P" Chrisr. Dawson & Chrisr. Neal; book 11 p. 75.

3378. Apr. 8, 1763 James Parkinson esq (Craven Co) to Samuel Cornell esq (same); for £245 proclamation money sold 0.5 ac in lot #510 in New Bern; border: begins at Broad Street & Queen Street & joins lot #271. (signed) James Parkinson; (witness) John Dellahuntee & John Pittman; Apr. 1763 acknowledged; book 11 p. 77.

3379. May 19, 1762 Nathaniel Hubble, gentleman (Newbern, Craven Co) to James Parkinson, merchant (Craven Co); for £245 proclamation money sold 0.5 ac in lot #510 in New Bern; border: begins at Broad Street & Queen Street & joins lot #271. (signed) Nathn. Hubble; (witness) "Johnr." Miller & Richd Fenner; [note at end indicates Parkinson paid Hubble £24 on May 29, 1762 (sic); [no wit. oath mentioned]; book 11 p. 78

3380. May 8, 1762 Richard Cogdell, high sheriff (Craven Co) first part, Nathaniel Hubble, gentleman (same) second part, & John Smith, administrator of John Lovett [or Lovall] merchant deceased (Newbern, NC) third part; for £240 [£52.4 also mentioned] proclamation money sold border: begins at Broad Street & Quuen Street & joins lot #510; sold Nov. 7, 1757 by town commissioners to James Davis who sold Feb. 28, 1758 to John Lovett; sold due to writ of fieri facias from New Bern Dist Superior Court of Pleas & Grand Sessions Nov. 9 second year of reign of "present" king and returnable to court May 2 "instant" directing sheriff to sell goods & chattels of John Lovett (late of New Bern) in hands of John Smith; writ for £84.16.4 [£184.16.4 also mentioned] proclamation money due to suit by James Green jr & cost of £3.15.2; and sold due to act of Parliament of Great Britain passed in fifth year of reign of King George II concerning collection of debts in America. (signed) Richard Cogdell, Jno Smith, & Nathn. "Hubbell"; (witness) Richard Fenner & Peter Conway; [note at end indicates Hubble paid Cogdell £55.4 (sic) on May 8, 1762; [no wit. oath mentioned]; book 11 p. 80.

3381. Feb. 22, 1763 Francis Nicholls, cooper, & wife Mary (Newbern, NC) to Joseph Leech, merchant (same); for £7.10 proclamation money sold 0.25 ac in half of lot #127 in New Bern; border: begins at corner of Union Street & Craven Street; land is 6.5 by 6.5 poles; sold by town commissioners to Nicholas Purify who "saved" the land "according to law" and sold half Aug. 11, 1753 to John Pearce who sold Jul. 6, 1761 to Francis "Nichols" recorded in book O p. 116 & 320 (sic). (signed) Francis Nichols' mark "X", Mary's mark "X", & Joseph Leech (sic); (witness) Martin Worsley & John Kennedy; wit. oath Apr. 1763 to Martin "Worsly"; book 11 p. 82.

3382. Sept. [or Dept.] 30, 1762 Joseph Gilbert, planter (Craven Co) to Isaac Barans, planter (same); for £15 proclamation money sold 150 ac on S side of Trent R about 0.25 miles above the upper bridge; border: begins at Jonathan Sanderson's corner tree. (signed) Joseph Gilbert's mark "Ʇ"; (witness) John Gilbert & Arthur Barans; Oct. 1762 (sic) acknowledged; book 11 p. 84.

3383. Jan. 6, 1763 Joseph Leech (Craven Co) to Martin Fuch, planter (same); for £20 proclamation money sold 100 ac; border: begins at a corner of "the" tract, joins a patent line, a branch, & Mr. "Hornegg"; part of grant Oct. 21, 1758 to said Joseph Leech. (signed) Joseph Leech; (witness) Josiah Ridgeway & James Hill; Apr. 1763 acknowledged; book 11 p. 85.

3384. Dec. 16, 1762 Thomas Simmons (Craven Co) to William Simmons (same); for £23 proclamation money sold 80 ac on E side of "said" run of Cypress Swamp [no more description]; part of 160 ac on N side of Nuce R & W side of head of Lower Broad Cr grant which was sold Nov. 6, 1724 to Henry Harford & "by conveyances" became property of Thomas Simmons. (signed) Thos Simmons' mark "X"; (witness) John Carruthers, Thomas Delamore, & Wm Brooks; wit. oath Apr. 1763 by John Carruthers; book 11 p. 87.

3385. Apr. 5, 1763 James Davis esq (Craven Co) to Joseph Leech [or Leach], merchant (same); for £75 proclamation money sold 250 ac in the Great Pocoson at head of Brices Cr; border: begins at an old marked corner pine in a point above Johnson's rice ground; granted Jun. 30, 1758 to James Davis recorded in Secretary's office book No. 11 p. 208. (signed) James Davis, Prudence Davis, & Joseph Leech (sic); (witness) William Carruthers [only one witness]; [note at end indicates Leech paid Davis £75 (witness) John Williams & John Carruthers (sic)]; [no wit. oath mentioned]; book 11 p. 88.

3386. Nov. 20, 1762 Adam Tooley (Princess Anne Co, Virginia), son of James Tooley & wife Sarah who was daughter of Adam Ferguson "and Elder" deceased (of Bath Co, NC), to my friends John Carney, William White, & Christopher Neal (all of Craven Co, NC) & their survivor; power of attorney to receive from anyone in North Carolina any Negro slaves, goods, chattels, or money that were property of Adam Ferguson deceased to which I am entitled. (signed) Adam "Tooly"; (witness) Richd Caswell & John "Sheepard"; wit. oath Apr. 1763 by Richd Caswell; book 11 p. 89.

3387. May 1, 1761 Newman Dunn (Craven Co) to my well beloved son William Dunn (same); for mutual love & affection gave, after my death, 100 ac on S side of Nuce R; border: begins at Arthur Johnson's line, joins Waterhole Br, & Earnest Grinade; part of "plantation" where I live. (signed) "Numan" Dunn; (witness) Perrigan Cox & Jos Fisher; wit. oath Oct. 1762 (sic) by Perrigan Cox; book 11 p. 90.

3388. Apr. 8, 1763 James Parkinson esq (Craven Co) to Longfield Cox, planter (same); for £86.10 sold 300 ac on S side of Nuce R & on upper side of Moseleys Cr; border: begins at John Benner's corner [no more description]; known at "the" State Landing; being upper part of grant Mar. 23, 1727 by Lords Proprietor to John Lovick esq who willed it [date blank] to James Parkinson. (signed) James Parkinson; (witness) John Bemers & David Gordon; Apr. 1763 acknowledged; book 11 p. 91.

3389. Oct. 22, 1762 Thomas Franklin (Craven Co) to Benjamin Williams (same); for £32 proclamation money sold 175 ac in 2 tracts: (a) 125 ac; border: begins at a pine at John "Akes" line at hed of Deep Run, joins "the" main road, John Franklin deceased; granted NOv. 25, 1754 to John Franklin; & (b) 50 ac on westermost side of Deep Run; includes places where Charles Well lately lived; being lower part of land purchased by John Franklin deceased from John Bedscot; both tracts owned by John Franklin when he died intestate and land became property of his heir Thos Franklin. (signed) Thoams Franklin; (witness) Thomas Green & Chrisr. Neal; [note at end indicates Williams paid Franklin £32 on Oct. 22, 1762]; [no wit. oath mentioned]; book 11 p. 93.

3390. Apr. 8, 1763 Gabriel Pickren, planter (Craven Co) to Benjamin Pickren; for

£50 proclamation money sold 90 ac on S side of Trent R; border: begins at a gum on the river, joins a patent line, Pocoson Swamp, & "Ingen" graves. (signed) Gabriel Pickren; (witness) John Gilbert & Ezekiel Mears; Apr. 1763 acknowledged; book 11 p. 95.

3391. Mar. 5, 1763 Solomon Smith (Craven Co) to Owin Daughity (same); for £15 sold 17 ac on S side of Nuce R; border: begins at a pine on "the" meadow side & joins mouth of a little branch. (signed) Solomon Smith's mark "X"; (witness) Richd Blackledge & Thomas "Wingott"; Apr. 1763 acknowledged; book 11 p. 96.

3392. Jul. 3, 1762 [2nd year of reign of King George III] "Abell" Deal (Craven Co) to John "Moglaughon"; for £20 NC money sold 100 ac; border: begins at a pine on N side of Little Contentney Cr, joins a patent line, Peter Manners, Levin Alderson; part of grant Jul. 7, 1750 to Joseph Jackson. (signed) Abel Deal's mark "X"; (witness) Major Griffin & James "Jurner"; wit. oath Oct. 1762 to James Turner; book 11 p. 97.

3393. Apr. 7, 1762 (Quaker style date) Levi Bush (Clubfoots Cr, Craven Co) to Mathew Moore (White oak R, Carteret Co, NC); for £25 proclamation money sold 100 ac on W side of Clubfoots Cr, at head of a creek that makes out of said Clubfoots Cr, & between land of Roger Jones & "broad Nockor Reed's" land; border: begins at mouth of a gut near the house where said Levi Bush formerly lived, joins a branch, "the" head line, Snake Br; part of a small grant for 200 ac to Edmund Mitchell. (signed) Levi Bush's mark "n"; (witness) John Thomlinson & John "Anyhill"; book 11 p. 98.

3394. Feb. 9, 1763 William Stringer, planter (Craven Co) to Christopher Reynolds (same); for £51 proclamation money sold 100 ac on S side of Nuce R at a place called Indian "Wills"; border: begins at a white oak at mouth of a little branch between "said" John Jones deceased & Christopher Reynolds. (signed) William "Stringe"; (witness) William McMurrin & George Stringe; wit. oath Oct. 1762 by William McMurrin; book 11 p. 100.

3395. Dec. 10, 1762 John Corney, planter (Craven Co) to John Guss, "laborur" (same); for £12 proclamation money sold 40 ac on E side of Adams Cr in fork of Lewises Cr; border: begin at John Frulidge's corner on E side of N branch of said creek, joins Nelson's old patent line, Adam Nelson, Thos Lewis' patent, E branch of the creek, & a swamp. (signed) John Corney's mark "D"; (witness) James Jones & Willobey Bartlett; wit. oath Apr. 1763 by James Willobey; book 11 p. 101.

3396. Nov. 17, 1762 Vinson Amyet, planter, to Edward Kinsey; for £100 sold 100 ac on S side of "Tuchoho" [Swamp]; border: begins at said Chs Kinsey's lower line & joins the lines of the patent; part of survey where Christian Kinsey formerly lived "on the remainder part thereof". (signed) Vincent Amyet; (witness) Joseph Kinsey & Peter "Amiet"; Dec. 1762 acknowledged by Vincent "Amiet"; book 11

p. 102.

3397. Nov. 11, 1762 Elizabeth Martin, widow (Craven Co) to my loving grand child Adam Forguson (same); for love & good will gave 150 ac on S side of Nuce R & on South R; border: joins a branch; formerly surveyed for Matthew "Resnover" & elapsed by him for nonpayment of purchase money and "now become due" to Elizabeth Martin due to act of Assembly. (signed) Elizabeth Martin's mark "X"; (witness) Jo Jones, Wittoby Bartlett, & Solcumb Farguson; wit. oath Dec. 1762 by Jo Jones; book 11 p. 103.

3398. Feb. 7, 1763 Thomas Sitgreaves, inn keeper, & wife "John Cady Sitgraves" (Craven Co) to William Sitgreaves, merchant (Philadelphia, Pennsylvania); for £400 proclamation money sold 0.5 ac in lot #17 in New Bern; border: between John Cambell's lot where Richd Cogdell lives & James Parkinson's lot; sold Sept. 19, 1759 by John Bryan & wife Ann Cady Bryan to Thomas Sitgreaves. (signed) Thos Sitgreaves; (witness) Jacob Blount & John Green; Apr. 1763 acknowledged by Thos Sitgreaves & John Cady Sitgraves; book 11 p. 104.

3399. Jun. 26, 1762 Mary Guttery, widow (Craven Co) to my 2 children Ebenezer Guttery & Esther Guttery; for natural love & affection gave 2 cows & calves, a 2 year old stear, a bay horse, 7 sheep, all my hogs, household furntirue, goods & chattels, & estate of whatever nature. (signed) Maray Guttery's mark "X"; (witness) Chrisr. Neal & Mary Neal; wit. oath Jul. 1762 by "Chris" Neal; book 11 p. 105.

3400. Oct. 30, 1762 Joseph Anderson (Craven Co) to Charles Webb (same); for £20 proclamation money sold 80 ac on N side of Nuce R & E side of Great Swamp; border: begins at a white oak & hickory at mouth of a small branch that makes out of said swamp, joins a branch, & Great Swamp; part of grant Sept. 26, 1753 to William Beesley. (signed) Joseph Anderson's mark "Ɵ"; (witness) Jacob Miller, William Williams, & Charles James; wit. oath Oct. 1762 by Jacob Miller; book 11 p. 106.

3401. Nov. 5, 1762 Thomas Simson, planter (Craven Co) to Wm Wickfield, planter (same); for £4 proclamation money sold 5 ac on W side of Punch Bowl Br; border: begins at a red oak in said Wickfield's own line, joins William Wickfield's old former line, joins land where he lives, lower corner of said Simson's corn field, & joins Bean. (signed) Thomas Simson's mark "X"; (witness) Katharine Wickfield & John Lee; Dec. 1762 acknowledged; book 11 p. 107.

3402. Oct. 24, 1761 Richard Cogdell, high sheriff (Craven Co) to John Carruthers, planter (same); for £29 proclamation money sold 0.5 ac in lot #72 in New Bern on E side of [blank] street; sold due to writ of fieri facias from New Bern Dist Superior Court of Pleas & Grand Sessions May 11 first year of reign of King George III & returnable to court Nov. 2 next ordering sheriff to sell property of

Abia "Baugs" deceased (late of Craven Co) in hands of William Carruthers executor of will of Abia baugs, for £9.10.0½ proclamation money due to suit by Abia Baugs against John Hill which action abated on plaintiff's death; and sold due to act of Parliament of Great Britain passed in fifth year of reign of King George II concerning collection of debts in America. (signed) R Cogdell; (witness) James Green & Charles Dundee; [not at end indicates Carruthers paid Cogdell £29 on Oct. 24, 1761]; [no wit. oath mentioned]; book 11 p. 108.

3403. Oct. 9, 1762 Richard Cogdell, high sheriff (Craven Co) to Peter Conway, gentleman (New Bern, NC); for £41 proclamation money sold 50 ac on N side of Neuse R & W side of Dawsons Cr; border: joins Thomas Carraway & Valintine Bowers; formerly estate of Valintine Bowers deceased who devised it to Sarah Bowers his widow who later married Nathan Baum and it "come" into hands of his administrator Joseph Crispin; sold due to writ of fieri facias from New Bern Inferior Court of Pleas & Quarter Sessions Jul. 10 second year of reign of King George II & returnable to court first Tuesday in Oct. next ordering sheriff to sell property of Nathan Baum in hands of his administrator Joseph Crispin for £12 proclamation money damages & £3.12.2 costs due to suit by administratrix of John Franklin; and sold due to act of Parliament of Great Britain passed in fifth year of reign of King George II concerning collection of debts in America; when sheriff advertised the land, John Pender sr claimed the land due to deed to him by Christian Bowers, won & heir of "Vallintine" Bowers; so sheriff summoned a "jewray" of 12 free holders who said the land was property of Nathaniel "Bunn" deceased; so sheriff sold it. (signed) R Cogdell, sher; (witness) Jno Smith & Garrard Sharp; [note at end indicates Conway paid Cogdell £41 on Oct. 9, 1762]; [no wit. oath mentioned]; book 11 p. 110;
   Oct. 9, 1762 Peter Conway says within £41 proclamation money was "proper money" of Joseph Crispin; SO for £0.5 Conway sold within land to Crispin. (signed) Peter Conway; (witness) Jno Smith & Garrard Sharp; [no wit. oath mentioned]; book 11 p. 112.

3404. Oct. 30, 1762 Elisabeth Martin, widow (Craven Co) to John Pittman, Robert Wallis, & Joseph Pittman (same); for £500 proclamation money sold "a parcel" of Negroes: Abigail, young Abigail, George, Rachel, Dinah, Simon, Ostiriah, Peter, Mimia, Patt, Juda, & Phebe. (signed) Elisabeth Martin's mark "E"; (witness) Jas Jones, Saml Masters, John Salmons, & Charles Rew; [note at end indicates Pittman, Pittman, & Wallis paid Elizabeth "full satisfaction" on Apr. 2, 1763; wit. oath May 2, 1763 by James Jones; [Charles Berry is clerk of court now]; book 11 p. 112.

3405. Apr. 18, 1763 (Quaker style date) John Thomlinson (Clubfoots Cr, Craven Co) to Christopher Neal (Dawsons Creek) & John Carney (NC), attorneys for Adam Tooley "the rnt"; for £500 proclamation money sold 6 Negroes: a wench Lacy & her child Lillyha, Johnson, Ben, "Ass", & Joshua the younger. (signed) John Thomlinson; (witness) John Pittman & Adam Forguson; [note at end indicates Thomlinson received consideration money]; wit. oath May 2, 1763 by

John Pittman; book 11 p. 113.

3406. Oct. 3, 1759 John Jones, planter (Duplin Co, NC) to George Kornegy, planter (Craven Co); for £36.18.9 proclamation money sold a horse & 50 ac which he "had" of Samuel Herring and 60 ac on Keepee Cr and everything "wherein am now possest"; sale void if Jones pays Kornegy £36.18.9 by "the twenty". (signed) John Jones; (witness) George Kornegy (sic) & William Kornegy; wit. oath "May 3" by George Kornegy jr; book 11 p. 114.

3407. Mar. 20, 1763 deposition of Francis Brice 60 years old: in 1723 or 1724 he went up Trent [R] with Thomas Pollock & John Baptist Ash, a surveyor, to survey land for said Pollock; they went to an old field called Holsters and began at a tree at the river, then ran out to a pine under a hill, then various courses of the marsh to the river, along the river to a pine close to the river side about 150 yards below an old field called Frenchman's old field which he said he marked at request of said Pollock as his upper corner tree; to day Brice went with Thomas Pollock & John Williams esqs, Lamuel "Katch", Daniel Simmons, Emmanuel Simmons, Baset, Simmons, John Granade, "John John" Knotts, Amos Small, James Frazer, Edmond Hatch, & John Hatch to the place he believe the upper corner tree stood; they found a dead pine and the sap rotten off which Brice believes was the corner pine he marked on above date for Thomas Pollock; Brice says he was one of chain bearers when the land was surveyed. (signed) Fran. Brice & John Williams; [no witness oath mentioned];
     Mar. 28, 1763 Emmanuel Simmons & Daniel Simmons, of "full" age swear: they know a certain dead pine that Francis Brice made oath he believed to be the tree he marked for Mr. Pollock's corner [blank] marked like a corner tree was called [blank] brought forward & known as Pollock's corner about 20 years as they "rember". (signed) "Emanuel" Simmons, Daniel Simmons, & John Williams [no wit. oath mentioned]; book 11 p. 115.

3408. May 31, 1762 George Pollock esq gentleman (Bertie Co, NC) to Thomas Leech, merchant (Newbern, Craven Co); for £20 proclamation money sold 2 ac joins New Bern at upper end of Front or Water Street on Nuce R; border: begins at upper or NW corner of said street, runs S60W 13 poles on bounds of said town, N33W 26 poles, then parallel with said town to Nuce R, & along the river to town bounds; part of 900 ac granted Jan. 22, 1713/4 to Daniel Richardson esq who sold Apr. 14, 1714 to Honb. Thos Pollock esq who bequeathed it to his son Cullen Pollock esq who left it to his son George Pollock esq. (signed) George Pollock & Thos Leech (sic); (witness) Rr. Cogdell & Jos Leech; wit. oath May 5, 1763 by Richard Cogdell esq; book 11 p. 116.

3409. May 7, 1763 then entered a "covet" for John Pittman against Charles Rew & Benjamin Wallis for bill of sale from Elizabeth martin for "said" Negro slaves: old Abigail, young Abigail, George, Simon, Peter, Rachel, Osteriah, Patt, Mimiah, Dinah, Phebe, & Jude. (signed) "Peet" Conway, CJC; book 11 p. 117.

3410. Apr. 13, 1763 James Parkinson, merchant (Craven Co) to Bernard Parkinson, merchant (same); on Mar. 6, 1746 by Cullen Pollock (then of "Tyrall" Co, NC) to John Bryan sold 0.25 ac in front of lot #18 opposite lot #18 and was sold Jan. 10, 1758 John Bryan & wife Ann Cade Bryan (of Craven Co) to James Parkinson for £75 proclamation money and on Jul. 25, 1761 James Parkinson (Craven Co) sold to Bernard Parkinson merchant (same) for £250 proclamation money 0.5 ac (sic) or all of front of said lot with warehouse & warf now possessed by John Redman and the new house erecting on said land with "remainder" of the front & all other improvements thereon; SO now to better secure the title and for £0.10 sterling Great Britain money sold 0.25 ac or land opposite or facing lot #18 being land in foregoing deeds sold by Cullen Pollock to John Bryan and by John & Ann Cade Bryan to James Parkinson with dwelling house, stores & wharf. (signed) James Parkinson; (witness) Gibbons Fawning & Richd Fenner; [note at end indicates B Parkinson paid J Parkinson £0.10 on Apr. 13, 1763; wit. oath Apr. 20, 1763 by Gibbons Jennings; book 11 p. 118.

3411. Feb. 22, 1763 [3rd year of reign of King George III] Andrew "Bailie", gentleman (NC) to John Campbell esq (of Lazyhill, Bertie Co, NC); for £200 proclamation money sold [or released] a third part of an undivided lot #3 in New Bern "in front H" Street and a third of a tan yard with buildings & improvements; land was sold Dec. 5, 1760 by Richard Spaight & Hugh Waddell esq (NC) to Andrew Bailie for £333.10.8 proclamation money. (signed) Andw Bailie; (witness) Edmd "Fenning" & Thos McGuire; [note at end indicates Campbell paid Bailie consideration money; wit. oath May 14, 1763 by Chief Justice Thomas McGuire; book 11 p. 121.

3412. Feb. 21, 1763 [2nd year of reign of King George III] Andrew Bailie, gentleman (NC) to John Campbell esq (of Lazyhill, Bertie Co, NC); for "shillings" Great Britain money leased for a year a third of an undivided lot #3 in New Bern "in" Front Street and a third of a tan yard thereon with buildings & improvements; sold De. 1, 1760 by Richard Spaight & Hugh Waddell esqs (of NC) to Andrew Bailie for £333.10.8 proclamation money; yearly rent is a "peper" corn, if lawfully demanded. (signed) Andw Bailie; (witness) Edmd Fenning & Thos McGuire; wit. oath May 11, 1763 by Chief Justice Thomas McGuire; book 11 p. 123.

3413. Apr. 11, 1763 James Parkinson, merchant (New Bern, NC) to Samuel Cornell esq merchant (same); for £175.8.11 proclamation money sold Negro man Will and Negro Parthana & her child. (signed) James Parkinson; (witness) John Williams & R Cogdell; [note at end indicates Cornell paid Parkinson £175.8.11 on Apr. 11, 1763; wit. oath May 13, 1763 by Richd Cogdell; book 11 p. 125.

3414. Oct. 9, 1762 Richard Cogdell, high sheriff (Craven Co) to William Ewin [or Euin], merchant (Newbern, Craven Co); for £39.1 proclamation money sold 0.5 ac in lot #287 in New Bern on New Street; sold Jan. 31, 1758 by New Bern town commissioners to Robert Herbin; sale is subject to mortgage Nov. 7, 1760 by Robert Herbin to M Johnson Smith (of New Bern) for £107.6 proclamation money; sold due to 3 writs of fieri facias from New Bern Dist Superior Court of Pleas & Grand Sessions May 2, 1762 [2nd year of reign of King George III] against Robert Herbin, inn holder (of New Bern) (a) for £120.4 proclamation money debt & £4.16.6 cost due to suit by Barnaby Coffie, (b) writ for £87.8.8 proclamation money due to suit by William "Ewen", & (c) writ for £114.8 proclamation money debt & £5.9.3 costs due to suit by William Ramsey & William Witton; and sold due to act of Parliament of Great Britain passed in fifth year of reign of King George II concerning collection of debts in America; writs were returnable to court May 2 next. (signed) Rd Cogdell, shr; (witness) Rd Caswell & Richd Blackledge; May 5, 1763 acknowledged; book 11 p. 125.

3415. Jan. 3, 1763 George Hays, carpenter (Newbern, Craven Co) to William Euen, merchant (same); for £13 proclamation money sold 0.5 ac in lot #189 in New Bern on Metcalf Street; sold Aug. 22, 1760 by town commissioners to George Hays; town has privilege of getting fire wood & timber from the land & pasture for common use; "Euin" to pay Cullen Pollock esq a pepper corn per year, if demanded. (signed) George Hays; (witness) John Williams & Rd Cogdell; [note at end indicates Euen paid Hays £13 on Jan. 3, 1763]; wit. oath May 3, 1763 by Richard Cogdell; book 11 p. 128.

3416. Mar. 20, 1761 [2nd year of reign of King George III] John Redman, merchant (Newbern, Craven Co) to James Parkinson, merchant (same); for £420 proclamation money sold or quit claimed a clock & a book case both mahogany, 2 large looking glasses, 2 tables, 12 leather bottom chairs, 2 large "Dione" lazy chair lined with blue, 2 tea tables, 3 servers, a tea chest, 19 pictures, 4 feather beds & bedsteads, 10 pair of sheets, 2 pair of blanketts, 3 ruggs, 6 counterpanes, 6 bed quilts, 4 boulsters, 8 pillows, 2 large & 6 small tables, a large beaufett in the hall or passage with 7 china bowls, 24 china plates, 24 cups & sassars, "sundry" glasses & earthenware, 7 large & 6 small silver spoons, a silver punch ladle, a pair shugar tonges, light mesh bottom chairs, 2 small writing desks, 36 puter plates, 6 dishes, 2 small looking glasses, 2 whips, a cross cut saw, 12 knives & forks, 2 pair of doggs, 2 large skilletts, 3 pots, 2 sauce pans, 4 window curtains, a flat & a large boat, a riding chair, a horse, 10 cows, 2 saddles & bridles, pair of mill stones & mill, a cart, a stage, a guardwine, 12 table cloths, 12 fourt candle sticks, 2 tea kettles, 2 great guns, indentures" of Gabriel Moore with his right of Negro Salem, & all the utensells in his possession when bill of sale was made Jul. 20, 1761 to said John Redman by James Parkinson for securing payment of £420 proclamation money. (signed) Jno Redman; (witness) Peter Conway & Wm Heritage; wit. oath Nov. 2, 1762 by Wm Heritage; book 11 p. 130.

3417. [blank] 1763 John Starkey jr, planter ("Corterete" Co, NC) to Wm Wharton; for £80 proclamation money sold 116 ac on Vine Swamp; border: begins at upper corner pine of "the' home tract on the swamp near "the" plantation fence & joins "the" back line; part of 580 ac known as St. James Park lately owned by Joseph Wharton deceased, father in law of John Starkey (sic); said 580 ac was part of

2,540 ac granted in 1727 to Thos Jones who sold in Apr. 1730 to Walter Lane who sold in Oct. 1731 to William "Handcock" who sold in 1734 to William "Turnarlift" who died intestate & land descended to his only child Jane now wife of John "Carathurs" jr. (signed) John Starkey jr; (witness) Joseph Wharton & Richd Wallace; wit. oath May 4, 1763 by Richard Wallace; book 11 p. 131.

3418. Jul. 18, 1761 Thomas Wharton (Carteret Co, NC) to John Starkey jr; for £100 proclamation money sold 116 ac on Vine Swamp; border: begins at upper corner of the whole tract on the swamp near "the" plantation fence & joins "the" back line; part of 580 ac St. James Park lately owned by Joseph Wharton deceased father in law of above Thomas Wharton which was part of 2,540 ac granted in 1727 to Thos Jones who sold in Apr. 1730 to Walter Lane who sold in Oct. 1731 to William "Handcock" who sold in 1734 to William "Turnerlift" who died intestate & land descended to his only child Jane now wife of John "Carothers" jr. (signed) Thomas Wharton; (witness) Richd Wallace & Joseph Jones; [note at end indicates Starkey paid Wharton £10 on Jul. 18, 1761]; wit. oath Nov. 7, 1761 by Richard Wallace; book 11 p. 133.

3419. [blank], 1762 Samuel Robert Hall, printer (Newbern, NC) to James Coor [or Core] (same); for £3 proclamation money sold 0.5 ac in lot #362 in New Bern on Pollocks Street & Norwoods Street; sold Jun. 6, 1753 by the commissioners to Susannah West. (signed) Samuel Robert Hall; (witness) Mathew Arthur jurat & Mary West; [note at end indicates Hall received consideration money Jul. 22, 1762]; [no wit. oath mentioned]; book 11 p. 135.

3420. Mar. 5, 1763 Owen Owens, planter (Craven Co) to Robert Orme, merchant (same); for £20 proclamation money sold 100 ac; border: begins at a corner red oak, joins Steel, & Emanuel. (signed) Owen Owens; (witness) Phil Ambrose & Thomas McLin; wit. oath May 9, 1763 by Chief Justice Phil Ambrose; book 11 p. 135.

3421. Nov. 27, 1762 John Yeats, planter (Craven Co) to Patrick Stanaland, planter; for £40 proclamation money sold 70 ac on S side of Neuse R; border: begins at Mr. Becton's corner pine; granted Oct. 3, 1755 to John Yeats. (signed) John Yeats' mark "Ƚ"; (witness) Matin "Fach" & Joseph Chilles; [no wit. oath mentioned]; book 11 p. 137.

3422. Mar. 17, 1763 Joseph Leech, merchant (Craven Co) to Frederick Isler, merchant (same); for £300 proclamation money sold land [no lot number mentioned] in New Bern on Front or Water Street; border: begins at a stake on the street 30 feet S of the house where Stephen Yorke formerly dwelt now occupied by Joseph Chaddick, runs N30W 90 feet to stake, S60W 100 feet to stake, S30E 90 feet, & N60E 100 feet to Front or Water Street. (signed) Joseph Leech; (witness) Fredk. Becton & Thos Leech; [no wit. oath mentioned]; book 11 p. 138.

3423. Dec. 8, 1762 [2nd year of reign of King George III] Mary Jones before Henry

Ward esq Secretary & notary public (Newport, in "English colony" of Rhode Island & Providence plantations in New England) acknowledged annexed "warrant of attorney" as her free act; Ward is justice of peach for Newport & certified in such matters. (signed) Henry Ward; [no witness];

Dec. 5, 1761 Mary Jones, widow (Newport, Newport Co, Rhode Island & Providence plantations) to John Whiting, gentleman (Newport); power of attorney to receive from anyone money & merchandize owed to her where ever it is found. (signed) Mary Jones; (witness) Martin Howard & Amos Whiting; (Newport) Nov. 8, 1764 acknowledged by Mrs. Mary Jones before Martin Howard, JP;

Apr. 21, 1762 John Whiting, attorney for Mary Jones, to John Fonville (Craven Co); power of attorney to receive from anyone money & merchandize owed to Mary Jones. (signed) John Whiting; (witness) James Reed & Hannah Reed; [no wit. oath mentioned]; book 11 p. 139.

3424. Sept. 16, 1762 Bennoni Loftin (Craven Co) to my well beloved son John Loftin; for natural love & affection gave all my land on Strawberry Br & Southwest [Cr] [no more description]; Bennoni reserves lifetime use of the land and John can't sell it until after Bennoni's death. (signed) Bennoni Loftin; (witness) Frederick Becton, Saml Calvitt, & Frederick Isler; [no wit. oath mentioned]; book 11 p. 142.

3425. [no date] inventory of goods & chattels of Herelus Bacon deceased (late of Craven Co) taken by George Hays, administrator: a horse, 4 pains of glass, a paint stone, 7 year lease of a house in New Bern. (signed) George Hays, adm; book 11 p. 142.

3426. Sept. 26, 1760 account of goods sold at public auction belonging to estate of Charles Preson deceased: buyers are Mary Reason, Charles Shanawoollf, Arthur Carriway, Joseph Wright, William Vaughan, Francis Dawson, Christian Bowers, James Carraway, John Nelson, & Joseph Edmondson; most expensive items are 8 cattle for £11.1, feather bed & furniture £8.4, feather bed & furniture £6, & feather bed & furniture £3.10 all bought by Mary Reason and 50 yards of homespun cloth £6.5 to Joseph Wright; total is £62.16.3. (signed) Jos "Carrthers", sher; book 11 p. 142.

3427. [no date] inventory of estate of Cornelious Loftin deceased: 2 small pad locks, a hone, 2 linnen wheels, a woolling do, pair shot mould, pair bulletts, claw hamer, saw set, pair steele spurs, pair horse shoes & gimblett, carpenter's rule, 4 joyner's plain irons & stocks, parcel of cooper's tools, parcel of shoe maker's tools, 2 augers & chizell, 2 pair clamps, round shave, hand saw, iron square, whip saw, cross cut saw, hatchett, 3 ches, parcel of books, 2 pair cotton cards, 3 beds & blanketts, "reg" & sheet 16.5 "feathers", 3 bedsteads& cards, 6 puter basons, 14 do plates, 6 puter dishes, 10 chairs, a rockoon hat, a frow, 3 iron wedges, 2 drawing knives, pewter tea pot, an iron skillet, 3 earthen porangers, a stone jub, 3 weeding hoes, 2 grubbing hoes, 4 club axes, a braod axe, 2 old hoes, 2 tables, a "rephell" gun, smooth board gun, 4 iron pots, an iron kittle, 2 frying pans, 4 pot hooks, pair tongues, pair large sitllards, 3 reap hooks, 2 close boded coates, a bare skin jacket, 2 compass saddle plates, a grind stone & crank, pracel of old wooden ware, lomb & gears & slays, 4 sides of leather, a bar plow, small petteagree, 4 mugs, punch bowl, 4 bottles, 2 old pewter tankards, 3 sugar boxes, parcel of old barrels, stone chamber pot, small parcel of tallow, parcel of wool & cotton, 6 sheep, 18 pewter spoons, 18 "ouamy" spoons, parcel of woolen "you", 5 cows & calves, 2 cows & yearlings, 3 two year old heifers, 4 barren cows, 5 yearlings, a mare & yearling, 2 broke horses, a "two old" horse, a bay mare, 4 bee hives, asiften, hand mill, 4 bells, an old saddle, 8 case, parcel of cooper's timber, 2 pair old wool cards. (signed) John Turner, exr; book 11 p. 144.

3428. [no date] inventory of goods & chattels of Lazaras Pearce deceased by Ann Pearce, executrix, & John Pearce, executor: 8 Negroes—2 old fellows, a wench, 3 boys, 3 girls, 4 beds & furniture, 2 single beds, household & farming items, cooper's tools, carpenter's tools, smith's tools, 22 yards broad cloth, kitchen items, book of Bunyan's works, 10 horses, 2 mares, 27 cattle, 14 sheep, & 38 hogs; debts due to the estate £27 proclamation money; debts due by estate £31.8 proclamation money. (signed) John Pearce [Ann doesn't sign]; book 11 p. 145.

3429. sale "Oct. 16-Nov. 1" [not signed] & no estate mentioned: all gills, tody, clubs, bowls; [total may be] £2.9.2; most expensive is £0.6.8. [not signed] book 11 p. 146.

3430. Sept. 24, 1760 inventory of estate of Thomas Flybus eceased by Thomas Sitgreaves, administrator: 2 mares & a colt, "parcel" of hogs running in the woods number unknown, household items, farming tools, weavers lomb, cooper's tools, & shoemaker's tools. [not signed]; book 11 p. 147.

3431. Oct. 10, 1760 inventory of goods & chattels of Moses Davis deceased: includes linen wheel, kitchen utensils, carpenter tools, cooper's tools, household items, shoe maker's tools, farming utensils, 2 "broak" horses, a sow & pigs, 15 year old hogs, 3 barrows, a boar, 5 sheep, 2 geese, & 4 fowls. (signed) Andrew Scott; book 11 p. 147.

3432. inventory of goods & chattels of John Lovett, merchant deceased (late of Newbern, Craven Co): [hand writen] lots of cloth, wearing apparel, kitchen utensils, household items, 20 or 30 gallons of West India rum, 2 feather beds, 4 large Bibles, 3 small Bibles, 2 large Common Prayer books, & 5 testaments. (signed) Jno Smith; certified Jun. 21, 1760 by Joseph Leech; book 11 p. 148.

3433. Jul. 11, 1760 sale of sundrys belonging to estate of John Lovett deceased: buyers are William Border, John Benners, Henry Chew [or Chue], "Neal", William Borden, William Routledge, Negro man Pearo" to John Benners for £43.1.7, Negro Anthony to John Sheppard for £85.4, Negro Primus to John Benners for £95, Negro woman to Roger Jones for £20.3, William Borden, Andr

Bell, Roger Jones, Frederick Acreman, & Lewis Welch. (signed) Christ. Neal, vendue master; book 11 p. 151.

3434. Aug. 12, 1756 inventors of goods & chattels of John Carruthers deceased (late of Craven Co) by John Starkey, executor: 4 Negro men, Negro woman, Negro girl, 2 Negro children, "some" mares & colts in the woods, a horse, 3 cows, 2 calves, sow, 4 shoots, 3 feather beds & furniture, household items, milk pot, mustard pot, kitchen items, linen wheel, 3 Bibles, a prayer book, a parianger, farming utensils, & tools for mill house. sworn by John Starkey, executor before a justice of the peace (signed) Jas Davis; book 11 p. 152.

3435. Sept. 1, 1752 household goods & chattels sold from estate of Jeremiah Murphy deceased (late of Craven Co) [mostly household items except 2 Negroes Saul & Harry to John Murphey for £57.6 and some livestock]: buyers are Thomas Murphey, Ann Murphey, John Murphey, James Lepsly [or Lipty], Manuel Simmons, John "Maedanel" [or Meadanell], Edward Frank, Mark Meavis, & Thomas Burnett;
　　　　vendue continued to Nov. 1, 1752 [mostly livestock: buyers are John "Murphery", Elizabeth Farrold, Nathan Benston, A M Murphey, D O Murphery, "Marshn Mevis", Bridgle Murphery, Elizabeth "Earrold", John Jones, Jam. Leepsy. sold by Edward Frank, vendue master; book 11 p. 153.

3436. May 31, 1794 (sic) appraisement of estate of McLiniery Lee deceased: feather bed £16, carpenter tools, household items, bolsters & pillows £10, "piece" of a wig £10, 4 blankets £10, 2 "bedttels" 15, woolen wheel £2, linen wheel £6, kitchen items, farming utensils, 2 Bibles £4, 3 three year old steers £30, 5 two year old heifers 125, 6 yearling heifers £24, 2 yearling stears £8, yearling bull £3, mare & colt £27, 10 cows & calves £100, 8 cows & 9 calves £5, 8 barren cows £64, 4 six year old stears £64, 2 five year old stears £28, 4 four old stears £48, & a horse £35 [total] £787.15.7 plus three year old bull £5, "old ball" £7, & 2 bulls £14. (signed) Hardy Bryan, William Barbour, & John "Follinsworth"; book 11 p. 155.

3437. Jul. 6, 1750 sales of estate of Lionett Leech deceased: buyers are Thomas Yeamons 12 cows & calves £101.01, 6 barren cows £36, 11 young calves & bulls £45.5, red 6 years old stear £16, red stear £16, 2 six year old a five year old & 4 year old heifer £50, 2 feather beds £38.5, horse £25, bell £2.5, & hand saw £2.10.6; James Leigh 13 heifers £49; Harris Yeamons yellow stear £10; George Charleton black year old stear £15; Hardy Bryan red 4 year old stear £8 & horse £15; John "Folliensworth" red stear £16 & horse £44; Lewis Bryant red stear £11; John Phillips small branded stear £7; James Leach red stead £8.10, Hozeiah Smith an old bull £7; household items, kitchen utensils, & farming tools [total] £677.17.9. (signed) Mar. 12, 1750 William Charleton before Lewis Bryan; book 11 p. 157.

3438. Apr. 13, 1762 sundrys of estate of John Sanders deceased sold at public vendue: buyers are Margaret McDaniels, Sarah Sanders, James Pecal sr, John Bryan, James McDaniel, Thomas Wood, Peter Mallard, James Heal, Thomas "Williocks", Michael Branes, Arthur Barrins, William Harberts, & James Noble; mostly household & farming items; and 9 cattle for £10, 10 year old hogs for £5, horse bell & coller £3.10, & sorrel horse £6.19 to Sarah Sanders; 3 sows & pigs £1.12 to Arthur Barris; mare £2.13 to Isaac Barrins; & young horse £3.3 to James Noble; [total] £35.5.10 with some items added. (signed) R Cogdell, sheriff; book 11 p. 157.

3439. Aug. 10, 1757 goods & chattels of Garret Machinson deceased sold: wagon & gear £10.10, 4 beds and 3 bedsteads £22, 3 mares & horse £25.10.10, tin callender & puter pot £80.10.4, Negro woman Rose & Negro boy Basue £150 and other household items to Margaret "Machinne"; other buyer: Charles Fellonsworth; [total] £277.12.2. (signed) Shadrach Allen jr; book 11 p. 161.

3440. May 6, 1756 sundry goods sold from estate of Martin "Willis" deceased: buyers are Edmond Collins, Jno Williams, Robert Wallis, John Berry, Chas Brown, William Mills, Jon. Kerney, Edmond Cullen, Jeremiah Parsons, James Dukes, Benjamin Williams, William Glover, Peter Dukes, & Mrs. Wallis; [total] £14.15. (signed) Chris Neal, vendue master, & Elizabeth Wallis; book 11 p. 161.

3441. Jul. 20, 1751 inventory of another part of estate of Thomas Nelson deceased sold by court order: Negro boy Toby to John Hill £40.5; Negro man Harry to John Carney £57.5; Negro man Tommy for £26, Negro wench Cate £50, horse £3.15, & 109 gallons run £22.12 to Martin Wallis; 5 sheep £1.5 to Isaac Gold, 2 horses £3.15 to "Elvze Helse Tun"; & a mare £2.15 to Theophilus Man; [total] £207.12.4. (signed) John Davis, vendue master; book 11 p. 162.

3442. Jul. 13(?), 1760 inventory of estate "of sale" of Margaret "Dand": buyers are Parrigon Cox, Thomas Setgreaves, Arthur Johnston, George Hays, Thomas Swafford, & Benjamin Price; household items & a horse; [total] £4.11.9. (signed) George Hays, admr; book 11 p. 162.

3443. Sept. 13, 1757 estate of Daniel Shine deceased "to" Jas Shine, executor: (final settlement); action by Rip V Dan against deceased £2.1.4, action by deceased against "witnesses, executors" £1.12.6, action against estate of Joseph Crispin £73.15, action at sale of Mr. Starkey Mar. 1750: £4.1.10, action against estate by Rev. James Reed & W Glavin Feb. 15, 1759 £21.11.6, cash to Robert Carruthers Oct. 7, 1750 £10.11, cash to James Davis for taxes in 1754 £3.16, cash to Joseph Carruthers for taxes in 1755 £3.12, cash to jacob Blunt taxes in 1756 £6.7, cash to Christopher Neal taxes in 1757 £6.4.8, cash to John Oliver £13, rum & sugar at vendue £2.4.4, copy of judgment against William Mouate, & paid clerk John Smith & James Davis and sheriff; [subtotal] £188.6.8 + balance due £57.8.11 [total] £255.15.1. inventory of goods & chattels of John West deceased: household items, kitchen items, & clothes; whole amount at estate sale £255.15.1; (signed) James Shine; book 11 p. 163.

3444. [no name of deceased & no date] household & kitchen items, farming tools, 3 cows & calves, 2 bulls, three year old steer, a heifer, 2 year old hogs, 14 two year old barrows, 9 breeding sows, 4 sheep, a Bible, spelling book, "Reefeells" seven sermons, the duty of man, 2 primers, the Christian Monster, & 300 nails. (signed) T Rachel West's mark "X', executor; book 11 p. 164.

3445. Dec. 26, 1760 inventory of estate of John Padgett deceased: 4 beds & furniture, 2 horses, 9 cattle, kitchen items, carpenter tools, household items, a large Bible, & farming tools. (signed) Mary Padgett, adm; book 11 p. 165.

3446. Jun. 12, 1756 sale of estate of Stephen Salley deceased about 12 o'clock with 8 months credit & good security: Capt. John Isler a cow & yearling steer £1.7.4; [same to following about same price] John Parker, E Carlis, Tenas Parker, M Williocks, Str Blair, John Williocks; and other livestock to John Isler, widow Swilley, & "Jon" Isler; a gun £2.6 to John Parker, gun £0.14 to Tenas Parker, horse £3.11.8 to John Conce, horse £5.11 to Hanable Swilley, black mare £5.16 to John Gilbert, & yearling mare £1.3 to Nuholass Swilley; [total] £32.13.6. (signed) John Stanaland, vendue master by order of Joseph "Crowdas"; book 11 p. 166.

3447. Oct. 20, 1762 inventory of goods & chattels of Henry Magill deceased by Arthur Johnston, adm: horse, bridle & saddle, gun, house clock, chest, some clothes, cow & calf, table & 6 chairs, hone & case & razors, parcel of books, "a few" wigs, & a few brushes. (signed) Arthur Johnston; book 11 p. 167.

3448. Mar. 20, 1758 inventory of sale of goods & chattels of Thomas Walden deceased: [no names of buyers]; mostly clothes; [subtotal] £2.18.8 + £13.18.8 = £16.17.4. [not signed]; book 11 p. 166.

3449. Nov. 8, 1762 inventory of goods & chattels of estate of Charles "Gorden" deceased by Richard Blackledge, adm: bond Feb. 24, 1759 from Jacob Wiley to David Palmer, adm. of deceased conditioned on payment of £490.12.3 proclamation money & received "said David Palmer" £46.16.2 on Mar. 15, 1759 from "sold" to Jacob Wiley sr; bond Jul. 8, 1756 from Isaac Vandam for payment of £170.7.9 with credit of £88; May 11, 1758 Kittrell Mundline bond conditioned on payment of £106.2.5½ & received by William Palmer £62; received of William Herritage for note of Richard Williams for £8 & judgment against estate of John Forrister deceased about £7 & judgment against Edward Carter for £3.7 Jun. 20, 1757, & order by Isaac Vandam, one Kittrell Mundine for £100 accepted & all paid "of not all to pd" Charles Gordon deceased on old book of accounts. (signed) Richard Blackledge, adm; book 11 p. 167.

3450. account of sale of estate of Thomas Phillips deceased by William Duberly: buyers are William Duberly, Sarah Tire, Ruben Phillips, & Francis Pope; most items sold to W Duberly; [total] £22.18.6. (signed) Jos Carruthers, sher; book 11 p. 168.

3451. Mar. 18, 1756 inventory of goods & chattels of John Steverson deceased (late of New Bern, Craven Co) by John Starkey, executor: house hold items, 2 feather beds & furniture, bottom of a barrel of rum, brass clock, farming items, kitchen items, a horse & cart, Negro boy, 2 Negro men, Negro woman, 72 "pipe" of wine, 294 hides in work in tan yard, 2,625 lbs tan leather, 2,047 shipped to Boston, remnant of store goods returned by Mr. Hollinsworth as by agreement value £97.14.9, debts received for Nov. 15, 1750 £660.7.1, & tan yard with tools & front lot £250. (no date) John Starkey, executor of will of John Steverson, swears above is true inventory before T A Davis; book 11 p. 169.

3452. Dec. 8, 1752 sale of goods & chattels of Jacc. Sheets deceased (late of Craven Co) sold by Sevit Sheets, amd: buyers are John Franks, Hardy Bush, John Isler, "Swille Sheet", George Coonce, & John Dillahunte; mostly household & farming items except 6 cattle sold for £2.3 and "Dutch" books to Swile Sheets; [total] £16.5.5. [not signed]; book 11 p. 170.

3453. goods & chattels of estate of Grigery Hobs deceases sold: leather briches £10 to Thomas Green; cloth breches £14 to John Godner jr; money "seals" £10 to James Calf; dishes £23.01 to James Durham; man's saddle, pair silver knee buckles, & shoes £30 to Jas Carruthers; clothes & 2 pair pumps £18.20 to [blank]; 3 dimity jackets £13.5 to Jas Harris, old coat £15 to Andrew Mansfield, "dish" £25 to John Campbell; coat £17 to Samuel Griffis; 2 cloth coats £59 to Mr. Grandine; coat & jacket £44 to John Carruthers; an old hoop £375 to John Williams esq; "old hoe" £40; dressing glass, bed & 9 chairs to Soloman Rew £719.5; other buyers: Richard Caswell, James Carraway, & Abrah Bangs; [total] £2175.15.6; "errors excepted from" Prudence Davis. (signed) Sol. Rees, vendue master; book 11 p. 172.

3454. Apr. 20, 1758 inventory of goods & chattels of Honorable Peter Stanly (sic) esq: deed from commissioners of Edenton for lots #201, 202, & 203 in new plan £51; deed from Moses Moore for 320 ac in New Hanover Co; deed from Robert Jones for 500 ac in Orange Co; grant for 400 ac in Anson Co; grant for 300 ac in Anson Co; grant for 300 ac in Anson Co; bond from Geo Dosbrow for £95 due Aug. 1, 1758; 11 quires of "gitt" paper; 6 quirres of gut paper; roan horse; long list of books including Statutes at Large; 29 table cloths; household items, clothes; 2 mahogany bedsteads & 3 other bedsteads; kitchen items; cooper's tools, Negro man Peter Colley, 3 Negro boys, Negro girl Pegg; coins amounting to £83.3 Virginia currency & treasurers notes of £1216.5.8; note of Capt. Chas M Harris for £27; 9 horses, a "charriott"; 4 riding saddles; 4 cows, 2 yearlings, 2 calves, a stear, 3 sheep & lambs, 13 ducks, 5 geese, & a turkey; farming tools; kitchen items; 5 busts of royal family, print of Gov. Dobbs, silver watch key & shoe buckles; doesn't include salary due Peter Hensley (sic) esq deceased at his death. (signed) Dec. 23, 1758 (Edenton, Chowan [Co)] inventory of Peter Hensley deceased by John Campbell, executor of the will, before J "Rieustet" AJ; book 11 p. 173.

3455. Jan. 30, 1762 inventory of estate of George Barbor, deceased: 2 feather beds; cooper's tools; household & kitchen items; wooden pistle; 5 young hogs, a sow & pigs; 2 hogs; 2 cows; 3 yearlings; & a stear. (signed) William Barbour; book 11 p. 175.

3456. Jan. 24, 1761 estate of John West deceased sold by order of court by James Steverson, vendue master: buyers are Zacket West, James White, Frederick "Beeton", Rachel West, Jacob Griffin, Thomas Harrison, & Thomas Tooks; mostly household & farm items; white horse £6 to Zachell West; bay horse £6.17.4 to Frederick "Bucton"; cow & calves and 2 year old bull £4.16 & 4 hogs for £7 to R West; legacy left by Daniel West decd of £4.16 to John West sold by John West's executor £0.19. (signed) [total] £53.7. (signed) R Cogdell, sheriff; book 11 p. 176.

3457. Feb. 11, 1762 inventory of household goods of Gregg "Ipartrongh" deceased by Thomas "McGow": includes bed "executed" by Richard Cogdell; house old items; "parcel" of apothecary drugs; carpenter tools; kitchen items; & "sundry" papers the balance "not yet determined". [not signed]; book 11 p. 177.

3458. Mar. 20, 1758 sales of estate of William Whaley: 30 cattle for £30, mare for £4.6, 8 hogs £2.7, a sheep £0.7 & household items to Thos Little; other buyers of household items, shoe marker's tools, & a canoe: John Arkis, Chas Shanawoolf, William Wahon, Benjamin Guthery, James Carney, John Bidscote, Joseph "Write". (signed) sold by John "Bedseet" for Jos Carruthers sheriff; book 11 p. 178.

3459. Apr. 15, 1758 goods of Joseph Fulsher deceased sold at public vendue by James Brinson with order of Joseph Carruthers from Craven Co sheriff: Cason Brinson jr 2 beds & bolsters £4.1.4 & household items; other buyers are John Baker & John Boyd; total £8.1.2. [not signed]; book 11 p. 178.

3460. Aug. 10, 1761 sales by Craven Co sheriff of goods & chattels of Herculas Bacon deceased: Hannah Bacon a horse £4.17; Richard Cogdell 4 pair of glasses £0.4; George Hays paint stone £0.17; & Richard Fanner 7 years lease of a house £17; [total] £22.18; sheriff's 2% commission £0.11. (signed) R Cogdell, sher; book 11 p. 179.

3461. May 9, 1761 inventory of estate of Edmond Becton deceased: Negro wench & 6 children, Negro boy, mare & cost, mare & yearling, 12 year old mare, 5 cows & calves, 5 cows & yearlings, 5 yearlings, a cow, 2 year old bull, 4 heifers, 3 three year old stears, 2 four year old stears, 5 old stears, 2 old stears, & small yearling, & "cast" in hand £47.19.9. (signed) proved by Frederick Becton before Andrew Scott; book 11 p. 179.
3462. Dec. 8, 1760 inventory of estate of John Quartermees deceased: a mare, a saddle & bridle, pair of shoe buckles, pair shoes, hat, old coat, pair leather

breeches, oznabrings" shird, 2 old jackets, old pair stockings, pair garters, cutless, & pocket book. (signed) Samuel Collins, adm Jun. 5, 1758 (sic); book 11 p. 179.

3463. Aug. 7, 1760 sales of part of estate of Martin Kilgo deceased: buyers are John Mason [or Maison], John Pittman, Joseph Masters, William "Glever", Thos Cooke, James Cummings, Elizabeth "Linnch", & Thomas Parsons [mostly household, kitchen, & farming items]; [no buyer mentioned for about half of items]. (signed) Elizabeth Kilgo, adm's mark "X"; book 11 p. 180.

3464. Aug. 10, 1758 sales of estate of John Fountain deceased: [no buyers mentioned]; household items, long list of carpenter tools; kitchen items; a mare & meal tub £4.3; Negro wench Hebe £10; Negro girl Lucy £12; house & lot £10. (signed) Jas Carruthers, sher; book 11 p. 180.

3465. [no date] inventory of goods & chattels of Leonard Outerbridge deceased: black walnut table, 8 chairs, household items, kitchen items, pair silver shoe buckles, silver knee buckles, a wig, a cow, & billard table with tacks & balls. (signed) "the" administrator; book 11 p. 182.

3466. [no date] inventory of goods & chattels of estate of William "Killgs" deceased 2 feather beds & 2 bolsters, spinning wheel, woolen wheel, household items, & kitchen items. [not signed]; book 11 p. 182.

3467. [no date] inventory of goods & chattels of estate of John Jones deceased: 2 beds & bedsteads, household items, kitchen items, 7 wooden plates, carpenter tools, & farming tools. (signed) proved by "the" administrator; book 11 p. 182.

3468. [no date] remainder of sale of Martin Wallis estate from page 175 balance copies on p. 180: Solomon Northan bedstead £0.6, Thomas Maison 2 large brass kettles £16 & pair "line trn" £04; Thomas Parsons old smith's hammer £4.11. (signed) Joseph Master, vendue master, & Elizabeth Wallis; book 11 p. 183.

3469. Jul. 30, 1761 inventory of estate of Benjamin Simmons: 3 mares "3 two old", 3 horse colts, 2 young horses, 12 barrels corn at the plantation not sold, 3 cattle, 2 cows, a heifer, 32 hogs sows & shotes "in kind port" sold £41.15, an old hogshead sold at £0.5. (signed) Alexander Blacke, sheriff; book 11 p. 183.

3470. [no date] inventory of goods & chattels of Thomas & Mary Fisher deceased (late of Craven Co) by their administrators & given by Christopher Dawson, one of administrators: Apr. 1756 cash from John Lingfield one of the Sec'y of Mary Fisher for her administrators to Thomas Fisher's estate £30.11.8, a mare in the woods, cattle, "householl furniture, plantation tools", bee hives, part of sales here with cattle & hogs in woods not known, & Negroes: Sam, Ben, Tom, & Abigale & her 2 children. [not signed]; book 11 p. 183;
       inventory of goods & chattels of Thomas & Mary Fisher deceased (late of Craven Co) & prices at sale Jun. 19, 1756 by Samuel M Cabbins, deputy sheriff

to enable John "Elithert" & Christopher Dawson to pay debts: buyers are William Powell cows, calves, & stear £5.13.2; William Spaight, Peter Reel "a stag" £2.5, John Williams, Zeblson Rice, [blank] Hegan, John Hill, James Peel's wife, John Hartley, Peter Peele for his sister Mary, Jeremiah King, George Fisher, Benjamin Fordham Negro Sam £20, & John Hill Negro Ben & his wife Abigail & 2 children £193.18; [total] £233.10; "no settlement" found, there are 7 small claims against the estate & judgment Jul. 8, 1753 payable Dec. 10 "following" Thomas Fisher to William Payton with power from Rob. Jones esq for £80.11.6, & suit now in superior court against William Payton for "farr kiln" sold to him at vendue; cash received of John Leinfield Apr. 1751 £30; cash from "the William" for goods £1; balance received of "the Clitherall" £0.22; to Thomas Fisher & Rob Payton note due Sept. 21, 1751 for £16.20 with 4.5 year interest 6% £4.5; charges paid "Larane part Thos Fisher; Thomas Fisher note Jun. 24, 1749 due now; to William Powel "sisters of administration paid him"; rum at vendue at Peter Reel's £0.2.5; [total] £32.0.3. (signed) Aug. 18, 1759 Christopher Dawson, one of administrators of Thomas & Mary Fisher, swears above is true before Joseph "Seuth" JP & Andrew Scott JP; book 11 p. 184;

estate of Thomas & Mary Fisher with John Clitherall, one of administrators: 1756 by Benjamin Fordham for Negro Sam sold to him Jun. 19, 1756 £20; John Hill for Negro man Ben, his wife Abrigaile", & 2 children sold £193.10; Samuel M Cubbins, deputy sheriff his part of sale Jun. 19, 1756 £3.11.2 [total] £217.7.2; Feb. 19, 1757 Clitherall & "Sitareavision Comp" £0.11.5; William Herritage judgment £0.30.19; Costsin rect. £1.10.2; others paid: Peter Conway, William "Nuhotson", John Smith, Jacob Blunt taxe for 1755 £1, William Powell caveat against Rob Payton, Joseph Carruthers sheriff, Christopher Dawson, & James Davis. (signed) John Clitherall; Aug. 18, 1795 John Clitherall swears above is true before Joseph "Sueh" JP & Andrew Scott JP; book 11 p. 185.

3471. John Berry to orphans of John Nelson deceased goods sold & used: money £136.19.3, orphans part of a still £40, cattle sold at Marramasuit £11.11.8, judgment against Jas Smith £6.13.10, received as per books £16.3.4; 4 mares & 6 old blankets & sheets £6.15, sundries at pt books & £5.0.9; debts received of Rich Whitehouse £5; cash £5; stears Mrs. Berry killed white she was widow £30 or £2.10 valued by James Nelson; cash received in "No" county £2; [total] £273.14.6; portage sold by former order of court still standing £42.13. [not signed]; book 11 p. 186.

3472. Dec. 28, 1762 sale of estate of Southey Rees deceased by Willsby Bartlet & wife Mary, adm. & admx: 2 cows & calves & 2 heifers for £4.12 and 8 cattle for £10.7 to Willsby Bartlet; 2 cows & a yearling for £2.10 and parcel of cattle in woods between Adams Cr & South R for £18.2.6 to Chris Neal; a cow & yearlings for £3 to Will Mill; parcel of cattle "over" South R for £17.7 to John Kerney; other buyers: Stephen Mahain, John Guess, Samuel Warner, Roger Jones, & John Pittman. [not signed]; book 11 p. 187.

3473. [no date] John Berry to orphans of John Nelson deceased for goods sold &

used: [same as list on p. 186 by John Berry]; book 11 p. 187.

3474. Dec. 28, 1762 Dec. 28, 1762 sale of estate of Southey Rees deceased by Willsby Bartlet & wife Mary, adm. & admx: [same as list on p. 187 for same estate]; book 11 p. 188.

3475. [no date] [probably John Nelson estate] sundries per book account £172.16.4; sundries per account £5.11.10; sundries cash £2.14.8; cash paid Benjamin Hall £8.16; caps paid orphans in their lot £13.13.6; paid off cattle on the banks allowed by James Nelson £2.11.8; commissions for receiving £434.3.5 = £21.14; commissions for paying £218 to orphans of Nathaniel Hall deceased at 5% = £10.18; [total] £239.5.7; balance due orphans £34.5.11; [new total] £273.14.6; we were appointed to settle estate of John Nelson deceased & set the orphan's shares apart & we find it as above (signed) Jno Mill & John Oliver; book 11 p. 188.

3476. [sale list, no estate mentioned] buyers are Chris Neal, Wills Bartlet, Wm Fulcher, John Kerney [or Kaeney] £11.5 for chest drawers, large chest, tea chest, & 6 silver tea spoons (also bought other items), James Fulford, Willsby Bartlet £11.1 for horse, mare, cart, & wheels and £7.5.4 for 15 sheet & £112.1 for 2 beds, 2 pair sheets, rug, 2 bedsteads, malls, & carts (also bought other items); John Pittman £3.13 for 10 cattle (also bought other items); William Good; Step. Mahain; Abner Neal jr; Wm Mill; Robert Berney [or Burney]; Robt Willis; James Physor; Adam Wallis; John Forguson; John Cumins; & Thomas Mason; [total] £190.10.5 (mostly household & farming items). (signed) R Cogdell, sheriff; book 11 p. 189.

3477. [no date] account of sales of part of estate of Stephen Wallis deceased by Robert Wallis executor: buyers are James Edmonson, Rob Wallis, Stephen Wallis, Ben Hall, Abner Neal sr £11.5.6 for cow & calf (and bought other items), Abner Neal jr, John Weymouth, Mary Rees, Thomas Tegnor, Susanna Wallis, William Mills, John Kerney £3.17 for bed, bolster, bedstead, & cord, & Rich Elderidge; total £27.0.8. (signed) Chris Neal, vendue master;

[no date] further account of sales of Stephen Wallis' estate: 2 cows, calves, heifer, sow, 7 shotes, & old weaving loom £6.5 to Abner Neal jr; 3 year old horse £3 to Stephen Wallis; feather bed, boulster, bedstead, & cord £4 to John Cook; "puoter" dish & bason £1.10 to Rob Wallis; [total] £13.15; "whole sale" £40.15.8. (signed) Robert Wallis, executors; book 11 p. 192.

3478. Feb. 13, 1759 inventory of goods & effects of James Fulford deceased: 2 feather beds, 2 boulsters, 10 old chairs, household items, kitchen items, woolen & linen wheels, carpenter's tools, farming items, & fishing net. (signed) James Conaway before Samuel Cornell swears above is true; book 11 p. 193.

3479. Apr. 6, 1760 account of sundries sold from estate of Mary McCubbins deceased: buyers are Wm Whitford, John Smith, Samuel McCubbins, Edward

Frank, Mackinney, William Barren, George Powel jr, Benjamin Lewis, James Grun, David Farnville, James Green, Joseph Leach, Samuel Slade "deceased", Mary Fardson, David Fonerell, William Brown, Henry Black, Rebecca Morgan, Isaac Fornville, Mrs. Coward, Benjamin "Tomsan", Peter Conway, Eck. Bogey, Eliah Bogey, Moses Taylor, William Snead, John Tomlinson, Farnefold Green, mallatto Jane £20 to Conway; [no total indicated] mostly household & kitchen items and livestock. (signed) Jas Carrathers; book 11 p. 194.

3480. Mar. 7, 1763 will of Deeme Dunn (Craven Co): in name of God Amen; (a) soul to God & body to be buried in Christian manner; (b) all my estate to be sold & after paying debts remainder to be divided between cousins Samuel Robert, & Margert Himan; (c) Samuel Robert [or Samuel, Robert] to be sole executor. (signed) Deeme Dunn; (witness) Thomas Whitford, "guard"; book 11 p. 196.

3481. Aug. 22, 1761 will of William Palmer, merchant (Newbern, Craven Co): in name of God Amen; (a) debts & funeral charges to be paid; (b) all my real & personal estate to be sold by executors to pay debts & funeral charges; (c) remainder go to my "next heirs"; (d) Joseph Leech (of New Bern) is executor to settle affairs in North Carolina and Abel James (of Philadelphia) is executor of will & settle affairs in Pennsylvania. (signed) Will Palmer; (witness) Nathl. Richardson, James Cook, & James David; book 11 p. 197.

3482. Nov. 1758 court ordered John "Clethereall", Joseph Leach esq, & James Parkinson or 2 of them to examine accounts of Deborah Outerbridge, admx of Leonard Outerbridge deceased, & report to Feb. Next court. (signed) Peter Conway, PC;

Feb. 1759 John Cletherall & Joseph Leech report they examined account of Deborah Outerbridge & find balance of £8.11.1 besides her commission which comes to £6.6.3; £8.11.1½ (sic) + £6.6.3 = £14.17.4½ (signed) John Cletherall & Joseph Leech; book 11 p. 197;

Deborah Outerbridge, adm. of "Genl" deceased: she paid Jno Fonville, John Callahan, Fountain, Joshua Bryant, Carruthers, Munelien, Saml Cornell, Thomas Graves, Rev. Reed, Fisher's company for funeral charges £1.11.8, Peter Knight for house rent £14.7.6½, James Parkinson, sheriff, & "burying Patt" & attendance £1.10; her commission on £126.6.1½ was £6.63; book 11 p. 198.

3483. [no date] estate of Samuel McCubbin deceased: "reem" at funeral £3, sugar at vendue £0.5, sheriff's commission at sale £1.14.4, cash to Sam Starkey £33, cash to Tom Carrathers £2.17.2, cash to Jacob Blunt £4.10.6, Mr. Powel bought at vendue £5.6,8, cash to Jas Leech £0.14.2, letters of administration £0.16.8, paid Samuel Lawson for judgment £0.6.4, commission £5.8; [total] £59.8.10 + "to balance" £9.10.4 = £68.19.2; fees paid Jas Hall May 11, 1758 £1.1; balance due estate £8.9; [final total] £11.10.4. [not signed]; book 11 p. 198.

3484. Nov. 16, 1758 "which" were "Lenord" Outerbridge (of Craven Co) account of administrator: sale of billard table £27.10; sales of inventory £25.6.6; by cash of John "Bouds" £5; balance due adm. £8.11.1½. (signed) Deborah Outerbridge; [total] £67.8.7 ½; Nov. 1758 foregoing account proved by adm. (signed) Peter Conway, CIC; book 11 p. 199.

3485. Feb. 17, 1758 Mary Mackubbin, adm: sales at vendue £68.1.2; sundries sold after £68.19. (signed) Mary "McUbbin", adm; balance "due brought down due" the estate £9.10.4; paid Elinor "Wilch" "as pact." £2.6.5; fees "Elioner" Welch as adm £1.1; paid Jas Hall, Pres. £3; balance due estate £3.1. book 11 p. 200.

3486. [no date] inventory of goods & chattels of Patrick Doyle deceased (late of Craven Co) by John Kemedy, adm: a "Taylor" goose" & shears, 8 yards checked linen; clothes; sewing items; 1 quire of tobacco; 3 cows & calves; cow & yearling; 2 barron cows; heifer; & £5 of old tinner bills [or bells]. (not signed); book 11 p. 200.

3487. Nov. 12, 1762 Elizabeth Martin, widow (Craven Co) to my loving grand child Adam Forguson, planter (same); for love & good will gave 320 ac on W side of South R & S side of Neuse R; border: begins at his own & Isaac Gould's corner gum at head of Martin Cr and joins "Martin boundarys"; granted Sept. 21, 1741 to Thoams Martin. (signed) Elizabeth Martin; (witness) J A Jones jurat, Macumb Forguson, & Lydia Latemore; [no wit. oath mentioned]; book 11 p. 200.

3488. Dec. 7, 1762 Levin Lane, planter (Craven Co) to Stephen Duey, gentleman (Halifax Co, NC); for £120 proclamation money sold house & 0.5 ac in lot #256 in New Bern; border: begins at corner of Broad Street & Hancock Street; lot is 6.5 by [omitted]; sold Jun. 6, 1753 by New Bern commissioners to "Sollomon Rue" who sold Oct. 4, 1754 to Levin Lane. (signed) Levin Lane; (witness) Andrew Scott & James Steverson jurat; [note at end indicates Lane received £120]; [no wit. oath mentioned]; book 11 p. 201.

3489. Dec. 4, 1762 James Combs (Craven Co) to Richard Blackledge, merchant (same); for £35 proclamation money sold Negro man Cesar. (signed) James Combs; (witness) Benj Corle jurat & Isaac Tull; book 11 p. 203.

3490. Sept. 13, 1759 Benjamin Hall, planter (New River, Craven Co) to Joseph Edmondson, planter (same river & county); for £2.4 proclamation money sold 100 ac on E side of head of Cashaw Cr & N side of plantation where Joseph Edmondson lives; border: begins at a white oak 25 poles N of said Joseph Edmondson's corner tree, joins a "pocosion", & run of Cashaw Cr. (signed) Benjamin Hall; (witness) Thomas Edmondson, James Edmondson, Samuel Barclift, & John Mill jurat; [no wit. oath mentioned]; book 11 p. 203.

3491. Mar. 14, 1763 James Herring, planter (Craven Co) to my son James Herring jr (same); for love & "eximation" gave, immediately after my death, 131.5 ac on S side of "Jo" [South] West Cr; includes "plantation" where I dwell; part of half of grant Apr. 24, 1762 to 263 ac Joseph Mason who sold to me; 263 ac is equally divided by line from "the" spring branch to "the" back line; upper part "for" southermost is the part given to my son. (signed) James "Hearon's" mark "X"; (witness) Thos Hays jurat & Armwell "Horon"; wit. oath 1763 (superior court) by Thos Hays; book 11 p. 204.

3492. Mar. 15, 1762 Jonas Ives, planter (Craven Co) to Isaac Simmons, planter (same); for l25 proclamation money sold 50 ac on N side of Neuse R & on N side of Lower Broad Cr; border: begins at mouth of Whittises Cr, joins Broad Cr, mouth of Little Cr above Fork Point, head of Little Cr, Jacob Jones, & a branch that makes out of Whites Cr; where Jonas Ives lives. (signed) Jonas Ives' mark "X"; (witness) Thomas Martin & Thomas Simmons jurat; wit. oath 1763 by Thomas Simmons; book 11 p. 205.

3493. Apr. 14, 1763 James Sheith, planter (SC) to Benjamin Sheith, planter (same); for £100 proclamation money sold 170 ac on N side of Neuse R; border: begins at a white oak near mouth of Beaverdam [Cr] and joins Bass; part of grant Feb. 10, 1737 to [omitted]. (signed) James Sheith; (witness) John Allen jurat & Isaac Carter; [no wit. oath mentioned]; book 11 p. 207.

3494. Jul. 4, 1761 Robert Wallace [or Wallis], planter (South River, Craven Co) to John Booth, waterman (Craven Co); for £20 proclamation money sold 100 ac on E side of South R; border: begins at a small black gum on "the" West side, joins John Thomlinson's line that parts Thomlinson's land from land of Stephen Wallace deceased, & land where widow Wallis lives; part of Mulberry Point land & "presently" known as Muriek's place. (signed) Robert Wallace's mark "R W"; (witness) Joseph Pettman [or Petman] & Robert Williams; [note at end indicates Booth paid Wallace £20 on Sept. 4, 1761]; book 11 p. 208.

3495. Nov. 25, 3rd year of reign of King George III [1763] Joseph Mason, planter (Onslow Co, NC) to James Herring, planter (Craven Co); for £5 proclamation money sold 260 [263 at end of deed] ac; border: begins at Jacob Griffin's corner pine and joins James Herring; granted Apr. 24, 1762 to said Jos Mason. (signed) Joseph Mason's mark "X"; (witness) Mathew Mason & Jas Herring jurat; wit. oath Jul. 1763 (superior court) by Jas "Herreing"; book 11 p. 210.

3496. Sept. 24, 1762 Jane Tear, widow (Craven Co) to my beloved sons Richard & William Tear; for natural love gave: 2 beds & beds with all the furniture belonging, 3 puter dishes, 17 puter plates, a puter bason, 3 iron potts, an iron kettle, 5 legged chairs, a linen wheel, a chest & small trunk, black walnut "coel" table, water pale, small pan, stone mugg, coffee pot & funnel, & an old logwood axe; property to be equally divided between them. (signed) Jane Tear's mark "X"; (witness) Sarbrough Tankard & Sam Griffis; wit. oath Apr. 1763 by [blank]; book 11 p. 211.

3497. Dec. 28, 1761 John Norwood, planter (Craven Co) to John Coor [or Core] (Newbern, Craven Co); for £8 proclamation money sold 0.5 ac in lot #43 in New Bern; border: joins Front Street & Bryan Street. (signed) John Norwood; (witness) Mary Coor & Jacob Shepard jurat; wit. oath Apr. 1763 by Jacob Shepard; [note at end indicates Coor paid Norwood £8 on Dec. 28, 1761]; book 11 p. 211.

3498. Apr. 7, 1763 John Starkey esq (Onslow Co, NC) & Mary Crawford, formerly Mary Carruthers, executor & executrix of will of Joseph Carruthers esq deceased ([late] of Craven Co) to William Powell, gentleman (New Bern, NC); for Joseph Carruthers signed his will in 1759 appointing above executors; for £1 sold 190 ac below forks of the 2 new roads above Mr. Powell's; border: begins at John Fonvill's lower corner, joins Samuel Griffis, & Mrs. Powell. (signed) John Starkey & Mary Crawford; (witness) Sarah Rice & James Davis jurat; [note at end indicates Powell paid Starkey £20]; wit. oath Jul. 1763 by James Davis; book 11 p. 212.

3499. May 12, 1763 John Williams esq (Newbern, Craven Co) to William Powell (same); for £16 proclamation money sold front of lot #114 on Water Street in New Bern; sold Mar. 5, 1749 by Cullen Pollock to John Williams. (signed) John Williams; (witness) Richard Cogdell & James Steverson; wit. oath Jul. 1763 by Richard Cogdell; [note at end indicates Powell paid Williams £16 on May 12, 1763]; book 11 p. 213.

3500. Apr. 15, 1760 Elizabeth Martin (Craven Co) to Joseph Pittman, planter (same); for [amount omitted] sold Negro boy Luke, son of Negro woman Abb "in whose hands, custody, possession, or keeping so ever he can or may be found". (signed) Elizabeth Martin's mark "X"; (witness) John Pittman jr, Prudence Wallis, & Nancy N Wallis; wit. oath Jul. 1763 by John Pittman; book 11 p. 214.

3501. Mar. 26, 1763 Thomas Davis (Craven Co) to John White (same); for £20 proclamation money sold 100 ac on White Oak Pocosin; border: begins at a white oak, joins a dividing line, & "the" home line; part of 212 ac tract. (signed) Thomas Davis; (witness) John Tuton, Robt White jr, & William White; wit. oath Jul. 1763 by "Robert White"; book 11 p. 214.

3502. Jan. 20, 1763 [3rd year of reign of George III] John Taylor, planter (Craven Co) to Thomas Wilson, planter (same); for £40 proclamation money sold [blank] & 70 ac on [blank]; border: begins at a white oak on said creek; granted [blank] 1736 to Henry Roberts [blank spaces in part of deed]. (signed) John Taylor; (witness) Thomas Hays jr & Christian Leary; wit. oath Jul. 1763 by "Thomas Hays"; book 11 p. 215.

3503. Dec. 10, 1756 Thomas Pollock esq (Craven Co) to William Bourke (same); for rents mentioned leased 200 ac; formerly in possession of [blank]; Bourke to build a bridge as per his "engage 18 days of May last"; [also mentioned] profits enacted by act of Assembly for a bridge at [blank] by Michael Wigens who formerly lived on said plantation; rent [blank] for next 15 years. (signed) Thomas Pollock & William Bourke; (witness) Robert Jones & John Markett;

    Feb. 12, 1756 I assign my interest in within lease to Robert Come for £5 proclamation money (signed) William "Bourk"; (witness) John McGraw & J

Kennedy; wit. oath Jul. 1763 by John Markett; book 11 p. 216.

3504. Dec. 11, 1760 John Lavender, planter (Craven Co) to Philimon Morris, planter (same); for £4 proclamation money sold 20 ac on Trent R & N side of Little Chinkapin Cr; border: begins at a gum on the river 45 poles below mouth of Little Chinkapin Cr, joins a branch, & joins mouth of the creek. (signed) John Lavender; (witness) William Morris & George Koonce jr; wit. oath Jul. 1763 by "George Koonce"; book 11 p. 216.

3505. Nov. 9, 1762 [2nd year of reign of George III] Elizabeth Martin (Craven Co) to Stephen Wallis, planter (same); for £5 sterling Great Britain money sold 150 ac on W side of South R between Keeling's Cr & Log House Cr; border: joins William Mill & John Pittman [no more description]. (signed) Elizabeth "E" Martin's mark "X"; (witness) Robert R Wallis, Lyda Lattamore, & John Cummings; wit. oath Jul. 1763 by Robert Wallis; book 11 p. 217.

3506. Jun. 17, 1762 Jeremiah Taylor [or Tailor], planter (Craven Co) to Stephen Wallis, planter (same); for £20 proclamation money sold 30 ac on head of Savannah Cr & on S side of South R making out of Neuse R; border: begins at an ash near mouth of a branch, runs up middle of the branch to "the" fork, "through" a chinkapin bridge, & joins "the" head line; part of tract Abner Neal sold to me. (signed) Jeremiah Taylor; (witness) William Davis, Solomon W Davis, & Robt R Wallis jr; wit. oath Jul. 1763 by "Robert Wallis"; book 11 p. 218.

3507. Apr. 5, 1763 Edward Gatlin, planter (Craven Co) to Thomas Gaskins [Gaskin] (same); for £20 proclamation money sold 80 ac on N side of Neuse R; border: begins at a pine near Pamlico Road & joins a branch; called "the" thoroughfare land; granted to John Gatlin sr; except 6 ac laid out for Ann Bright. (signed) Edward Gatlin; (witness) James Coor jr & James Arthur; wit. oath Jul. 1763 by "James Coor"; book 11 p. 219.

3508. Jan. 27, 1763 John Pearce, planter (Craven Co) to Edward Gatlin (same); for £37 proclamation money sold 200 ac on N side of Neuse R; border: begins at a pine on the pocosin side. (signed) John Pearce; (witness) James Coor jr, Mrs. West, & James Pearce; [note at end indicates Gatlin paid £37 in 1763] [not signed]; wit. oath Jul. 1763 by James "Coor"; book 11 p. 220.

3509. Apr. 25, 1763 Thomas Hays, planter (Craven Co) to Solomon Gray, planter (same); for £25 proclamation money sold 81 ac on E side of Southwest Cr; border: begins at a hickory on side of Signal Br, joins a meadow near Southwest Cr, mouth of Great Br; granted Sept. 29, 176 to Abram Taylor. (signed) Thomas Hays; (witness) Christian "Teange" & A W Heron; Jul. 1763 acknowledged; book 11 p. 221.

3510. Jul. 4, 1763 Edmond Hatch (Craven Co) to Robert Grimes (same); for £5 proclamation money sold 500 ac on S side of Trent R; border: begins at James

Frazier's corner pine and joins John Lee; granted Oct. 22, 1762 to [omitted]. (signed) Edmond Hatch; (witness) Laura Hatch & Benj Hatch; Jul. 1763 acknowledged; book 11 p. 221.

3511. Jul. 27, 1762 Stephen Wallace, planter (Craven Co) to John Dixon (Carteret Co, NC); for £20 proclamation money sold 100 ac; border: begins at mouth of a branch that makes out of a creek "up" South R on E side which parts "Benry" Nelson & the premises & runs up the swamp to a cypress swamp. (signed) Stephen Wallace's mark "X"; (witness) John Brage & William Davis; Jul. 1763 acknowledged; book 11 p. 222.

3512. Ju. 10, 1762 Isaac Simmons to John Fulcher, planter; for £20 proclamation money sold 60 ac on S side of Lower Broad Cr; border: begins at [blank] formerly owned by Lemenett Harvey, joins Francis Dawson, Harvey's Pocosin, Giddous Cr, Thomas Simmons, & "the" main line; granted Nov. 11 [blank]19 to Rice Price. (signed) Isaac Simmons' mark "X"; (witness) William Fulcher, Thos Simmons, & Robert Barney jr; [no wit. oath mentioned; blank spaces at beginning of deed]; book 11 p. 223.

3513. Apr. 16, 1763 William Pratt (Craven Co) to George Phenny Lovich (same); for £60 proclamation money sold 100 ac on S side of Neuse R & on Golves [blank] out of Slocumbs Cr; border: begins at mouth of a branch at head of a large cove making out of said creek, joins Riggs, & "the" head line. (signed) William Pratt; Joseph Wall & Jacob Taylor; wit. oath Jul. 1763 by Joseph Wall; [note at end:] George P Lovich's mark [is] a crop staple fork in each ear [not signed]; [blank spaces at beginning of deed]; book 11 p. 224.

3514. Apr. 5, 1762 James Frazier, planter (Craven Co) to Robert Grimes, planter (same); for £10 proclamation money sold 46 ac; border: begins at an oak in a branch between his "plantation" & Daniel Beniar & joins Reedy Br. (signed) James Frazier; (witness) James M "Danale" & Edmond Hatch jr; Jul. 1763 by "Edmond Hatch"; book 11 p. 225.

3515. Apr. 22, 1763 Joseph Reasonover (Craven Co) to William Lipsey (same); for £50 proclamation money sold 100 ac on N side of Trent R; border: begins at a black gum between said Joseph Reasonover & "carper granted" land and joins Trent R. (signed) Joseph Reasonover; (witness) John Hatch, Benj Hatch, & Edmond Hatch jr; wit. oath Jul. 1763 by "Edmond Hatch"; book 11 p. 226.

3516. Jul. 6, 1763 John Lingfield sr, planter (Craven Co) to my beloved son John Lingfield (same); for natural love & affection and £1,000 proclamation sold Negro man Peter, Negro woman Sude, all my working tools "to bellander" farming or hand craft, all my wearing apparell, all my water crafts, a gray horse called Whistler, my own riding ridge & saddle, a breading mare called Pleasure, a gun, pair of "and" irons, a bell, "mettle" spice morter & pestle, pair of spoon "milds", a saddle, & grinding hand mill. (signed) John Lingfield's mark

"X"; (witness) Jno Rice & Benj Williams; wit. oath Jul. 1763 acknowledged; book 11 p. 227.

3517. Jul. 26, 1762 Thomas Green (Nacin, Craven Co) to Thomas Franklin (Craven Co); for £25 sold 150 ac on N side of Neuse R at head of Dochams Cr; border: joins Garrott & Hyman; granted Sept. 1, 1759 to [omitted]. (signed) Thomas Green's mark "X"; (witness) Joseph Wright, Benj Rice, & Benj Williams jr; wit. oath Jul. 1763   by "Benj Williams"; book 11 p. 227.

3518. Apr. 9, 1763 John Lingfield (Craven Co) to James Tingle; for £15 sold 100 ac on N side of Neuse R & S side of Upper Broad Cr; border: begins at a gum at mouth of Murry Br, joins head of the branch, William Case, "the" back line, & Andrew Grinder; being land Christopher Dawson "got a deed for". (signed) John Lingfield's mark "X"; (witness) David Lewis & Edward Williams jr; wit. oath Jul. 1763 by "Edward Williams"; book 11 p. 228.

3519. Apr. 19, 1763 John Gess (Craven Co) to John Carney (same); for £12 proclamation money sold 40 ac on E side of Adams Cr & in fork of Lewis Cr; border: begins at John Frabody's corner oak on E side of N branch of said creek, joins Nelson's old patent, Abner Neal jr, & E branch of said creek; where said John Gess lives. (signed) John Gess' mark "X"; (witness) Elias Justice & James "Godfery"; Jul. 1763 acknowledged; book 11 p. 229.

3520. Apr. 7, 1763 John Heath, before John Williams JP, swears he bought from "Middlesex in Virginia" Martin Black, a "free" Negro, who faithfully served his time to best of Heath's knowledge who was bound by his mother to him for 21 years. (signed) John "T" Heath & John Williams; wit. oath Apr. 1763 (inferior court) deposed in open court (signed) Peter Conway, CIC; book 11 p. 230.

3521. Apr. 10, 1763 Mary Heborn (Craven Co) to my loving children: (a) to James and Steven [Stewart ?]; for love, good will, & affection gave, after my death, 2 blankets, 2 potts, pair of pot hooks, moving dresser, 2 puter dishes, 8 puter plates, 6 deep plates, 2 puter basons, 4 basons, 4 wooden dishes turned, 4 chairs, 6 "ditto" of cups & sausers, 2 tea pots, 4 deep dishes, an ovell table; (b) to son Charles Stewart (sic), after my death, an iron kettle, an ovell table, a cubbard dresser, 4 puter dishes, 8 puter plates, 6 deep plates, 6 deep dishes, a skillett, pair of tongs, 4 wooden dishes, a feather bed, bedstead, & boalster, 2 pillows, 4 chairs, pine table, 6 cups & saucers, a tea pot & cream jug, blanket, 2 iron pots, 2 pair pot hooks; (c) to son George Stewart, after my death, a walnut table, feather bed, bolster, & 2 pillows, pair of sheets, 12 puter plates, 3 deep dishes, a tea kettle, 3 washing tubs, 3 plates; & (d) to grandchild Mary Pope a side saddle & 2 silver tea spoons. (signed) Mary Hebron's mark "X"; (witness) Searborough Tankard & Hugh Moore; Jul. 1763 acknowledged; book 11 p. 230.

3522. Mar. 5, 1763 (Quaker style date) John Bishop sr (Clubfoot Cr, Craven Co) to Henry Stanton & Joseph Stanton (Core Cr, Carteret Co, NC) & John

Thomlinson (Clubfoots Cr, Craven Co), in trust for Quakers; for love & regard I have for people of God called Quakers gave 1 ac on W side of Clubfoot Cr; border: begins at a cedar post on side of a branch near SE corner of said John Bishop's Bridge, runs S29E 135 feet along the branch to Bishop & Horton's corner pine, S63W 236 feet on dividing line between said John Bishop & Parmenius Horton to a cedar post, N 84 feet to cedar post, N52E 202 feet to first station; land sold for "executing" a meeting house for "waiting upon & worshiping" Almighty God and laying out a burying yard for burying their dead and no other purpose; if any of the trustees die or are removed, then the 2 remaining trustees can choose a successor at the monthly meeting. (signed) John Bishop; (witness) Roger Jones & John Bishop jr; [no wit. oath mentioned]; book 11 p. 230.

3523. May 28, 1763 Abner Neale (Craven Co) to William Fulcher (same); for £50 proclamation money sold 150 ac on N side of Neuse R, S side of Orchard Cr, & on mouth of said creek; border: begins at a marked pine at mouth of Orchard Cr, joins a point, Thomas Fulcher, Elias Martin deceased, a branch, & head of a small creek. (signed) Abner Neal; (witness) John Carney & Robert "Barney" jr; wit. oath Jul. 1763 by "Robert Barney"; book 11 p. 231.

3524. Mar. 21, [1762 ?] 2nd year of reign of George III John Fillyaw, wheelright (Craven Co) to William Perry (same); for £84 proclamation money sold 200 ac in 2 tracts: (a) 100 ac on S side of Tuckeho Cr; border: begins at a red oak on "the" river side; & granted Nov. 11, 1743 to John Fillyaw; & (b) upper tract is 100 ac; border: begins at a red oak on "the" river side & joins a swamp; granted May 7, 1754 to John Fillyaw. (signed) John Fillyaw; (witness) Daniel Shine, James Green, & Wm Waddell; Jul. 1763 acknowledged; book 11 p. 232.

3525. Mar. 5, 1763 (Quaker style date) Parmenas Horton, merchant & distiller (Clubfoot Cr, Craven Co) to Henry Stanton & Joseph Stanton (Core Cr, Carteret Co, NC) & John Thomlinson (Clubfoots Cr, Craven Co), trustees for Quakers; for love & regard I have for sorship of Almighty God & his people called Quakers gave 1 ac on W side of Clubfoots Cr; border: begins at said Horton's & John Bishop's corner pine near a branch side, runs S 142 feet to cedar post, W 215 feet to cedar post, N 24 feet to dividing line [with J Bishop], & N63E 236 feet along said line to first station; sold for executing" a meeting house for worshiping Almighty God & laying out burying yard to bury their dead & no other; if any of the trustees die or are removed, then the 2 remaining trustees can choose a successor at the monthly meeting. (signed) "Permenus" Horton; (witness) Roger Jones & John Bishop jr; [no wit. oath mentioned]; book 11 p. 233.

3526. Aug. 21, 1762 John Deep (Craven Co) to Benjamin Foscue (same); for £40 proclamation money sold 200 ac on W side of Brice's Cr; border: begins at corner red oak next to Robert Coleman and runs up the creek & "out into the woods" [no more description]; part of 500 ac grant to William Brice esq. (signed) John Deep's mark "X"; (witness) John Brown & Bazell Smith; Jul. 1763 acknowledged; book 11 p. 234.

3527. Aug. 28, 1759 sales of [estate of] Jeremiah Parson deceased: buyers are David Reasonover a gun £0.5, Daniel Smith jr a gun £0.19.4, John Mitc. powder 4 lbs shot £0.7.8, Ross Simpson a gun £2.1.4, Richard Smith sword & carterage box £0.9, John Oliver, Robert Blake, James Duke, Mary Roe, Sarah Masters, Sarah Parsons, John Mason, John Pittman, John Parsons, Thomas Mason, Jeremiah Taylor, Francis Hill, Thos Parsons a mare £4, John Bishop, Joseph Masters, John Burnes, James Bell, William West, Elijah Tognest, John Benners, Adam Wallis, Rolin Moor, John Russell, Huphrey Smith, Solln. Northan, Edmond Mitchell, John Carney, John Mill, Edmond Cullen, John Williams, Thos Pittman, Thos Cook, James Jones, Thos Rue, Thos Duke, Charles Rue, James Cummins 2 large hogs £1.13, John Staton 4 hogs £2.1 & a mare £3.2, John Pender 4 hogs £1.3.8 & 5 hogs £1.13, John Carney 4 hogs £2.2.4, Arthur Johnston 11 hogs £2.2.4, John Cook, William Northan a mare £4, John Cook a horse £4.2, James Jones, "Rimond" Cullen, Easther Parsons, James Phenny, Jane Margin, Abner Neal sr, Nathan Huddle, John Weymouth, S Dixon, W Martin, Richard Graham, John Horton, Ben Williams, Sarah Masters, Patrick Cannon, Henry Stanton 7 sheep £3, Thos Bishop 7 sheep £4.4, John Pender 14 sheep £7.7, Mary Rue, John Mill, John Oliver, J Barrenton, N Dunn Negro man £82.10, & Jas Hancock Negro woman £106.5 [mostly household & farming items];

3527b. sale of "last part" of estate of Jeremiah Parsons deceased: buyers are John Carney, John Pittman, John Russell, Abner Neal sr, Thos Parsons, Joseph Royal, Thos Cook, John Wamouth, James Jones, John Williams, John Stanton, Patrick Coner, John Parsons, John Russell, Thomas Parsons jr, William Dunn, Jane Morgan, Betty Hill, James Cummins, Berry Nelson, John Mill, Richard Graham, Francis Hill, William West, Sarah Parsons, Thos Rue, Solomon Northan, J Taylor, Chas Rue, John "Esquires", Abner Neal jr, Solomon Dixon, Edmond Cullen, Elijah Jackevers [or Jackwost], William Churcheron, Lewis "Witch", Thos Gassops, John Benners, H Smith, David Reef, Adam Farguson, S Dickson, Nathan Hudwell, Daniel Smith jr, John Lingfield, & Nathan Hurdle [mostly household & farming items];

3527c. Apr. 1761 inferior court sales of estate returned by administrator: buyers are John Mill, Arthur Johnston, Richard Graham, John Pender, Jno Smith, L Thomas, Thoms Parsons, James Bell, S Masters, John Mill, Elijah "Jackive", & Francis Hill [mostly livestock]. (signed) Thomas Parsons' mark "X" "proved by adm"; book 11 p. 234.

3528. Dec. 28, 1762 John Willcocks (Craven Co) to Stephen Willcocks (same); for £350 proclamation money sold set of saw mills & a tract of land [omitted] ac on N side of Crooked Run; border: at head of the saw mill, runs down "the runs", joins the river, Hatch, & head of the mill pond [no distances in description]. (signed) John Willcocks; (witness) Isaiah Wood & Thos Willcocks jr; wit. oath Apr. 1763 by Thomas Willcocks;

[no date} David Dunn's mark is a crop & under keele in left ear & crop & over keele & slit in right ear [not singed]; book 11 p. 239.

3529. May 18, 1763 James Parkinson esq (Craven Co) to John Levingston esq, merchant (New York City, NY); for £700 proclamation money sold 0.5 ac lot #18 in New Bern; border: begins at corner of Front Street & [blank] street; lot is 13 by 6.5 poles; sold Oct. 15, 1741 by William Wilson esq (of Craven Co) to John Bryan who with wife Amanda sold Jan. 10, 1758 to James Parkinson. (signed) James Parkinson; (witness) John Kennedy & John Rice; [note at end indicates "Livingston" paid Parkinson £700]; (Edenton, NC) wit. oath May 23, 1763 by John Kennedy before Charles Berry; book 11 p. 240.

3530. Aug. 7, 1761 account of sale of residue to estate of Stephen Wallis deceased: buyers are John Kerney Negro man (no name) £100, Stephen Wallis, John Benners, Edmond Cullen, Joseph Pittman, James Fulford, Adam Wallis, Sam Warner, William Mill, Jas Pittman, John Sallman, Rawlens Williams, Sarah Tignor, Jas Bell, John Pittman [sub total] £124.17.8; more buyers S Forguson, Robert Wallis, Abner Carter, Edmond Mitchell, George Parkins, Abner Neal sr, John Taylor, Adam Forguson, John "Danners", & Chas Rew; [total] £145.11.2. (signed) Chrisr. Neal, vendue master; book 11 p. 241.

3531. May 15, 1753 goods & chattels sold from estate of Mr. Evan Jones deceased: buyers are John Buck bay horse £6.6, 3 cows & calves £6.12, John Barrows dark bay horse 14.12, John Bonner 3 cows & calves £5.2 & 3 cows & yearlings £5.5 & 2 yearling stears & 2 yearling heifers £2.10, Jas Jones, Edmond Cullen, John Lovett, Lewis Welch, Saml Masters, Jon. Tunneyville, George Lee, Grigg Yarborough, Ben Cummins, Mrs. Masters, Thos Lovick esq, John "Physion", Jas Griffith, John Taunyhill, John Lovick, Roger Jones, Benj Small, John Bishop [mostly household & kitchen items]. (signed) Thos Lovick & "Rodger" Jones before Jas Jones; book 11 p. 242.

3532. Sept. 5, 1759 inventory of goods of Joseph Lee deceased: set of pump tools, set of carpenter tools, 2 beds, parcel of walnut planks & some timber, and household & kitchen items. (signed) Christian Lee, widow of Joseph, before Andrew Scott, JP; book 11 p. 243.

3533. Jun. 20, 1763 James Parkinson esq (Newbern, NC) to Richard Hamilton, merchant (same); for £95 proclamation money sold Negro woman Betty; sale void if Parkinson pays Hamilton £95 proclamation money by Jul. 1, 1762. (signed) Jas Parkinson; (witness) John Rice & Robt Gordner; [note at end indicates Hamilton paid Parkinson £95 on Jun. 20, 1763]; wit. oath Jul. 21, 1763 by Robert Gordner before Fras "Corber" AJ; book 11 p. 244.

3534. Apr. 2, 1763 John Stanton (Craven Co) to John "Papsons" (same); for £8 proclamation money sold 100 ac on head of Back Cr [no more description]; granted Apr. 24, 1762 to John Stanton. (signed) John "S" Stanton's mark "X"; (witness) Chas Rice jr, John Pittman, & Wm James; wit. oath Apr. 1763 by Chas Rice; book 11 p. 245.

3535. Sept. 1, 1762 Jacob Taylor, planter (Craven Co) to my beloved son William Taylor; for love & good will gave, after my death, 200 ac; border: begins at a sloping hickory on a "pount" on SE side of main branch of Southwest Cr above said Taylor's house, joins Taylor's pasture, & Southwest Creek Swamp; where said William Taylor lives. (signed) Jacob Taylor's mark "X"; (witness) Thos Hayes & Christian Judge; [no wit. oath mentioned]; book 11 p. 245.

3536. account of estate of Capt. William Marsh deceased by Robert Gordon: amount of Richd Hamilton account paid him £304.14.9 ½, amount of Vallentine Wade's account 111.3, balance of Capt. "and" Bryan's account £4.1, Hannah Tolson for attendance of Capt. Marsh in his sickness at Portsmouth £1, paid Robert M Lane for care of Capt. Marsh £2, Chas "Dunde" for a gun £0.6, Peter Conway clerk £6.3.8, Wm Herritage attorney £0.1.10, Peter Conway for action against Stephen Cade for $21 & cost £3, Wm Herritage & Richard Caswell attorneys 12.5, Martha Hayes £1.13.8, John Callough "on" barber £0.2, Richard Daves constable £0.8, my commission on sale of £32.6.19 at 10% is £32.13.10 (sic), [total] £371.2.42; balance "on other side" £25.16.12. (signed) Robert Gordon; Apr. 1762 (inferior court) John Williams, John Cuthrell, Jas Davis, Saml Carroll, & Thos Haslen or 2 of them to settle with Robert Gordon as executor of will of William Marsh deceased & report to next inferior court. (signed) Peter Conway, clerk; book 11 p. 246;

Oct. 22, 1764 Joshua Cemp's mark is upper slop & a slit in right ear and crop & nick in left ear (signed) Peter Conway, register; book 11 p. 246;

Feb. 25, 1762 [Robert] Gordon esq [further accounty]: sales of sundries by Mr. Cogdell £319.9.4, "emmeated dutys" received from Richard Hamilton of £224.11.6 that Capt. Marsh paid him in "W I" £11.3, cash from Mr. Hamilton for commissions on £291.1.11 that Capt. Marsh bought for him in West Indies £71.5.9, cash received from Capt. John Mill £5.10, cash on 1 gunery 37/6 proc. £1.18.8, [total] £345.6.3, balance due Robert Gordon £25.16.12, Williams order to Jas Parkinson £27, William Bourke's note £3.10 "this" was a gambling account as he has gone out of the county & no effect; (New Bern) Jul. 16, 1763 John Williams, John "Edthridge", Thos Haslen, & Jas Davis examined vouchers & account & find balance of £22.16.1 ½ to Robert Gordon executor & £30 due to estate of William Marsh; book 11 p. 246;

Nov. 7, 1764 Isaac Cemp's marks is crop & 2 slits in right ear and slit & nick in left ear (signed) Peter Conway, register; book 11 p. 247.

3537. Jul. 8, 1763 John Williams, residing chairman of Craven Co Inferior Court, "put" as apprentice Jacob Fulcher, orphan of Joseph Fulcher deceased age 15, to Robert Burney (of Craven Co); Jacob to dwell until age 21 according to act of Assembly in such cases & be obedient to his master; Burney agrees to provide apprentice with "convenient & sufficient" meat, drink, lodging, & apparel, and do his best to "interest" Jacob in art of "shop" joiner and teach him to read & write. (signed) Robert Burney (sic); (witness) Chas Cogdell [only one witness]; [no wit. oath mentioned]; book 11 p. 247.

3538. Jul. 8, 1763 John Williams, residing chairman of Craven Co Inferior Court, bound as apprentice John "Marvis", orphan of Mark Mavis deceased age 14, to James Cunningham (of Craven Co); John to reside with Cunningham until age 21 as by act of Assembly in such cases and be faithful to his master; Cunningham will "allow" John "convenient & sufficient" meat, drink, lodging, & apparel, do his best to "interest" John in art of a taylor, & teach him to read & write. (signed) Jas Cunningham (sic); (witness) Richard Hamilton [only one witness]; [no wit. oath mentioned]; book 11 p. 247.

3539. Apr. 8, 1763 John Williams, residing chairman of Craven Co Inferior Court, bound as apprentice Walter Dunn, orphan of Newman Dunn age 12, to John Miller (of Craven Co); Walter to reside with master until he is 21 according to act of Assembly in such cases and be obedient in all things during that time; Miller will provide "convenient & sufficient" meat, drink, lodging, & apparel, do his best to "interest" Walter in art of a taylor, & teach Walter to read & write. (signed) John Miller & John Williams; (witness) P Ambrose & John Dudly; [no wit. oath mentioned]; book 11 p. 248.

3540. Jan. 7, 1764 John Williams, residing chairman of Craven Co Inferior Court, bound as apprentice Richard Daves, orphan of Richard Daves deceased age 9, to Joseph Jones (of Craven Co); Richard to reside with master until he is 21 according to act of Assembly in such cases and be obedient in all things during that time; Jones will provide "convenient & sufficient" meat, drink, lodging, & apparel, do his best to "interest" Richard in art of a mariner, & teach Richard to read & write. (signed) John Williams & Joseph Jones; (witness) Peter Conway [only one witness]; [no wit. oath mentioned]; book 11 p. 248.

3541. Apr. 4, 1764 John Williams, residing chairman of Craven Co Inferior Court, bound as apprentice William Bush, orphan of Levi Bush deceased age 18, to Frederick "Areman" (of Craven Co); William to reside with master until he is 21 according to act of Assembly in such cases and be obedient in all things during that time; Areman will provide "convenient & sufficient" meat, drink, lodging, & apparel, do his best to "interest" William in art of a cooper, & teach William to read & write. (signed) "Frederick Arehman's" mark "X" & John Williams; (witness) Isaac Patridge [only one witness]; [no wit. oath mentioned]; book 11 p. 248.

3542. Apr. 4, 1764 John Williams, residing chairman of Craven Co Inferior Court, bound as apprentice Daniel Bush, orphan of Levi Bush deceased age 7, to Frederick Acreman (of Craven Co); Daniel to reside with master until he is 21 according to act of Assembly in such cases Deed be obedient in all things during that time; Acreman will provide "convenient & sufficient" meat, drink, lodging, & apparel, do his best to "interest" Daniel in art of a cooper, & teach Daniel to read & write. (signed) John Williams & "Frederick" Acreman's mark "X"; (witness) Isaac Patridge [only one witness]; [no wit. oath mentioned]; book 11 p. 249.

3543. Apr. 4, 1764 John Williams, residing chairman of Craven Co Inferior Court, bound as apprentice William Bush, orphan of Levi Bush deceased age 18, to Frederick Acreman (of Craven Co); Daniel to reside with master until he is 21 according to act of Assembly in such cases and be obedient in all things during that time; Acreman will provide "convenient & sufficient" meat, drink, lodging, & apparel, do his best to "interest" William in art of a cooper, & teach William to read & write. (signed) John Williams & "Frederick" Acreman's mark "X"; (witness) Isaac Patridge [only one witness]; [no wit. oath mentioned]; [same as #2540 above]; book 11 p. 249.

3544. Apr. 4, 1764 John Williams, residing chairman of Craven Co Inferior Court, bound as apprentice Daniel Bush, orphan of Levi Bush deceased age 7, to Frederick Acreman (of Craven Co); Daniel to reside with master until he is 21 according to act of Assembly in such cases and be obedient in all things during that time; Acreman will provide "convenient & sufficient" meat, drink, lodging, & apparel, do his best to "interest" Daniel in art of a cooper, & teach Daniel to read & write. (signed) John Williams & "Frederick" Acreman's mark "X"; (witness) Isaac Patridge [only one witness]; [no wit. oath mentioned]; [same as #2541 above]; book 11 p. 250.

3545. Jan. 6, 1764 John Williams, residing chairman of Craven Co Inferior Court, bound as apprentice Esney [or Esiney] Beesley [female], orphan of [blank] deceased age 7, to Phillip Miller (of Craven Co); Esney to reside with master until he is 21 according to act of Assembly in such cases and be obedient in all things during that time; Miller will provide "convenient & sufficient" meat, drink, lodging, & apparel, do his best to "interest" Esney in art of reading & writing (sic), & teach Esney to read & write. (signed) Phillip Miller & John Williams; (witness) Isaac Patridge [only one witness]; [no wit. oath mentioned]; book 11 p. 250.

3546. Apr. 4, 1764 John Williams, residing chairman of Craven Co Inferior Court, bound as apprentice Hardy Allard, orphan of [blank] deceased age 17, to Thomas Fish (of Craven Co); Hardy to reside with master until he is 21 according to act of Assembly in such cases and be obedient in all things during that time; Fish will provide "convenient & sufficient" meat, drink, lodging, & apparel, do his best to "interest" Esney in art of a cooper, & teach Hardy to read & write. (signed) Phillip Miller & John Williams; (witness) Isaac Patridge [only one witness]; [no wit. oath mentioned]; book 11 p. 250.

3547. Oct. 4, 1762 John Rice, coroner (Craven Co) to Richard Cogdell esq (Newbern, Craven Co); for £40 proclamation money sold (a) 0.5 ac in lot #44 (in the old plan or 50 in new plan) in New Bern; sold in 1731 by Cullen Pollock & Walter Lane, New Bern commissioners, to John Rodgers who with wife Sarah sold Dec. 15, 1738 to William Norwood who sold "sometime" in Dec. 1739 to Thomas Norwood who sold Mar. 30, 1750 to John Bryan for £50 old tenner or

£6.13.4 proclamation money; & (b) front of lot #17 in New Bern; sold Mar. 6, 1746 by Cullen Pollock (of Tyrrell Co, NC) to John Bryan for £12; sold due to writ of fieri facias from Craven Co Inferior Court of Pleas & Quarter Sessions Jul. 10 2nd year of reign of George [III ?] & returnable to court first Tuesday in Oct. instant against John Bryan for £35.15 proclamation money debt & £2.4.5 costs due to suit by Richard Cogdell; and sold due to act of Parliament of Great Britain passed in 5th year of reign of King George II concerning collection of debts in America. (signed) John Rice, coroner; (witness) A M Fenner & Richd Fenner; [(unsigned) note at end indicates Cogdell paid £40 on Oct. 4, 1762]; Nov. 13, 1762 acknowledged by John Rice before Chas Berry, JP;

Jul. 14, 1764 mark of Joseph McKime is crop & under bit in right ear and crop & slit in left ear. (signed) Peter Conwar, register; book 11 p. 251.

3548. due to act in 7th & 8th years (sic) [1696 or 1697 ?] of King William III "intitated part for providing frand & registration abeses in the plantation trade", William Stewart, master of sloop Dispatch, sworn the sloop Dispatch of Carolina is square stearned vessel of burthen 20 tons or thereabouts was "someally" by same name being a price condened here in 1758 as appears by a "jayner" registered now delivered up & cancelled an amount of tons or of property & he with Wm Gasten are present owners thereof; no "younger" directly or indirectly has any part or interest therein. (signed) William Stewart; "Walter Murry—D #6%"; May 25, 1763 (Custom House, "Kingston") [blank] "made oath to the above register" (signed) W H Syath; Sept. 17, 1763 recorded (signed) Peter Conway, register; book 11 p. 252.

3549. Oct. 4, 1762 Jacob Taylor, carpenter (Craven Co) to Benjamin Telson, cooper (same); for £15 proclamation money sold 300 ac on S side of Neuse R & opposite head of Otter Cr; border: begins at a gum in a small branch "at" Beards Cr. (signed) Jacob Taylor; (witness) John Jones & Rebecca Jones "jr"; wit. oath Oct. 1762 by Rebecca Jones; book 11 p. 253.

3550. Nov. 22, 1761 Owen Daugherty, planter (Craven Co) to Solomon Carmack, planter (same); for £50 NC money sold 100 ac on S side of Neuse R; border: begins at a pine on upper side of Mosley Cr & joins a branch; part of a "quarter tract" granted [date blank] to Levi Trenwith. (signed) Owen Daugherty; (witness) John Carmack & Jas Carmack; "1761" acknowledged; book 11 p. 253.

3551. Apr. 15, 1758 inventory of estate of John Mare & May Mare, due to order of court from John "Thomlison" executor & Elizabeth Martin executrix of Thomas Martin deceased, "to our" plantation on South R & 8 Negroes: Sarah, Luke, Sam, Primas, Juda, Tamar, Sarah, & Samuel all received into my care (signed) Jacob Blount; book 11 p. 254.

3552. Jun. 25, 160 inventory of estate of Joseph "Masters State" deceased: kitchen items, farming items, horse, mare, household items, carpenter tools, 4 feather beds, 79 bee hives, note for £15.10.1, note for £26.5.4, "Negroes & half of three more", 54 cattle, 15 hogs, & 9 sheep. (signed) Thomas Cook jr & Saml Masters jr; book 11 p. 254.

3553. May 26, 1763 John Relf, merchant (Philadelphia) to my loving friend Saml Cornell (New Bern, NC); power of attorney to receive money & good due to me by anyone. (signed) John Relf; (witness) Peter Knight & John Frank; wit. oath Jul. 1763 by Peter Knight; book 11 p. 255.

3554. Aug. 25, 1765 William Miller, planter ("North-folk" Co, Virginia) to John Carney, gentleman (Craven Co); for £50 proclamation money sold 200 ac on S side of Neuse R & on W side of Adams Cr; border: begins at a pine at mouth of an Alligator Pond on W side of the river, joins Capt. Neal's line of land he bought of Matthew Godfrey to "the head", & another of Neal's lines; "taken out" of a large grant to J Smith. (signed) William Miller; (witness) Jas Godfrey & Jas Jones jr; [note at end indicates Carney paid Miller consideration money on Aug. 25, 1763]; wit. oath Oct. 1763 by "Jacob" Jones; book 11 p. 255.

3555. Apr. 16, 1763 John Nelson (Craven Co) to Charles Rue (same); for 110 proclamation money sold 40 ac on S side of Neuse R & E side of Adams Cr; border: begins at a pine at mouth of a little creek that parts said land from Adam Lewis "the land" that now belongs to Mr. John Frabody, joins head of head of a branch, Shad Br, & head of a gut; part of grant to Thomas Lewis sr. (signed) John Nelson; (witness) Jab. Jones, B Rue, & Wm James; wit. oath Oct. 1763 by Jacob Jones; book 11 p. 256.
3556. Sept. 28, 1763 Jas Frazier (Carteret Co, NC) to Jas Simmons (Craven Co); for 140 proclamation money sold 60 ac on S side of Trent R; border: begins at John Simmons' corner pine & joins a branch; part of granted to said Jas Frazier. (signed) Jas Frazier; (witness) John Hatch, Robt Grimes, & Edward Hatch; wit. oath Oct. 1763 by Robert Grimes; book 11 p. 257.

3557. Oct. 5, 1763 Robert Grimes (Craven Co) to Jas Simmons (same); for £1.3 proclamation money sold 100 ac on S side of Trent R; border: begins at a white oak near head of a small branch in Jas Frazier's patent line and joins "Edmnd patent" line; part of grant to Edmond Hatch and sold to Robert Grimes. (signed) Robert Grimes; (witness) Anderson Gillett William Banan; Oct. 1763 acknowledged; book 11 p. 258.

3558. May 21, 1763 "for some time past" there hae been disputes between Thomas Pollock & Edmond Hatch & Daniel Simmons about bounds of 1,500 ac formerly granted to "Honorable" Thomas Pollock esq deceased; the parties mutually agreed to refer matter to following arbitrators: Francis Brice, John Physon, Jas Hancock, John Smith, Jas Green, John Bryan, Jas Williams, Peter Rhem, William Baston Whitford, John Franks, John Williams, & Moses Hoston; SO arbitrators met on the premises and were qualified; they "tried" lines of Pollock's patent and found: begins at an ash beside of Trent R near "and" Indian old field being upper corner of land formerly patented by Barron D Graffinreid, runs S59W 264 poles up the river to a pine stump on the river bank proved to be upper corner by oath of Francis Brice who was present at the survey, runs S31E 430 poles into the woods, N59E 332 poles to Barron D "Griffin's" line, & then to bound by said line to beginning agreeable to survey & marked lines made today; we award lines of patent now settled to be proper bounds. (signed) Francis Brice, Jno Physon, Jas Hancock, John Smith, Jas Green, John Bryan, Jas Williams, Peter Rhem, W B Whitford, John Franks, John Williams, & Moses "Houston"; (witness) Christopher Neal & Farnifold Green, surveyors;

"Mar. 28" Emanuel Simmons & Daniel Simmons swear a certain dead pine that Francis Brice swears he believed to be the tree he marked for Mr. Pollock's corner when it was green & it was marked like a corner tree and was called & known as Pollock's corner tree above 20 years as they remember (signed) Emanuel Simmons & Daniel Simmons before John Williams;

Mar. 28, 1763 Francis Brice, age 60, swears sometime in 1723 or 1724 he went "up test" with Thomas Pollock & John Baptist Ash, a surveyor, to survey some land for Thomas Pollock, they went to an old field called Adsters and began at a tree at the river, then ran out to a pine under a hill, then various courses of the "mast" to the river, then along the river to a pine close to the river about 150 yards below an old field called Franchmen old field and be marked the pine at request of Pollock as upper corner, today Brice went with Thomas Pollock, John Williams esq, Lemuel Hatch, Daniel Simmons, Emanuel Simmons, "Basset" Simmons, John Granade, John Johnston, Amos Small, Jas Edmond Hatch, & John Hatch to place he believed the upper corner tree stood & found a dead pine with rotten stump, Brice believes this was the corner pine he marked on above date for Thomas Pollock, Brice says he was chain barrier when land was surveyed (signed) Francis Brice & John Williams;

Apr. 28, 1763 Thomas Pollock, gentleman (Craven Co) to Edmond Hatch & Daniel Simmons; a bond for £1,000 proclamation money; bond void if Pollock abides by final determination of arbitrators: Francis Brice, John Physon, Jas Hancock, John Smith, Jas Green, John Bryan, Jas Williams, Peter "Rhen", Wm Whitford, John Franks, John Williams, & Moses "Holston". (signed) Thomas Pollock; (witness) John Granade & John Hatch; book 11 p. 259.

3559. Aug. 1, 1763 Jesse Holton sr, planter (Beaufort Co, NC) to George Holton, planter (same); for £12 proclamation money sold 75 ac on S side of Bay R; border: divided from other part by the river "direct crossing to the back line" [no more description]; being upper half of 150 ac sold Apr. 9, 1761 by Jos Martin to Jesse Holton sr & part of grant Nov. 14, 1730 to Daniel Shine. (signed) Jesse Holton; (witness) Jas "Willocks" & Thos Cuthrell; wit. oath Oct. 1763 by Thos Cuthrell; book 11 p. 260.

3560. Oct. 7, 1763 Isaac Van "Dum" & John Smith (Newbern, Craven Co) and Joseph Crispin (Craven Co) to "warship of all trustees" or Justices of Craven Co; a bond for £1,500 proclamation money; Van Dum was appointed guardian of Mary Lester, orphan & minor (of Craven Co); bond void if Van Dum brings Mary up during her minority & "non age" with necessary meat, drink, washing, lodging, apparel, & learning "according to her degree" and guard her goods & land from goods & chattels of William Lester "or" Joseph Black deceased or anyone else; Van Dum to give the property to Mary when Mary is 21 or marries & account for all loss. (signed) Isaac Van Dum, John Smith, & Joseph Crispin; (witness) Peter Conway [only one witness]; Oct. 1763 by acknowledged; book 11 p. 261.

3561. Mar. 8, 1763 Charles Holton (Craven Co) to Edward Gatlin (same); for £50 proclamation money sold 150 ac on E side of Swift Cr; border: begins at a red oak; half of 300 ac "equally divided" and sold by executors of will of Edward Bryan to [omitted] "of the same half to be taken at the eastward" & near Joseph Dawson; granted in 1742. (signed) Charles Holton; (witness) Jas Gatlin & Harry Jones; wit. oath Oct. 1763 by Jas Gatlin; book 11 p. 262.

3562. Jul. 8, 1763 Richard Cogdell, high sheriff (Craven Co) to Andrew Scott esq, doctor in physic; for £101 proclamation money sold 0.5 ac in lot #82 on Hancocks Street in New Bern; sold Feb. 20, 1756 by Walter Lane & John Bryan, late New Bern commissioners, to Joseph Carruthers; being house where Joseph Carruthers lived; sold due to writ of fieri facias from New Bern Dist Superior Court May 11, 1763 & returnable to court Nov. 2 next against Joseph Carruthers deceased (late of Craven Co) in hands of John Starkey, Chas Crawford, & Mary Crawford "otherwise" Carruthers his wife executrix of will of Joseph Carruthers for £399.15.10 proclamation money & £3.12 costs due to suit by Andrew Scott & John Rice for "non performance of certain promises & appurtenances" by Joseph Carruthers in his lifetime; and sold due to act of Parliament of Great Britain passed in 5th year of reign of King George II concerning collection of debts in America. (signed) Richard Cogdell; (witness) Peter Conway & Richard Fenner; [note at end indicates Scott paid Cogdell £101 on Jul. 8, 1763; Oct. 1763 acknowledged; book 11 p. 263.

3563. Aug. 23, 1763 Andrew Scott esq, doctor of physic, to John Green, merchant (Newbern, Craven Co); for £120 proclamation money sold 0.5 ac in lot #82 on Hancock Street in New Bern; sold Feb. 20, "1746" by Walter Lane & John Bryan, late New Bern commissioners, to Joseph Carruthers; being house where Joseph Carruthers lived; sold by Craven Co sheriff for £101 proclamation money due to writ of fieri facias from New Bern Dist Superior Court May 11, 1763 & returnable to court Nov. 2 next against Joseph Carruthers deceased (late of Craven Co) in hands of John Starkey, Chas Crawford, & Mary Crawford "otherwise" Carruthers his wife executrix of will of Joseph Carruthers for £399.15.10 proclamation money & £3.12 costs due to suit by Andrew Scott & John Rice for "non performance of certain promises & appurtenances" by Joseph Carruthers in his lifetime; and sold due to act of Parliament of Great Britain passed in 5th year of reign of King George II concerning collection of debts in America. (signed) Andrew Scott; (witness) Richard Cogdell & Richard Fenner; [note at end indicates Green paid Scott £120 on Aug. 23, 1763; wit. oath Oct. 1763 by Richard Cogdell; book 11 p. 264.

3564. Aug. 1, 1761 John A Brice, planter (Craven Co) to John Pender, mariner (same); for £100 sterling Great Britain money sold 500 ac on N side of Neuse R & on Brices' Cr; border: begins at mouth of Adeston's Br of the creek, joins Francis Brice jr, back line of the patent, Rigdon Brice's patent; known as "the" Rich Land; part of land left by "C" Williams Brice at his death to his 2 sons Francis & William Brice now deceased. (signed) John A Brice; (witness) John Jones & John "Pendor" jr; wit. oath Oct. 1763 by John Pendor jr; book 11 p. 266.

3565. Jan. 20, 1763 Joseph Crispin, mariner (Craven Co) to Jas Roberts, planter (same); for £35 proclamation money sold 2 tracts: (a) 200 ac on N side of Neuse R & upper side of Dawsons Cr; where said Roberts dwells; border: begins at Christopher Dawson's patent corner of land where Joseph Atherly dwells, joins said of Dawsons Cr, & back line of the patent; being lower part of grant to Richard Johnson and by "sundry conveyances" became Joseph Crispin's property; & (b) 90 ac on S side of above 200 ac & includes land between "the same" & Miry Br; granted to Jos Crispin [reference to grant for metes & bounds. (signed) Joseph Crispin; (witness) S "Justices", Thos Green, & Chris Neal; [note at end indicates Roberts paid Crispin £35 on Jan. 20, 1763; wit. oath Oct. 1763 by Christopher Neal; book 11 p. 267.

3566. Oct. 3, 1763 George Foy, planter (Craven Co) to Simon "Spight" (same): for £48 proclamation money sold 50 ac on N side of Trent R & W side of "Beavor" Cr; border: begins at a white oak near the creek; granted Sept. 14, 1737 to John Vandozent. (signed) George Foy; (witness) George Metts, Fred Becton, & F Becton; [note at end indicates Spight paid Foy consideration money Oct. 3, 1763]; wit. oath Oct. 1763 by Fred Becton; book 11 p. 267.

3567. Oct. 8, 1763 Richard Cogdell esq (Craven Co) to John Council Bryan, planter (same); for £30 proclamation money sold front of lot #16 in New Bern; border: 30 feet in front of "the" street; now in occupation of William Ervin merchant (of New Bern). (signed) Richard Cogdell; (witness) Isaac Vandam & David Gordon; Oct. 1763 acknowledged; book 11 p. 268.

3568. Jan. 20, 1763 Jas Roberts, planter (Craven Co) to Christopher Neal (same); for £10 proclamation money sold 2 tracts on N side of Neuse R & on upper side of Dawson's Cr: (a) 25 ac; border: begins at mouth of a small creek or gut where said Roberts lately dwelled, joins side of Dawsons Cr, "mouth" of the race path, head of western branch of the gut, & Joseph Crispin; part of Richard Graves' "old" patent; & (b) 60 ac; border: begins at corner oak of Graves & Randolph Fisher's patents near mouth of Dawson's Cr and joins eastermost branch of a gut; being eastern part of said Roberts' new patent where he lately dwelled. (signed) James Roberts; (witness) S Justice, Thos Green, & Joseph Crispin; [note at end indicates Neal paid Roberts consideration money Jan. 20, 1763; wit. oath [no date] by Joseph Crispin; book 11 p. 269.

3569. Feb. 25, 1763 Charles Holton, planter (Dobbs Co, NC) to John Harris, carpenter (Craven Co); for £50 proclamation money sold 150 ac on E side of Swift Cr; border: begins at a white oak in Mason's line. (signed) Chas Holton's mark "X"; (witness) Edward "Gottin", Jas Gallin, & Thos "Gallon"; "except Edward Bryan patent" [written at end of deed]; wit. oath Oct. 1763 by Edward Gallin; book 11 p. 270.

3570. May 28, 1763 James Herbert, planter (Dobbs Co, NC) to John Browning, planter (Craven Co); for £30 proclamation money sold 100 ac in fork of Neuse R & "Contentary" Cr; border: begins at a water oak on side of the creek low ground at mouth of a small meadow and joins river low grounds; part of grant Oct. 24, 1762 to James Herbert. (signed) James Herbert's mark "X"; (witness) John Allen jr, Benj Heath, & Isaac Carter; wit. oath Oct. 1763 by "John Allen"; book 11 p. 271.

3571. Oct. 9, 1762 Richard Cogdell, high sheriff (Craven Co) to William Ramsey & William Wilton, merchants in company (same); for £149 sold 0.5 ac opposite lot #20 in front of New Bern; border: begins on S side of Trent [R] at a post or boundary of Joseph Balhe lately deceased in front of lot #19, runs N80W 88.5 (sic) poles, S10W 6.5 poles to the river, S80E 6.5 poles along the river, & straight line to beginning; sold Apr. 21, 1747 by Fulder & Williams Powell to Mary Wilson who sold May 23, 1757 to Robert Herbin deceased; present sale subject to mortgage Nov. 7, 1760 by Robert Herbin to John Smith (of New Bern) for £107.6 proclamation money; sold due to 3 writs of fieri facias from New Bern Dist Superior Court & Grant sessions May 2, 1762 against Robert Herbin inn holder (late of New Bern, NC) for £120.4 proclamation money debt & £4.16.6 costs and writ against Robert Herbin for £87.8.8 proclamation money due to suit by William Ervin for debt & £3.15.2 costs and writ for £114.8 proclamation money against Robert Herbin due to suit by William Ramsey & William Wilton for debt & £9.9.3 costs; and sold due to act of Parliament of Great Britain passed in 5th year of reign of George II concerning collection of debts in America. (signed) Richard Cogdell, sheriff; (witness) Richard "Coswell" & John Smith; Sept. 6, 1763 I acknowledge I received, out of "neat pounds" of sale of Robert Herbin's estate, full satisfaction for mortgage mentioned in this deed (signed) John Smith; Oct. 1763 acknowledged; book 11 p. 272.

3572. Feb. 11, 1763 Henry Roberts, planter (Craven Co) to Nathan Ward, planter (same); for £20 proclamation money sold 250 ac on S side of Southwest Cr; border: "bounded by courses of the patent" & divided from remainder of "said" 350 ac by Great Br that Thomas Hays lives on, Great Br & course of said patent are on SW side of Great Br (sic) [no more description]; part of grant Apr. 10, 1761 to said Henry Roberts. (signed) Henry Roberts; (witness) Aaron Williams jr & Christian "Legry"; wit. oath Oct. 1763 by "Aaron Williams"; book 11 p. 273.

3573. Jul. 11, 1763 John Acton Brice, yeoman (Craven Co) to Elihue Hall, planter (same); an agreement: Brice to lease for 20 years to Hall (a) land & dwelling house near New Bern on Brice's Cr; known as Rich Land "plantation"; & (b) a good work horse and 12 cattle; for his "care" Hall can take a fourth of increase of the cattle every 3 years; if house needs repairing, then Hall to do repair & charge to account of Brice and this amount will be "discounted" from the rent; yearly rent is £6 proclamation money due Dec. 25 next "for the term"; Brice's "quiet wahing & lodging" [mentioned]; if Brice marries, then Hall is exempt from entertaining Brice and will release dwelling house to Brice and a "free" priviledge of the rent of land to clear & plat; Brice will deliver to Hall his 2 Negro men: Jane (sic) & Ralph on condition Hall finds Negroes sufficient clothing & diet & pay "all levys"; Hall will pay Brice £12 proclamation money per year for hire of Negroes; if Negroes become incapable of service by sickness or accident or be absent, then Hall will deduct the time lost; parties agree to bond for £1,000 proclamation money for faithful performance of agreement. (signed) John Acton Brice & Elihue Hall; (witness) Stephen Yorke & Jacob Sheppard; wit. oath Oct. 1763 by Jacob "Shepard"; book 11 p. 274.

3574. Jul. [blank], 1763 John Starkey, gentleman (Onslow Co, NC) and John Hollinsworth, planter (late of Craven Co & now of [blank] Co) to Joseph Bryan, gentleman (Craven Co); for £80 proclamation money sold 250 (sic) ac in 2 adjoining tracts on N side of Neuse R: (a) 100 ac on N side of Neuse R; border: begins at a pine on a pocosin, joins Cat tail Swamp, "the" main road, & Hickson; sold Aug. 13, 1753 by John Peters (of Craven Co) to John Hollinsworth; & (b) 145 ac; part of 300 ac granted May 2, 1744 by David Gurganus to John Hollinsworth and "not before" sold by Hollinsworth. (signed) John Starkey & John Hollinsworth; [no witness]; [note at end] both tracts formerly mortgaged Sept. 28, 1758 by John Hollinsworth to John Starkey recorded in Craven Co book N p. 118 (signed) Chas Hollinsworth & John Starkey (sic); Oct. 1763 acknowledged; book 11 p. 275.

3575. Oct. 3, 1763 Edward Williams, planter to Richard Hill, planter (same); for £40 proclamation money sold 100 ac on N side of Neuse R, on head of Goose Cr, & on both sides of the swamp on E & W "side" of the swamp; border: begins at beginning pine on edge of the pocosin, joins a dividing road, a small branch, the swamp, & "the" back line; part of 275 ac granted Sept. 26, 1751 to Amos Cuthrell who sold to Edward Williams who sold to Richard Hill. (signed) Edward Williams; (witness) Edward Gatlin, Thos Cook, & John Parsons; wit. oath Oct. 1763 by Thos Cook; book 11 p. 276.

3576. Jun. 27, 1761 William Palmer, Joseph Leech, & Barnaby Coffie, merchants (Craven Co) to David Smith (Newbern, Craven Co); a bond for £827.11.4 proclamation money; bond void if Palmer, Leech, & Coffie pay Smith £413.15.8 proclamation by Jan. 1 next with lawful interest. (signed) Will Palmer, Joseph Leech, & Barnaby Coffie; (witness) Rept. Lam & Phil Ambrose; [no wit. oath mentioned]; book 11 p. 277.

3577. Aug. 26, 1763 Samuel Berry, planter (Craven Co) to Henry Heath, planter (same); for £35 proclamation money sold 100 ac on S side of Neuse R; border:

begins at a cypress on the river, joins first branch, Williams Br, & Southwest Cr. (signed) Samuel Berry; (witness) John Heath & Thos Wetherington; wit. oath Oct. 1763 by John Slade (sic); book 11 p. 277.

3578. Mar. 20, 1763 John Heath sr to my well beloved son Thomas Heath; for natural love & affection gave 90 ac on S side of Neuse R & near Dudley Gordon's Br; border: near "plantation" where John Heath sr lives [no more description]. (signed) John Heath sr; (witness) John Heath "sr jr" & Henry Heath; "wit. oath" Oct. 1763 by John Heath sr; book 11 p. 278.

3579. May 8, 1763 James Herbert, planter (Dobbs Co, NC) to John Browning, planter (Craven Co); for £30 proclamation money sold 100 ac in fork between Neuse R & "Contentaray" Cr; border: begins at a water oak beside the creek low ground at mouth of a small meadow & joins river low ground; granted Oct. 24, 1761 to James Herbert. (signed) James Herbert's mark "X"; (witness) John Allen jr, Benj Heath, & Isaac Carter; [no wit. oath mentioned]; [almost same as deed on p. 271]; book 11 p. 279.

3580. Mar. 17, 1763 Edward Gatlin, planter (Craven Co) to Edmond Pierce (same); for £22 proclamation money sold 100 ac on N side of Neuse R [no more description]; granted Oct. 8, 1747 to Joseph Mason. (signed) Edward Gatlin; (witness) Zebulon Rile, John Gatlin, & Edward Gatlin (sic); wit. oath Oct. 1763 by Zebulon Rile; book 11 p. 279.

3581. Apr. 17, 1762 Solomon Smith (Craven Co) to Longfield Cox; for £20 proclamation money sold 300 ac on S side of Neuse R & upper side of "Mosles" Cr; border: begins at Trick's corner "live", joins John Lovick, Solomon Smith, & river low ground; known as Smith land; part of grant Feb. 18, 1737 to said Solomon Smith. (signed) Solomon Smith's mark "X"; (witness) Ephraim Lane, David Gordon, & Wm Arnold; Oct. 1763 acknowledged; book 11 p. 280.

3582. Dec. 23, 1762 Joseph Pledger, planter (Craven Co) to John Yates (same); for £25 proclamation money sold "either" half of 100 ac, which Yates chooses when he sees it, on S side of Neuse R, & W side of Hancock's Cr; border: begins at a pine in the fork of the creek and joins head of a small branch. (signed) Joseph Pledger's mark "X"; (witness) Isaac Wood, Graham Wood, & Dan Yates jr; wit. oath "Oct." by "Dan Yates"; book 11 p. 281.

3583. Nov. 3, 1763 Peter Conway, gentleman (Newbern, Craven Co) to John Fillyan, planter (Craven Co); for £20 proclamation money sold 200 ac on "Tuskahana" R & Trent R; border: begins at a white oak near Reedy Br, joins Sqr. "Tchnson", an old corner near Tuscahana [R], & Trent R. (signed) Peter Conway; (witness) "Cathrine" Foy & Isaac Patridge; [note at end indicates Fillyan paid Conway £20 on Nov. 3, 1763]; wit. oath Nov. 3, 1763 by Isaac Patridge before Frank Costin, AJ; book 11 p. 282.

3584. Feb. 25, 1763 Charles Hopton, planter (Dobbs Co, NC) to Edward Gatlin (Craven Co); for £50 proclamation money sold 100 ac on E side of Swift Cr; border: begins at Edward Bryan's "side" line & joins forks of 2 branches. (signed) Charles Hopton's mark "X"; (witness) John Harris, James Gatlin, & Thos Gatlin; wit. oath Oct. 1763 by James Gatlin; book 11 p. 283.

3585. Sept. 12, 1763 Solomon Carter (Duplin Co, NC) to Rebecca Davis (Craven Co); for £28 proclamation money sold 300 ac on N side of Tuckaho Cr; border: begins at a white oak on the creek side; known as the springs. (signed) Solomon Carter; (witness) Wm Cole & Jas Davis; wit. oath Oct. 1763 by Solomon Carter; book 11 p. 283.

3586. Sept. 26, 1763 Hinson Wright, planter (Craven Co) to James McCoy, planter (Beaufort Co, NC) & James McKling; for sold 100 ac on S side of Bay R & on Southwest Br; border: joins Mary Tompson [no more description]; granted in 1744 to John Homes [or "Tomson"], when land was in Beaufort Co, who willed it to Mary Thomson who sold to Hinson Wright; Wright & McKling agree to divide land so McKling will have 100 ac on SW prong of said creek that begins at a crossway & landing place in second small turn of SW prong of the creek, runs S20W with said crossway through the marsh & swamp to a beach on edge of the high ground, S35W 38 poles to marked poplar, S20W to a beach, & with said line to W corner of whole survey, & to beginning. (signed) Hinson Wright & Jas "McLeroy"; (witness) John Willcocks [only one witness]; wit. oath Oct. 1763 acknowledged by Hinson Wright & Jas McLeroy; book 11 p. 284.

3587. Jun. 28, 1762 John A Brice (Craven Co) to Chas Cogdell, gentleman (same); for £100 sold 170 ac on E side of Brices Cr; border: begins at Frances Bone's line tree on Halltons Br and joins "the" dividing line that was run across for Lewis Williams; includes the land & island on the creek sold to "him" and by him recovering to me by deed May 20, 1762; part of tract willed by William Brice to his son John A Brice. (signed) John A Brice; (witness) R Cogdell & Rigdon Brice; [note at end indicates Capt. Chas Cogdell paid Brice £100 on Jul. 3, 1762]; wit. oath Oct. 1763 by Richard Cogdell; book 11 p. 285.

3588. Apr. 13, 1763 Thomas Loftin (Craven Co) to Elkenah Loftin (same); for £20 proclamation money sold 120 ac on E side of Salesbury Br; border: begins at George Roberts' corner red oak & joins Cornelius Loftin; granted Oct. 23, 1761 to said Thomas Loftin. (signed) Thomas Loftin; (witness) John Loftin & Dan Hill; wit. oath Oct. 1763 by John Loftin; book 11 p. 286.

3589. Aug. 6, 1762 George Stringer jr [George King sr, also mentioned], planter (Craven Co) to Robt Reynolds (same); for £70 proclamation money sold 20 ac on E side of Goose Creek Swamp; border: begins at first corner red oak, joins mouth of Poplar bee tree Br, & John Stringer; part of grant Oct. 8, 1747 to Francis Stringer. (signed) George Stringer; (witness) Fred Becton & Wm Isler; wit. oath Oct. 1763 by William Isler; book 11 p. 287.

3590. Apr. 5, 1763 William "Heritage" & John Franks, executors of Hardy Bush deceased (Craven Co) to William Nelson (same); for £7 proclamation money sold 100 ac on N side of Trent R & E side of "Musseskee" [Swamp]; border: begins at a pine, joins "M" Swamp; part of grant Sept. 29, 1756 to Hardy Bush. (signed) Wm Herritage & John Franks; (witness) Samuel Hatch & Jas Green; [note at end indicates Franks received £7 on "Apr. 5"]; Oct. 1763 acknowledged by Wm Herritage & John Franks; book 11 p. 287.

3591. Jan. 20, 1763 James Roberts, planter (Craven Co) to Joseph Crispen, mariner (same); for £50 proclamation money sold 165 ac in 2 tracts: (a) 25 ac on N side of Neuse R & upper side of Dawson's Cr; border: begins at Joseph Atherly's corner on side of Dawson's Cr, joins Roberts' new patent, the gut where Roberts lives, land line that divides this land from land sold to Christopher Neal; & (b) 140 ac; border: begins at the gut that divides the land from land sold to Christopher Neal where Richard Graves' old patent line crosses, joins Atherley, Randolph, Fisher, & eastermost branch of the gut; being western part of said Roberts' new patent where he lately lived. (signed) James Roberts; (witness) S "Justices", Thos Golen, & Chris Neal; [note at end indicates "Crispin" paid Roberts £50 on Jan. 20, 1763]; wit. oath Oct. 1763 by Christopher Neal; book 11 p. 288.

3592. Oct. 23, 1762 George Hays, house carpenter (Newbern, Craven Co) to George "Mallattoe" boy about 9 months old, who I bought from Peter Conway gentleman (of New Bern, NC); for natural love & affection and for £0.10 proclamation money I emancipate George; I agree to a bond of £500 proclamation money to abide by this agreement. (signed) George Hays; (witness) R Cogdell & Peter Conway; wit. oath Nov. 5, 1763 by Peter Conway before Chas Berry; book 11 p. 289.

3593. Oct. 18, 1763 Horona Duncan, widow (Craven Co) to Peter Conway, gentleman (New Bern, NC); for £30 proclamation money sold house & 0.5 ac in lot #81 in New Bern; sold Jun. 29, 1759 by Wm Herritage esq to said Horona Duncan. (signed) Horona Duncan; (witness) Isaac Patridge, C Neal, & Mary Weeks; wit. oath Nov. 1763 by Isaac Patridge; book 11 p. 290.

3594. Oct. 29, 1761 Henry Vanpett, planter (Craven Co) to Anthony Vanpett, planter (same); for £18 proclamation money sold 100 ac between great & Little "Contentary" [Cr]; border: begins at a white oak on side of a small branch of Watery Br; granted to Jacob Vanpett. (signed) Henry Vanpett; (witness) Samuel Spencer & Jacob "Blound"; wit. oath "1761" by Jacob Blound; book 11 p. 290.

3595. Jul. 8, 1762 John Carrathers, planter (NC) to Joseph Leech, merchant (Newbern, Craven Co); for £25 proclamation money sold 60 ac; border: begins at a chincapin near Richard Elliott & Vandom's line, joins "the" road, Richard Elliott's grant, Wm Hern's grant, & W Rice; granted Sept. 1, 1759 by Thomas

Norwood who bequeathed it to Fran. Norwood his widow who sold to John Carrathers recorded in Secretary's office & register's office. (signed) John Carrathers; (witness) John Fenner & Stephen Yorke; wit. oath Oct. 1763 by Stephen Yorke; book 11 p. 291.

3596. Aug. 3, 1763 William Arnold, planter (Craven Co) to Longfield Cox; for £7.10 proclamation money sold 40 ac on S side of Neuse R & upper side of Flat Swamp; border: begins at a pine on Thomas Pollock's line and joins "Village Couch"; granted Oct. 7, 1756 to James Arnold. (signed) William Arnold & Elisabeth Arnold's mark "X" (sic); (witness) Solomon Smith & Moses Taylor; wit. oath Oct. 1763 by Solomon Smith; book 11 p. 292.

3597. May 6, 1763 John Williams, planter (Craven Co) to Nehemiah Cullen, planter; for "value received" sold 50 ac on W side of Adams Cr & S side of Neuse R; border: begins at a marked pine at the ferry landing on Duck Cr, & joins an old line; part of tract purchased by John Lovitt. (signed) John Williams; (witness) Richard Dukes, Peter Dukes, & Edmond Cullen; wit. oath Oct. 1763 by Edmond Cullen; book 11 p. 293.

3598. May 20, 1762 Lewis Williams, planter (Onslow Co, NC) to John A Brice (Craven Co); for "good causes" quit claim 170 ac on Brices' Cr; border: from Hallstain Br on said creek to Rigdon Brice's line and joins said creek; being land formerly belonging to said "A Brice" who sold to said Williams but deed has been mislaid in Craven Co clerk's office without being registered & now not to be found. (signed) Lewis Williams; (witness) Chas Cogdell & Francis "Godfre"; wit. oath Jul. 1763 by Chas Cogdell; book 11 p. 294.

3599. Jul. 3, 1762 John "Pendar", mariner (Craven Co) to for Charles Cogdell, gentleman (same); for "good causes" quit claim 170 ac on Brices Cr; border: from Hollstons Br on said creek to Rigdon Brice's line and joins said creek; formerly sold by John A Brice to Lewis Williams but deed was mislaid in Craven Co clerk's office without being registered & now not to be found. (signed) John Pendar; (witness) John Holland & Elizabeth Holland; wit. oath Jul. 1762 by John Holland; book 11 p. 294.

3600. Nov. 30, 1763 Peter Conway's mark is crop in left ear & poplar leaf in right ear (signed) Peter Conway, CS & register;
     Nov. 30, 1763 Ann Black's mark is crop in left ear and under hole & over hole in right (signed) Peter Conway, CS & register;
     Dec. 15, 1763 Willis McCoy's mark is crop and over bite in right ear & crop in left ear (signed) Peter Conway, CS & register; book 11 p. 295.

3601. Nov. 20, 1763 Samuel Purviance sr, merchant (Philadelphia, Pennsylvania) to my loving friend Matthew Scott, merchant (of Woodstock, near New Bern, NC); power of attorney to receive money & goods owed to me as copartner with David Caldwell deceased by anyone including John Nisbett, Andrew Wallace, Robt Gums, Hugh Thompson, William Street, Joseph Street, John Cunningham,

Craven County, NC Deed Books 11-13

Richard Sagers, Robert Dunber, Michael Dirmount, Thomas Galbreath, & William Steverson (all of Pennsylvania) late traders. (signed) Samuel Purviance sr; (witness) Jonathan Fielder & Thomas Galbraith; wit. oath Jan. 1764 by Thomas Galbraith; book 11 p. 296.

3602. Feb. 12, 1759 John Jones, planter (Craven Co) to Marmaduke Cox (same); for £21 proclamation money sold 150 ac in fork of Cabbin Br; border: begins at a black jack in William "Stoy's" [or Stroy] line. (signed) John Jones; (witness) A M Combs & Geo Becton; wit. oath Oct. 1759 by George Becton; book 11 p. 296.

3603. Dec. 28, 1763 Solomon Edwards (Craven Co) to James Whiting (same); for £3 proclamation money sold 100 ac on E side of Upper Broad Cr; border: begins at a lightwood post on the creek side below James Whiting's house, joins Clitherall, & Sitgreaves; part of 400 ac granted Oct. 23, 1761 to [omitted]. (signed) Solomon Edwards; (witness) David Lewis & W Speight; Jan. 1764 acknowledged; book 11 p. 297.

3604. Nov. 21, 1763 John Oliver, painter (Philadelphia, Pennsylvania) to my loving friend Robert Graham (now at Philadelphia & of New Bern); power of attorney to receive money & goods owed to me by anyone in North Carolina but especially Joseph Chadwick (residing in New Bern, NC) or bill of exchange drawn by Joseph Chadwick on "Cornwell lands, merchant" (in New York) payable to me also to recover of Edward Carter, farmer (living in "now" province aforesaid) the price of a house as by account to me. (signed) John Oliver; (witness) Isaac Anthum, Jos Pope jr, & Thos "Galbrith"; wit. oath Jan. 1764 by Thomas Galbrith; book 11 p. 298.

3605. Sept. 3, 1763 Charles Smith, planter (Craven Co) to George Smith, planter (same); for £20 proclamation money sold on N side of Neuse R; border: begins at a red oak marked by ourselves on John Dishman's line near "the" main road, joins a line concluded by ourselves, & "the" back line; half of 300 ac granted in 1762 to Chas Smith. (signed) Charles Smith; (witness) Lewis Bryan & Harvy Smith; [note at end:] Chas Smith "accepts a privilege" in above land for his natural life & "have wholy" to his "son" George as the deed directs; wit. oath Jan. 1762 by "Harvey" Smith; book 11 p. 299.

3606. Jul. 17, 1763 Joseph "Rehm" (Craven Co) to Michael Koonce, planter (same); for 1100 proclamation money sold 140 ac on N side of Trent R & on Williams Cr; border: begins at a red oak; granted Feb. 14, 1739 to William Suggs and sold Apr. 8, 1762 to Joseph Rehm. (signed) Joseph Rehm; (witness) John "Frank" & Jno Bryan; wit. oath Jan. 1764 by John Franks; book 11 p. 300.

3607. Dec. 31, 1763 John Robinson, planter (NC) to James Willis, planter (Craven Co); for £6 proclamation money sold 39 ac "in Beavordamn" Br where the line running N50W crosses said branch; border: joins Fisher & the run of Beaverdamn Br; part of 250 ac granted Apr. 22, 1763 to William Gatlin. (signed) John

Robinson's mark "X"; (witness) Dennis Pender, P Pender, & George Fisher; Jan. 1764 acknowledged; book 11 p. 300.

3608. [top of deed missing] William Gatlin to John Robinson; [remainder of details of deed missing]. (signed) William Gatlin; (witness) D Pender, Jas Willisms & Geo Fisher; wit. oath Jan. 1764 by George Fisher; book 11 p. 301.

3609. Dec. 17, 1763 Benjamin Williams, planter (Craven Co) to James McKleroy, planter (Beaufort Co, NC); for £12 proclamation money sold "9 ac laid out for 320" ac on S side of Bay R & lower side of Neals Cr; border: begins at corner oak of Neal's patent on the point on lower side of Neals Cr & joins back line of the patent; half of grant Nov. 27, 1762 to said Benjamin Williams. (signed) Benjamin Williams; (witness) Giles "G" Riggs, John Riggs, & Thos Franklin; wit. oath Jan. 1764 by Giles Riggs; book 11 p. 302.

3610. Dec. 17, 1760 Benjamin Williams, planter (Craven Co) to John Riggs sr, planter (Beaufort Co, NC); for £[blank] proclamation money sold 120 ac on S side of Bay R nea head of "Neales" Cr; border: begins at James McKelroy's corner marked beach on lower side of said land & joins "the" back line; part of grant Nov. 27, 1762 to said Benjamin Williams. (signed) Benjamin Williams; (witness) Giles "G" Riggs, Jas McKleroy, & Thos Franklin; wit. oath "Jan." by Giles Riggs; book 11 p. 303.

3611. Dec. 17, 1760 Benjamin Williams, planter (Craven Co) to Giles Riggs, planter (same); for £6 proclamation money sold 200 ac on S side of Bay R & W side of head of Alligator Cr; border: begins at John Riggs' corner gum, joins a patent line, & "the" back line; where said Giles Riggs lives; part of grant Nov. 27, 1762 to said Benjamin Williams. (signed) Benjamin Williams; (witness) Jas "McLeroy", Thos Franklin, & John Riggs; wit. oath Jan. 1764 by James McLeroy; book 11 p. 304.

3612. Sept. 3, 1763 Charles Smith, planter (Craven Co) to Harry Smith, planter (same); for £20 proclamation money sold on N side of Neuse R; border: begins at a red oak on John Dunham's line near "the" main road & joins "the" back line; being half of 300 ac granted in 1762 to said Chas Smith. (signed) Charles Smith; (witness) Lewis Bryan & George Smith; wit. oath Jan. 1764 by George Smith; book 11 p. 304.

3613. Apr. 2, 1763 Samuel Wingate, planter (Craven Co) to Rawley Williams (same); for £20 proclamation money sold 200 ac; border: begins at an ash in mouth of Cabbin Br and joins Wingate's back line; where said Rawley Williams lives; being lower part of grant Sept. 29, 1756 to said Samuel Wingate. (signed) Samuel Wingate; (witness) Reuben Phillips & Saml Spencer; wit. oath Jan. 1764 by Reuben Phillips; book 11 p. 305.

3614. Feb. 24, 1763 Orinphorus West & wife Margaret (New Bern, NC) to

Andrew Moyers, farmer (same); for £130 proclamation money sold 0.5 ac in lot #275 in New Bern; sold by New Bern commissioners to said Samuel Lawson who sold Jun. 13, 1751 to William Bastion Whitford who resold Feb. 5, 1754 to Samuel Lawson and lot was seized by Richard Cogdell, high sheriff of Craven Co, due to writ of fieri facias, and sold Jan. 4, 1763 to Orinphorus West for £95. (signed) Orinphorus West & Margaret's mark "X"; (witness) Arthur Blackman & Charles Evitt; dower renounced Feb. [blank], 1763 by Margaret West before Thomas Haslion; wit. oath 176[blank] by Chas Evitt; book 11 p. 306.

3615. Dec. 31, 1763 John Robinson, planter (Craven Co) to George Fisher, planter (same); for £5 proclamation money sold 85 ac; border: begins at a branch where "the" line running West crosses said branch called "Warnes", joins George Fisher, crosses "Beavordamn" Br, & Waines Br; where said Robinson lives; part of 250 ac granted Apr. 22, 1763 to William Gatlin. (signed) John Robinson's mark "X"; (witness) Dennis Pender, P Pender, & James Willis; Jan. 1764 acknowledged; book 11 p. 307.

3616. Dc. 20, 1762 John Pendar, mariner (Craven Co) to John Acton Brice, planter (same); for £100 sterling Great Britain money sold 200 ac on S side of Neuse R & on Brices Cr; border: begins at mouth of Holstons Br on the creek, joins Francis Brice jr, the back line of the patent, & Rigdon Brice's patent; known as Rich Land "plantation"; except 170 ac sold to Chas Cogdell; and "my" wife consented her dower; part of a patent left by "old" Col. William Brice at his death to his 2 sons Frank & William Brice now deceased. (signed) John Pendar; (witness) Benj Brice & B Brice; [note at end indicates Brice paid Pendar £100 sterling on Dec. 20, 1762; wit. oath Jan. 1764 by Betsey Brice; book 11 p. 308.

3617. Dec. 17, 1763 William Gatlin (Craven Co) to John Robinson, planter (same); for £3 proclamation money sold 250 ac on Swifts Cr & on James Neck; border: beside John James' line and includes oak ponds land [reference to patent for metes & bounds]; Robinson to pay yearly quit rent to the king of £0.4 proclamation money per 100 ac. (signed) William Gatlin; (witness) Dennis Pendar, James Williams & George Fisher; wit. oath Jan. 1764 by George Fisher; book 11 p. 309.

3618. Dec. 22, 1763 [3rd year of reign of King George III] William Smith (Craven Co) to Roger "Handcock" (same); for £150 proclamation money sold 340 ac on S side of Neuse R & E side of Slocombs Cr; border: begins at mouth of Duck Cr, joins head of main branch of the creek, Mark Furguson, a small pond, head of Grubby Neck Br, & Marks Cr; granted in 1716 to John Slocumb sr. (signed) William Smith's mark "X"; (witness) Joseph Loftin & Sarah Loftin; [note at end indicates Smith received "contents" on Dec. 2, 1763]; Jan. 1764 acknowledged; book 11 p. 310.

3619. Jan. 11, 1761 John Causway (Craven Co) to Thomas Tuten (same); for £16 proclamation money sold 113 in 2 tracts: (a) 83 ac on S side of Swift Cr; border:

begins at a white oak near Garroll's line, joins Willis Shipp, & Great Swamp; granted to James Hatch; & (b) 30 ac; border: joins "it [above tract] on lower side [reference to previous deed for metes & bounds]; "held by deed" dated Sept. 8, 1756 from James Godett. (signed) John Causway; (witness) John Tuten & Sarah Tuten; wit. oath Jan. 1764 by John Tuten; book 11 p. 311.

3620. Nov. 5, 1763 [3rd year of reign of (King George III)] Joseph Chadwick, merchant (Craven Co) to my trusty & loving friend Judah Smith (same); power of attorney to recover money & goods owed to me by anyone. (signed) Joseph Chadwick; (witness) Fred Becton & Fred Isler; wit. oath Jan. 1764 by Frederick Becton; book 11 p. 312.

3621. Jun. 25, 1763 John Clitheral jr, Peter Conway, & John Rice, New Bern Commissioners, to John Leech (New Bern, NC); for £0.20 sold front lot #410 in New Bern; sold due to act of Assembly passed Oct. 25, 1756 at New Bern to better regulate New Bern & secure titles to persons holding lots in town; John Clitheral, Joseph Leech, Peter Conway, Sam Carnell, & John Rice were chosen as commissioners to sell lots; town reserves right of getting fire wood & timber for town use and use part of lot as common pasturage; if Leech dies without heirs, land reverts to the town. (signed) John Clitheral jr, Peter Conway, & John Rice; (witness) Richard Cogdell [only one witness]; Jul. 1763 acknowledged;
        Aug. 2, 1764 Hardy Bryan's mark is a swallow fork in left ear and over slope in right (signed) Peter Conway, register; book 11 p. 312.

3622. Oct. 21, 1763 Joseph Leech, merchant (Craven Co) to Bryan Wilkinson (Philadelphia, Pennsylvania); for Leech is bound to Wilkinson for £836.8 Pennsylvania money conditioned on payment of £418.4 by Apr. 21, 165 in "one entire" payment with lawful interest; SO to better secure payment sold in trust 2 lots in New Bern: (a) lot #10 wher said "Leach" has a tan yard & (b) front lot #9 now in occupation of widow Hannah Langford; sale void if Leech pays debt on time. (signed) Joseph Leech; (witness) Richard Cogdell & John Green; wit. oath Nov. 7, 1763 by John green before Chas Berry; book 11 p. 313.

3623. [no date] inventory of goods & chattels of Edward Griffith deceased: clock, 2 watches, mahogony desk, 2 oak desks, household furniture, kitchen utensils, 24 earthen plates, 12 china plates, 10 butter pots, 3 "hair" brooms, carpenter tools, about 2 pounds of gun powder, farming tools, 14 shirt buttons, 2 Bibles, 2 testaments, English dictionary, English dispensatory, other books, the Lord's Prayer, a linen wheel & 2 pair cards, 18 small bars of lead, 132 doz (sic) taylor's tumblers, a chocolate mill, 95 bushels of salt, 3 pounds lard soap, [Negroes ?] Jackson, Murry, Tom, Sarah, Nan, Rose, Mark, Cloe, Jack, John, Sarah (sic), & little M Kate. (signed) "Mr" Rachael Griffith; book 11 p. 314.

3624. Sept. 17, 1762 John Tilghman, planter (Craven Co) to Jacob Taylor, planter (same); for £10 proclamation money sold 300 ac on S side of Trent R; border: begins at a red oak near "the" running branch; granted Oct. 28, 1761 to said John

Tilghman. (signed) John Tilghman; (witness) Thos Hays & C Ruggs; wit. oath Oct. 1762 by Christian Ruggs; book 11 p. 315.

3625. Nov. 20, 1762 Adam Tooley (Princess Ann Co, Virginia) to John Carney, William Mill, & Christopher Neal (Craven Co); a bond for £300 proclamation money; today Tooley signed power of attorney to Carney, Mill, & Neal for recovery of "a parcel of Negroes, goods & chattels, rights & credits" which were property of Adam Forguson the elder deceased and descended by "kniveship" to Adam Tooley & others, children of his mother Sarah Tooley who was daughter of Adam Forguson the elder; bond void if Carney, Mill, & Neal recover any of the Negroes & conveys them to Carney, Mill, & Neal (sic). (signed) Adam Tooley; (witness) Richard Cogdell & John Sheppard; [no wit. oath mentioned]; book 11 p. 316.

3626. Feb. 22, 1762 John Salmons, cooper (Craven Co) to John Carney & Samuel Masters, planters (same); for £18 proclamation money sold 100 ac on W side of South R; border: begins at mouth of a gut & the branch of the gut, joins Fulford, South R, mouth of Southwest Cr; "taken out" of patent owned by Thomas Martin deceased. (signed) John "Salmon"; (witness) Jas Jones, Lovick Jones, & Thomas Roe; wit. oath Apr. 1764 by James Jones; book 11 p. 317.

3627. Jan. 6, 1764 Abraham Bailey, planter (Onslow Co, NC) to Elisha Blackshear, planter (Craven Co); for £30 proclamation money sold 100 ac on S side of Tuckeho [Swamp]; border: begins at a white oak in an "angle" of a branch on Tuckeho [Swamp] and joins Johnson. (signed) Abraham Bailey; (witness) John Bryan & Alex Blackshear; Apr. 1764 acknowledged; book 11 p. 318.

3628. Mar. 31, 1764 [4th year of reign of King George III] Absalem Tuton (Craven Co) to Hugh Pugh (same); for £20 proclamation money sold 125 ac on Gum Swamp & S side of Swift Cr; being half of 250 ac granted Nov. 15, 1762 to Absalom Tuton which was divided by line of marked trees across the tract and part sold now is next to where said Hugh Pugh lives being land he bought of Thomas Tuton "at a place" known as the ridges [no more description]. (signed) Absalem Tuton; (witness) John Tuton, Thomas Tuton, & Jacob Blount; wit. oath Apr. 1764 by Jacob Blount esq; book 11 p. 318.

3629. Mar. 31, 1764 [4th year of reign of King George III] John Tuton (Craven Co) to Absalem Tuton (same); for £20 proclamation money sold 100 ac on S side of Swift Cr; half of 200 ac granted Mar. 5, 1747 to Henry Smith which was divided by line of marked trees and part now sold is upper part of said patent [no more description]. (signed) John Tuton; (witness) Thomas Tuton, Hugh Pugh, & Jacob Blount; wit. oath Apr. 1764 by Jacob Blount; book 11 p. 319.

3630. Mar. 31, 1764 [4th year of reign of King George III] Thomas Tuton (Craven Co) to Hugh Pugh (same); for £20 proclamation money sold 100 ac on N side of Neuse R & E side of Beasley Swamp; border: begins at a pine on Gum Swamp;

part of grant to Edward Mosley. (signed) Thomas Tuton's mark "X"; (witness) John Tuton, Absalem Tuton, & Jacob Blount; wit. oath Apr. 1764 by Jacob Blount; book 11 p. 320.

3631. Mar. 31, 1764 [4th year of reign of King George III] Henry Jarrell (Craven Co) to Hugh Pugh (same); for £30 proclamation money sold 100 ac on W side of Clay Root Swamp; border: begins at a white oak on the swamp side; where Joseph Gad formerly lived. (signed) Henry Jarrell's mark "X"; (witness) David Bell, James Lane, & Jacob Blount; wit. oath Apr. 1764 by Jacob Blount; book 11 p. 322.

3632. Mar. 31, 1764 [4th year of reign of King George III] Isaac Stocks (Pitt Co, NC) to Hugh Pugh (same, sic); for £10 proclamation money sold 100 ac on W side of Clay Root Swamp; border: begins at said Pugh's corner white oak & joins land he bought of said Hugh Pugh. (signed) Isaac Stocks' mark "X"; (witness) David Bell, James Lane, & Jacob Blount; wit. oath Apr. 1764 by Jacob Blount; book 11 p. 323.

3633. Mar. 27, 1763 William Charleton (Craven Co) to my well beloved son William Mazell Charleton; for natural love & affection gave all my goods, chattels, household stock & commodities. (signed) William Charleton's mark "X"; (witness) Lewis Bryan, Joseph Dearkman, & John Gailer; wit. oath Apr. 1764 by Lewis Bryan; book 11 p. 324.

3634. Apr. 9, 1736 George Lovick, gentleman (Craven Co) to William Pratt, yeoman (same); for £50 proclamation money sold 250 ac on S side of Neuse R; border: begins at a red oak on the river side; where John L Miller formerly lived & known as Mt. Pleasant. (signed) George "P" Lovick; (witness) Joseph Hall & Jacob Taylor; [note at end:] this is to certify Mr. Lovick isn't to pay any "rear" quit rents on land in above deed (signed) William Pratt; wit. oath Apr. 1764 by Joseph Hall; book 11 p. 325.

3635. Nov. 8, 1763 [3rd year of reign of King George III] Obediah Yarborough (Craven Co) to Bryan Cavener (same); for £25 proclamation money sold 300 ac on E side of Slocumbs Cr; border: begins at Forguson's corner white oak on a branch side & joins Winn. (signed) Obediah Yarborough; (witness) Jacob Taylor, Benj Cox, & Daniel Holland; wit. oath "Apr." by Benj Cox; book 11 p. 326.

3636. Apr. 9, 1763 George Lovick (Craven Co) to William Pratt (same); for £10 proclamation money sold 307 ac; border: beginsa t a red oak on side of a branch that makes into Brices Cr, joins patent line, Great Br, Jacob Taylor, John Ives, George Lovick's "great" tar kiln, & Brices Cr. (signed) George Lovick; (witness) Joseph Hall & Jacob Taylor; [note at end:] this is to certify Mr. Lovick isn't to pay any "rear" quit rents on land in above deed (signed) William Pratt; wit. oath Apr. 1764 by Jacob Taylor; book 11 p. 328.

3637. Mar. 30, 1764 Richard Blackledge, merchant (Craven Co) to John West, cooper (same); for £20 proclamation money sold 170 ac on S side of Neuse R & W side of Mosleys Cr; border: begins at a pine on said creek & joins his own survey; granted in 1762 to said Richard Blackledge. (signed) Richard Blackledge; (witness) Benj Blackledge & John Wetherington sr; Apr. 1764 acknowledged; book 11 p. 329.

3638. Apr. 10, 1763 James Handcock sr, cooper (Craven Co) to my 4 sons James Handcock jr, William Handcock, Evan Handcock, & John Handcock (same); for £0.20 sterling Great Britain money and for parental love & fatherly care sold 640 ac on S side of Neuse R & E side of Slocumbs Cr; border: begins at Sandy Point at mouth of said creek and joins head of Duck Cr; granted in 1766 to John Slocumb sr. (signed) James Handcock sr; (witness) J A Jones & Jos Loftin; wit. oath Apr. 1764 by "James" Jones; book 11 p. 330.

3639. Apr. 3, 1764 Samuel Branton, planter (Craven Co) to John Phillips, planter (same); for £6 proclamation money sold 50 ac on N side of Neuse R; border: begins at a red oak on his line "or" Caleb Wiggins and joins John Phillips; granted Apr. 22, 1763 to said Branton. (signed) Samuel Branton; (witness) Walter Jones & John Wetherington; Apr. 1764 acknowledged; book 11 p. 332.

3640. Apr. 29, 1763 Solomon Peters, planter (Craven Co) to John Phillips (same); for £20 proclamation money sold 100 ac on N side of Neuse R & on great "Contented" Cr near the mouth; border: begins at a water oak on the creek pocosin. (signed) Solomon Peters' mark "X"; (witness) Samuel Branton, Eliz Branton, & Adam Hyde; wit. oath Apr. 1764 by Samuel Branton; book 11 p. 333.

3641. Nov. 18, 1763 Humphry Wilks (Craven Co) to John Hatch (same); for £85 proclamation money sold 300 ac on S side of Trent R & on Crooked Meadow; border: begins at a red oak at head of Bachelor Br; granted Jun. 8, 1739 to John Richards who sold to Humphry Wilks. (signed) Huphrey Wilks; (witness) John Dillahunty, Benj Hatch, & Edmond Hatch; wit. oath Apr. 1764 by Edmond Hatch; book 11 p. 334.

3642. Mar. 24, 1764 Joel King, planter (Craven Co) to John Bedscott (same); for £45 proclamation money sold 164 ac on N side of Neuse R & W side of Upper Broad Cr, & between Christopher Dawson sr's line; border: begins at mouth of a branch next to the "plantation" where Joseph King deceased lived, joins "the" back line, John Hartley, & Christopher Dawson; part of 400 ac granted to William Whitford sr and sold Feb. 6, 1754 by his 2 sons William Whitford & William Bostin Whitford to my deceased father Jos King recorded in Craven Co clerk's office. (signed) Joel King's mark "X"; (witness) Peter Conway, Isaac Fonville, & Isaac Patridge; wit. oath Apr. 1764 by Peter Conway; book 11 p. 336.

3643. Jul. 8, 1763 John F Merkert, planter (Craven Co) to John Granade, planter (same); for £20 proclamation money sold 100 ac on W side of eastermost branch of Mill Cr; border: begins at corner of John Granade's 100 ac in Joseph Sanderson's line and joins land formerly sold by John F Merkert to John Granade; granted Apr. 7, 1750 by John F Merkert. (signed) John Frederick Merkert's mark "X"; (witness) Gordus Rickitson & Samuel Collins; wit. oath Apr. 1764 by Samuel Collins; book 11 p. 337.

3644. Apr. 4, 1764 Heziah Williams, widow (Craven Co) to my beloved children Jesse Williams, Zilpa Williams, & Euphema Williams (same); for love & affection gave Negro woman Florence, Negro girl Alley, Negro boy Charles, 2 cows & their increase, a 2 year old heifer, & a mare & colt & their increase to be divided among Jesse, Zilpa, & "Euphamia" Williams; Heziah retains "her right" in the Negroes for her natural life; Heziah put Jesse, Zilpa, & Euphamia Williams in possession of "the premises" by delivering to John Benners esq, for Jesse, Zilpa, & Euphamia Williams, a pisterun Spanish money valued at £0.1 sterling. (signed) Heziah Williams' mark "X"; (witness) Thos Sitgreaves & John Rice; wit. oath Apr. 1764 by John Rice; book 11 p. 339.

3645. Apr. 1, 1764 Joseph Leech esq, merchant (Newbern, Craven Co) to Peter Knight, merchant (Philadelphia, Pennsylvania); for £37.10 proclamation money sold 93 ac on S side of Neuse R; border: begins at Richard Graves' corner red oak near the river side; granted Nov. 18, 1743 by King George II to John Bryan and sold by Joseph Carrethers, Craven Co sheriff, to Peter Knight due to writ of fieri facias from New Bern Superior Court third Tuesday in Sept. 30th year of reign of George II & recorded in Craven Co register's office book K p. 366-368 and sold Nov. 1757 by Peter Knight to Joseph Leech recorded in "book L vol. 11" p. 151. (signed) Joseph Leech; (witness) Richard Cogdell & R Caswell; Apr. 1764 acknowledged; book 11 p. 340.

3646. Oct. 27, 1763 Henry Roberts, planter (Craven Co) to Thomas Wilson, planter (same); for £35 proclamation money sold 130 ac on E side of Southwest Cr; border: begins at a hickory on Hayes Br below Taylor's "plantation", joins Henry Roberts' corner on Southwest Cr, & mouth of a branch; granted in 1759 to John Taylor. (signed) "Henery" Roberts; (witness) Christian Lergray & Arnewell Heron; wit. oath Apr. 1764 by Arnewell Heron; [note at end:] Mar. 5, 1764 received fees for surveying Thos Wilson's land & returning the same (signed) Whitford Green; book 11 p. 341.

3647. Aug. 24, 1763 James Parkinson, merchant (Craven Co) to James Handcock, yeoman (same); for £52.2.7 proclamation money sold all goods, articles, & household stuff in annexed schedule now in possession of said Parkinson. (signed) James Parkinson; (witness) Robert Gordon & Elisha Doan; (no date) delivered into possession of John Rice, for James Handcock, a bed mentioned in annexed inventory in place of the absolute inventory of all articles (signed) James Parkinson (witness) Robert Gordon & Elisha Doan; Aug. 24, 1763 received of James Parkinson (sic) £52.2.7 (signed) James Parkinson; Aug. 24, 1763 inventory of James Parkinson's property: a black horse formerly owned by Mr. Cogdell, an old horse Jack, a bed, 6 blankets, 2 quilts, 4 counterpine, 6 pair sheets, 4 pillow cases, a bedstead cord & mat & curtains, a black walnut desk, round maple table, small walnut table, an armed & 2 small walnut chairs, an armed mohogony chair, a desk, 2 saddles & bridles, a chair without wheels, a steel "mill", a two mast boat called "the polly", & a large iron kettle (signed) James Parkinson (witness) Robt Gordon & Elisha Doan; Apr. 1764 acknowledged; book 11 p. 343.

3648. Nov. 4, 1763 Henry Roberts, planter (Craven Co) to "Arnwell Hern", planter (same); for £50 proclamation money sold 70 ac on S side of Southwest Cr; border: begins at a white oak, joins John Taylor's line now called Wilson's, & "the" back line; part of 350 ac granted Apr. 10, 161 to Henry Roberts. (signed) Henry Roberts; (witness) Thomas T Wilson & Christian Lergray; wit. oath Apr. 1764 by "Thomas Wilson"; book 11 p. 344.

3649. [blank] 1764 [4th year of reign of King George III] Jane Phillyan to my loving son James Phillyan, planter (Craven Co); for love, good will, & affection gave all my goods, wares, plates, jewels, ready money, household stuff, implements, chattels, leases, & "other" things that belong to me or all real & personal property; [note at end"] Jane "reserves" that above gift is in my hand & at my own will until my death. (signed) Jane Phillyan's mark "X"; (witness) Mathew Gregory & Alex Randall; wit. oath Apr. 1764 by Alexander Randall; book 11 p. 346.

3650. Nov. 21, 1763 Elizabeth Martin, widow (Craven Co) to John Salmons, cooper (same); for £10 proclamation money 100 ac on S side of South R; border: begins at mouth of a gut "up" Southwest Cr, joins a branch, Fulford, & South R; part of grant owned by Thomas Martin at his decease. (signed) Elizabeth Martin's mark "X"; (witness) Samuel Masters, Thos Roe, & Thos Parsons; wit. oath Apr. 1764 by Thomas Roe; book 11 p. 347.

3651. Mar. 5, 1764 Elias Martin (Craven Co) to James Edmondson (same); for £3 proclamation money 47 ac on N side of Neuse R; border: begins at John Riggs' corner beech in "the" pocosin at head of Great Point Run, joins Hall, & "the" main road; being NW part of said Martin's patent. (signed) Elias Martin's mark "X"; (witness) Chris Neal & William Riggs; wit. oath Apr. 1764 by Christopher Neal; book 11 p. 348.

3652. Mar. 13, 1764 John Jarmon, planter (Craven Co) to William Cole (same); for £50 proclamation money sold 200 ac on Beaverdam Br of Trent R; border: begins at a pine by head of a little branch on S of Beaverdam Br and joins Barnell Howard; granted Nov. 27, 1762 to John Jarmon. (signed) John Jarmon; (witness) John Knotts & William Jones; [note at end indicates Cole paid Jarmon £50]; Apr. 1764 acknowledged; book 11 p. 349.

3653. Jan. 20, 1764 Joseph Loftin, planter (Craven Co) to his son Leonard Loftin (same); for love & fatherly affection 200 ac on S side of Neuse R & W side of

Handcock's Cr; [being] "Manner plantation" where I live; border: begins at a pine at head of a marsh, joins head of the first branch, Abraham Jones, & the main creek; as by "patent & deed" dated 1717, 1757, & 1740. (signed) Joseph Loftin; (witness) James Handcock & Thomas Masters; wit. oath Apr. 1764 by James Handcock; book 11 p. 350.

3654. Feb. 2, 1764 Thomas Roe (Craven Co) to James Reed, planter (same); for £10 sold 50 ac on S side of Neuse R; border: begins at a white oak on the river side and joins a branch. (signed) Thomas Roe; (witness) James Handcock & James Handcock jr; wit. oath Apr. 1764 by James Handcock; book 11 p. 352.

3655. Jan. 23, 1764 Leonard Loftin, planter (Craven Co) to Jos Loftin, planter (same); for love & fatherly (sic) affection gave "several" tracts [omitted] ac on S side of Neuse R & W side of Handcock's Cr; being all the land that belongs to me by patent or deeds; except the filed & 2 points joined by the field I tend & liberty to get rail timber of any part of said land for my life and my wife Sarah's life and widowhood. (signed) Leonard Loftin; (witness) James Handcock & Thomas Masters; wit. oath Apr. 1764 by James Handcock; book 11 p. 353.

3656. Dec. 26, 1763 Jacob Taylor to my beloved son Joshua Taylor; for love & affection gave 80 ac on S side of Neuse R & on W side of Otter Cr; border: begins at my lower corner tree, joins mouth of a branch, a valley, & a small pond. (signed) Jacob Taylor; (witness) Bazil Smith & Abram Taylor; wit. oath Apr. 1764 by Bazil Smith; book 11 p. 354.

3657. Jan. 18, 1864 John Gailer (Craven Co) to Valentine King (same); for £25 proclamation money sold 100 ac on S side of Swift Cr; border: begins at an oak on side of Swift Creek Swamp; [granted] Sept. 1, 1759 [34th year of "his majesty's" reign]; V King to pay yearly quit rent of £0.4 proclamation money. (signed) John Gailer's mark "X"; (witness) Benj Hickman & Wm Browning; wit. oath Apr. 1764 by William Browning; book 11 p. 355.

3658. Dec. 30, 1763 Derham Leigh, planter (Craven Co) to Rawles Perry, planter (same); for £4 proclamation money sold 100 ac on N side of Trent R & both sides of Joshua Cr; border: begins at a pine in "Lee's" line, joins Hermon Howard, Adam Moore, Samuel King, & said Leigh; granted Apr. 10, 1761 to Derham Leigh. (signed) Derham Leigh; (witness) William Randall, William Perry, & Richard Gore; wit. oath Apr. 1764 by William Randall; book 11 p. 357.

3659. Mar. 22, 1764 Abram Bussett Simmons, planter (Craven Co) to Amos Small, planter (same); for £100 proclamation money sold 120 ac on S side of Trent R; border: begins at a black gum on E side of Crooked Run in Abram B Simmons' line, joins a small branch, Peter Andrews' beginning corner, & main swamp; part of 200 ac granted Oct. 3, 1755 to Benjamin Simmons. (signed) Abram Bussett Simmons; (witness) James Taylor & John Oliver; wit. oath Apr. 1764 by John Oliver; book 11 p. 358.

3660. Aug. 1, 1763 Mark Hesford to John Morris, planter (Craven Co); for £16 proclamation money sold 100 ac in Craven, formerly Beaufort, Co on S side of Bay R & head of Thomas Cr; border: begins at a pine on a point by the creek side and joins Humes; part of grant Oct. 23, 1761 to said Mark Hesford. (signed) Mark Hesford's mark "X"; (witness) James Willcocks sr & James Willcocks jr, & William Willcocks; wit. oath Apr. 1764 by William Willcocks; book 11 p. 359.

3661. Feb. 8, 1764 Henry Vanpetts, planter (Craven Co) to Thomas Moore, planter (same); for £40 proclamation money sold 166 ac on N side of Swift Cr; border: begins at a sweet gum on the creek & joins a swamp; part of grant May 21, 1741 to Samuel Jasper. (signed) Henry Vanpetts; (witness) William Browning & Benj Heckham; wit. oath Apr. 1764 by William Browning; book 11 p. 361.

3662. Apr. 2, 1764 Derham Leigh, planter (Duplin Co, NC) to Rawles Perry, planter (Craven Co); for £5 proclamaton money sold 70 ac on N side of Trent R in Paster Fork & on W side of Joshuas Cr; border: begins at an oak and joins Samuel King; part of grant Apr. 10, 1761 to Derham Leigh. (signed) Derham Leigh; (witness) William Randall, Robert White, & William Perry; wit. oath Apr. 1764 by William Randall; book 11 p. 362.

3663. Dec. 30, 1763 Derham Leigh (Craven Co) to Rawles Perry (same); for £100 proclamation money sold 100 ac; border: begins at Suggs' line on W side of Willson's Cr. (signed) Derham Leight; (witness) William Randall, William Perry, & Richard Gore; wit. oath Apr. 1764 by William Randall; book 11 p. 363.

3664. Nov. 17, 1762 John Owins, taylor (Onslow Co, NC) to John Oliver, planter (Craven Co); for £1 proclamation money sold 5 ac on S side of Trent R; border: begins at a water oak on said Owins' line on Poplar Br; part of 640 ac granted May 10, 1760 to William Wickliff. (signed) John Owins' mark "X"; (witness) James Daniels & A B Simons; wit. oath Apr. 1764 by James "McDaniels"; book 11 p. 364.

3665. Mar. 22, 1764 Jacob Taylor, planter (Craven Co) to Stephen Tilghman, planter (Somersett Co, Maryland); for £30 proclamation money sold 238 ac in the fork between Swift Cr & Turkey Br on S side of Swift Cr; border: begins at "great" Abram Taylor's corner pine & joins Turkey Br; granted Apr. 10, 1761 to Abram Taylor. (signed) Jacob Taylor's mark "X"; (witness) Thomas Willson, Christian Lergue, & John Tilghman; wit. oath Apr. 1764 by Thomas Willson; book 11 p. 366.

3666. Mar. 5, 1764 Elias Martin (Craven Co) to John Riggs (same); for £5 proclamation money sold 93 ac on N side of Neuse R; border: begins at "the" main road near the bridge on "Gree" Point Run in said Riggs' patent line, joins line of land sold by said Martin to James Edmondson, "the" patent line, & a savannah; being SE corner of Marin's patent. (signed) Elias Martin's mark "X"; (witness) Christopher Neale & William Riggs; wit. oath Apr. 1764 by Christopher Neale; book 11 p. 367.

3667. Nov. 27, 1762 Samuel Roberts, planter (Craven Co) to James Roberts, planter (same); for £6 proclamation money sold 100 ac on upper side of Dawsons Cr; border: begins at mouth of Run Path Gut, joins head of westermost branch on E side of "the Run Path", & "the" back line; being western part of Richard Graves' patent where said Samuel formerly lived. (signed) Samuel Roberts; (witness) Isaac Atherly & Joseph Atherly; [note at end indicates James paid Samuel £6 Nov. 27, 1762]; Apr. 1764 acknowledged; book 11 p. 369.

3668. Mar. 14, 1764 Joshua Hill (Pitt Co, NC) to Joel King, planter (same); for £100 proclamation money sold 400 ac; border: begins at a great pine on "the" western branch; part of grant in 1745 to Hardy Bryan. (signed) Joshua Hill; (witness) Joseph Bryan, Joseph Mosley, & Wm Gatlin; wit. oath Apr. 1764 by Joseph Bryan; book 11 p. 370.

3669. Jan. 2, 1764 John Hill (Craven Co) to Jeremiah King (same); for £150 proclamation money sold 100 ac on Parmeto Swamp; border: begins at a white oak on the swamp side below William Beasely & joins Parmeto Swamp; where Jeremiah King dwells; granted Mar. 3, 1759 to said John Hill. (signed) John Hill; (witness) Joseph Bryan, Wm Gatlin, & Mary Butler; wit. oath Apr. 1764 by Joseph Bryan; book 11 p. 371.

3670. Nov. 7, 1763 Philimore [or Philimon] Morris, planter (Craven Co) to William Morris, planter (same); for 20 ac on N side of Trent R & N side of Little Chinkapin [Cr]; border: begins at a gum on the river, joins Willow Br, & mouth of Little Chinkapin Cr. (signed) Philimore Morris; (witness) John Gilbert [or Gifbert] & Edward Marshburn; wit. oath Apr. 1764 by Edward Marshburn; book 11 p. 372.

3671. Mar. 10, 1762 Samuel McCubbins [or McCubbinson] (Trent River, Craven Co) to Jacob Tingle (Beaufort Co, NC); for £40 proclamation money sold between Neuse R & Trent R and on N side of Bachelors Cr; border: begins at a pine; includes land in the patent on N side of said creek & granted by Gov. Johnston to Samuel McCubbins sr. (signed) Samuel McCubbins; (witness) Edward Franks & Robert "Clitton"; wit. oath Apr. 1764 by Edward Franks; book 11 p. 374.

3672. Mar. 14, 1764 Joseph Bryan, planter (Craven Co) to William Gatlin, planter (same); for £50 proclamation money sold 100 ac on Parmeto Swamp & on N side of Swift Cr; border: begins at a white oak on "the" branch side, joins the swamp, "the" dividing line, & "the" head line; part of grant Oct. 20, 1740 to Joseph Bryan. (signed) Joseph Bryan; (witness) Joseph Mosley, Joel King, & Jeremiah King; Apr. 1764 acknowledged; book 11 p. 375.

3673. Jan. 7, 1764 William Barren, planter (Craven Co) to Thomas Fearn, planter (same); for 110 proclamation money sold [omitted] ac on W side of Beaver Cr; border: begins at a spanish oak on Jacobs Br & joins a swamp. (signed) William "Barron"; (witness) Peter Galvin & Wm Bryan; wit. oath Apr. 1764 by William Bryan; book 11 p. 376.

3674. Dec. 24, 1763 [3rd year of reign of King George III] Joshua Taylor (Craven Co) to Frederick Aerman (same); for £30 proclamation money sold 225 ac; border: begins at a white oak on the point in the fork, joins eastermost creek, & westermost creek. (signed) Joshua Taylor; (witness) Jacob Taylor & Joseph Gatlin; wit. oath Apr. 1764 by Joseph Gatlin; book 11 p. 378.

3675. Sept. 29, 1763 Martin Hagin, planter (Beaufort Co, NC) to Matthias Toler, planter (Craven Co); for L25 proclamation money sold 50 ac on E side of Swift Cr; border: begins at Pine tree Swamp on E side of Swift Cr [no more description]; includes "plantation" where said Matthias Toler lives; part of 300 ac on Swift Cr land surveyed for Jacob Robinson. (signed) Martin Hagin's mark "X"; (witness) Mark Noble, Francis Scales, & Peter Rule; [note at end indicates Toler paid (not signed) £25 on Sept. 20, 1763]; wit. oath Apr. 1764 by Francis Scales; book 11 p. 379.

3676. Dec. 1, 1763 John Reed & wife Margaret, late widow of James Wyn deceased to James Davis (New Bern, NC); for £20 sold their interest in Margaret Reed's dower in land where Jas Wyn lived. (signed) John Reed & Margaret Reed; (witness) Bryan Cavender [only one witness]; wit. oath Apr. 1764 by Bryan Cavender; book 11 p. 380.
3677. Jul. 13, 1763 Thomas Pollock to John Granade, planter (Craven Co); for £30 proclamation money quit claim land I may own in deed "whereof therewith is" a true copy [no more description]. (signed) Thomas Pollock; (witness) Edmond Hatch & James Williams; wit. oath Apr. 1764 by James Williams; book 11 p. 381.

3678. Jan. 10, 1764 Charles Shanewoolf [or Shanewolf] (Craven Co) to Benjamin Bush (same); for £10 proclamation money sold 100 ac; border: joins land formerly sold by said Everton to Benjamin Gatlin [reference to grant for metes & bounds]; part of grant to Thomas Everton who sold to Chas Shanewolf. (signed) Charles Shanewoolf; (witness) Christopher Dawson & Joseph Edmondson; wit. oath Apr. 1764 by Christopher Dawson; book 11 p. 382.

3679. Jun. 5, 1763 Elihu Hall, gentleman (Craven Co) to Bazill Smith, "sport" (same); for £4 proclamation money sold 300 ac on S side of Neuse R & head of Otter Cr; border: begins at James Hill's upper corner, joins said Elihu's back line, point of the "person", & Jacob Taylor's line on head of Otter Cr. (signed) Elihu Hall; (witness) John Pendar & William Pendar; Apr. 1764 acknowledged; [note at end indicates Smith paid Hall £4 on Jun. 5, 1763; book 11 p. 383.

3680. Jan. 8, 1764 Moses Cox & Martha C Cox (Craven Co) to John Bishop (same); for £12 proclamation money sold 100 ac on Pine tree Br; border: begins at a white oak in fork of Pine tree Br; being tract owned by Edward Masters deceased by grant Nov. 24, 1744. (signed) Moses Cox's mark "X" & Martha Corana Cox; (witness) David Lewis & Thomas Cuthrell; Apr. 1764 by acknowledged by Moses & Martha C Cox; book 11 p. 384.

3681. Mar. 5, 1763 John Hartley (Craven Co) to Thomas Whitford jr (same); for £5 proclamation money sold 50 ac on N side of Neuse R & On upper side of Upper Broad Cr; border: begins at mouth of Ready Glade & joins a small branch; part of 400 ac granted Mar. 24, 1747 to [omitted]. (signed) John Hartley; (witness) John Whitford, Joseph Horton, & Thos Whitford; wit. oath Apr. 1764 by John Whitford; book 11 p. 385.

3682. Apr. 4, 1763 John Pendar sr, mariner (Craven Co) to John Pendar jr, mariner (same); for £300 proclamation money sold Negro man Jack, Negro woman Rose, 8 cows & calves, yoke of oxen, 10 small "N" cattle marked with swallow fork in right ear & slit in left ear, 2 horses, 2 carts, 3 plows, 5 feather beds & their furniture, 12 chairs, 2 tables, 24 puter plates, 6 dishes, 6 puter basons, 6 iron pots, a bell mettle pot, tea kettle, 2 desks, 3 chests, 6 pair sheets, 6 table cloths, 6 tows, a "beaupret", all the corn in "ensuing" crop belonging to "said' Pendar, 30 small big hogs marked as above; sale void if John Pendar sr pays John Pendar jr £300 proclamation money by Apr. 4, 1765. (signed) John Pendar sr; (witness) John Holland & William Pendar; [note at end indicates John jr paid John sr £300 on Apr. 4, 1763]; wit. oath Apr. 1764 by John Holland; book 11 p. 386.

3683. Apr. 4, 1763 John Pendar sr, mariner (Craven Co) to John Pendar jr, mariner (same); for £100 proclamation money sold 272 ac known as the bluff of Broad Cr [no more description]; sale void if John Pendar sr pays John Pendar jr £100 proclamation money by Apr. 4, 1765. (signed) John Pendar sr; (witness) John Holland & William Pendar; wit. oath Apr. 1764 by John Holland; book 11 p. 387.

3684. May 11, 1756 Edward Griffith, gentleman (Craven Co) to my well beloved daughter Ann Griffith "yet an infant" (same); for affection gave 4 Negro girls: Abb, Rachel, Grace, & Little Rose and their increase and 2 Negro boys: George & Bob. (signed) Edward Griffith; (witness) Mary Moore & Joseph Leech; May 1756 (sic) acknowledged; book 11 p. 388.

3685. Jan. 30, 1762 [2nd year of reign of King George III] Thomas Pollock esq (Craven Co) to George Kornegy, planter (same); for rents mentioned leased for 40 years 400 ac on N side of Trent R; begins at a red oak in "the angle" of Duck Bridge Br & Trent R & joins "H Pocks" Br; now in "actual possession" of said Kornegy; surveyed by Henry "Skebbon"; yearly rent is £3 sterling due Mar. 1 of each year. (signed) Thomas Pollock & George Kornegy; (witness) Robert Owins & Daniel Simmons; [note at end:] George Kornegy agrees to pay £200 (sic) in above manner within 12 years "first to be expired of the above demised" in May 1764; (witness) [no dated] by Robert Owins before Charles Berry; book 11 p. 389.

3686. Apr. 26, 1764 (Quaker style date) George P Lovick esq (New River, Craven Co) to Parminus Horton, John Howard, & Bartholomew Howard, merchants & sons-in-law (sic) of Parminus Horton (of Cluboots Cr, Craven Co); for £30.13.4 proclamation money sold 460 ac at head of Clubfoots Cr; border: joins Tooks Cr on W "now" known as Blakes Cr; border: begins at Took's own corner cypress on Clubfoots Cr "or swamp", joins a pine below the landing on the creek above a small gut, & mouth of Took's Cr; granted Mar. 29, 1714 (Quaker style date) to James Tooke merchant. (signed) George P Lovick; (witness) Joseph Hall & Wm Porter; May 4, 1764 acknowledged before Chas Berry; book 11 p. 391.

3687. Oct. 23, 1762 Samuel Tindell (Dobbs Co, NC) Mark Hesford (same); for £20 proclamation money sold 270 ac; border: begins at a pine on westermost prong of Tilghman's Cr [reference to grant for metes & bounds]; where I lived; granted Nov. 20, 1739 [13th year of reign of King George II] to me; except 100 ac formerly granted to William Lewis. (signed) Samuel Tindell; (witness) William Willcocks & James Willcocks; wit. oath Apr. 1764 by James Willcocks; book 11 p. 392.

3688. May 10, 1764 William Wharton's mark is crop & 2 slits in each ear (signed) Peter Conway, register;

Jul. 30, 1764 Hugh Pate's mark is a crop & slit if left ear and crop & under bit in right ear (signed) Peter Conway, register; book 11 p. 394.

3689. May 9, 1764 William Crawford & Thomas Wishart (Virginia), surviving "executor" of will of Lewis Conner deceased (late of Norfolk Co, Virginia), to William Dry esq (Brunswick, NC); for Lewis Conner signed his will Oct. 25, 1752 empowering William Crawford & Thomas Wishart with Samuel Bush, Samuel Bush jr, & John Swann, attorneys at law since deceased [as executors ?] to sell all Lewis Conner's land in North Carolina; due to "said power" Crawford & Wishart & for £500 proclamation money sold 2 tracts: (a) 5,860 ac "now" near head of Neuse R in Onslow Co, NC; granted Apr. 9, 1730 by "deputies" of late Lords Proprietor to Lewis Conner; & (b) 500 ac on N side of Neuse R & on S side of "Contentary" Cr; granted Apr. 9, 1730 by deputies of Lords Proprietor to Lewis Conner [no more description for either tract; only one grant on this day to Lewis Conner for 10,000 ac on Saxapahaw R]; land doesn't include land or interest of Samuel Johnston, late of Poplar Spring, deceased within limits of said 4,860 ac (sic) near head of Neuse [R] in Onslow Co; signed by Alexander Easley esq (of Chowan Co, NC) due to power of attorney Sept. 21, 1758 to him by William Crawford & Thomas Wishart. (signed) William Crawford, Gales Easley (sic), & Thomas Wishart "by" Alex Easley; (witness) Samuel Johnston [only one witness]; May 10, 1764 acknowledged by Alexander Easley esq before Charles Berry; book 11 p. 394.

3690. May 9, 1764 John Rice, gentleman (Craven Co) to William Dry (Cape Fear, NC); for £150 proclamation money sold 3 tracts: (a) 196 ac on N side of Neuse

[R] & N side of "Horyton" Cr; border: begins at a hickory on the creek side; granted Nov. 18, 1738 to [omitted]; (b) 190 ac "then" in Craven Co, now Dobbs Cr; border: begins at a white oak on N side of Briery Br; granted Sept. 27, 1764 to [omitted]; & (c) 640 ac on N side of Neuse R; border: begins at a stake at mouth of a creek; granted Mar. 5, 1746 to [omitted]; [no more description for any of the tracts]; sale void if Rice pays Dry £150 proclamation money with legal interest by May 10, 1766. (signed) John Rice; (witness) Robert Ellis & John Daves; wit. oath May 11, 1764 by Robert Ellis before Charles Berry; May 11, 1764 recorded; book 11 p. 396.

3691. Jan. 1, 1763 Mark Hesford to Bond Veal, planter (same); for £10 proclamation money sold 85 ac; border: begins at James Bell's corner pine, joins "the" back line, head of Cabbin Cr, & Samuel Tindell, mouth of Tindells Cr, & head of Chappel Cr; part of a grant Nov. 20, 1739 to Samuel Tindell. (signed) Marka Hesford's mark "X"; (witness) John Willcocks sr & "William Wm Willcocks jr"; wit. oath Apr. 1764 by William Willcocks; book 11 p. 398.

3692. May 4, 1764 (Quaker style date) George P Lovick esq (New River, Craven Co) to Parmenas Horton, John Howard, & Bartholomew Howard, merchants & distillers in equal partnership (Clubfoots Cr, Craven Co); for £1.8 proclamation money sold 15.5 ac on S side of Neuse R & at head of Southwest Br of Clubfoots Cr; border: begins at corner white oak made by Parmenas Horton & John Bishop, joins Tooke, the river, the swamp, head of westermost branch, & "partly joining or near" Robert Blake's "plantation"; being "a small piece" left out when survey was made for Parmanas" Horton & John Bishop when partnership purchased from Thomas Lovick esq deceased; part of Tooke's Broad Creek patent. (signed) George P Lovick; (witness) Joseph Hall & James Jones; May 4, 1764 acknowledged before Charles Berry; book 11 p. 399.

3693. Oct. 10, 1763 Mary Moore, widow of Roger Moore esq deceased, to Joseph Leech, merchant (Newbern, Craven Co); for £30 proclamation money sold 0.5 ac lot #75 in New Bern on Middle Street; border: begins at corner of lot formerly Edward Bryan's on W side of the creek, runs N80W 13 poles, N10E 62 (sic) poles, S80E 13 poles to Middle Street, & down the street to beginning; sold Jun. 24, 1743 by the town commissioners to Nicholas Routledge who sold Dec. 20, 1745 to Samuel Griffis who sold Aug. 3, 1748 to Mary Moore recorded in register's office book B p. 217. (signed) Mary Moore; (witness) Mary Vaile & Thos C Howe; [note at end indicates Leech paid Mary £30 on Oct. 10, 1763]; wit. oath May 8, 1764 by Thomas "Clefford" Howe esq before Charles Berry; book 11 p. 401.

3694. Oct. 7, 1763 Joseph Leech, merchant (Newbern, Craven Co) to Thomas C Howe esq (New Bern, NC); for £750 proclamation money sold (a) 0.5 ac in lot #105 in New Bern; border: begins at corner of lot #106 on Water Street, runs N80W 13 poles, S10W 6.5 poles, S80E 13 poles, & to beginning; Leech has built a large dwelling house & out houses on this lot; sold Apr. 7, 1754 by New Bern commissioners to John Fonville who sold Dec. 20, 1750 to Arthur Johnston yeoman (of Craven Co) who sold Mar. 3, 1752 to Joseph Leech for £30 proclamation money along with front of lot #105 which [Johnston] purchased from C Pollock (sic); (b) 0.5 ac in water front of lot #105; border: begins at farther side of Water or "Trent" Street opposite upper corner of said lot, runs 13 poles on direct line to upper side of the lot to edge of the channel, S 6.5 poles down the channel to lower side of said lot, & 13 poles to the street opposite lower corner of the lot; sold Nov. 5, 1753 New Bern commissioners to Joseph Leech. (signed) Joseph Leech; (witness) James Sears & Richard Fenner; [note at end indicates Howe paid Leech £750 on Oct. 27, 1763 (sic)]; wit. oath May 10, 1764 by Richard Fenner esq before Charles Berry; book 11 p. 403.

3695. Dec. 9, 1763 Levin Scott, planter (Onslow Co, NC) to Ephraim Lain (Craven Co); for £10 proclamation money sold [omitted] ac left to me by John Dreading on W side of Core Cr; border: joins Robert Taylor & Thomas Pollock [reference to grant for metes & bounds]; surveyed for John Dreading. (signed) Levin Scott; (witness) "Lyiard Gelpray" & Stephen Rue; wit. oath May 8, 1764 by Stephen "Lee" before Charles Berry; book 11 p. 407.

3696. Jan. 28, 1763 John Pendar sr, mariner (Craven Co) to John Pendar jr (same); for £150 proclamation money sold a cedar built sloop called Sally formerly owned by William Cole with all her tacklings, furniture, & "boat". (signed) John Pendar sr; (witness) John Holland, William Pendar, & James Parkinson; [note at end indicates John jr paid John sr £150 on Jan. 28, 1763]; wit. oath (no date) by James Parkinson; [second] wit. oath Jan. 28, 1763 by John Holland before James Parkinson; book 11 p. 408.

3697. Jan. 2, 1763 Samuel Harvey to Manuel Harvey (Craven Co); for £50 proclamation money sold 50 ac on S side of Neuse R; border: begins at mouth of a branch [on] Daniel Daugherty's line, joins a hickory on the river "just" above "this" landing, Richard Harvey, & a pocosin. (signed) Samuel Harvey; (witness) Longfield Cox, Jonathan "Markforson", & John Clements; wit. oath Apr. 1764 by Longfield Cox; book 11 p. 409.

3698. Apr. 19, 1764 [4th year of reign of King George III] Rachael Houston, widow (Carteret Co, NC) to Samuel Noble, planter (same); in his will May 6, 1760 William Houston gave his wife Rachael the "plantation" where he lived with land he bought from James Noble; SO for £1.6 proclamation money sold "said plantation" [no more description]. (signed) Rachael Houston's mark [blank space]; (witness) James Ray, Sarah Williams, & Betty Noble; wit. oath May 8, 1764 by James Ray before Charles Berry; book 11 p. 410.

3699. Apr. 3, 1764 Samuel Smyth, John Smith, & Charles Crawford (Craven Co) to justices of Craven Co court; a bond for £1,000 proclamation money; Smyth is guardian of Ann Griffith during her minority or "nonage"; bond void if Smyth provides Ann with necessary meat, drink, washing, lodging, apparel, & learning "according to her degree" and tutor her; Smyth to manage Ann's goods & chattels from Edward Griffith esq deceased; bond void if Smyth performs his duties & makes return to the justices. (signed) Samuel Smyth, John Smith, & Chas Crawford; (witness) Peter Conway [only one witness]; Apr. 1764 acknowledged by Samuel "Smith", John Smith, & Charles Crawford; book 11 p. 412.

3700. Apr. 7, 1764 John Williams, residing chairman of Craven Co Inferior Court, put a free Negro girl Lettice age 11 with Patrick Gordon esq (of Craven Co); Lettice to "dwell & serve" until she is 21 years old according to act of Assembly in such cases; Lettice to be faithful & obedient servant to her master; Gordon agrees to provide Lettice sufficient meat, drink, lodging, & apparel. (signed) John Williams & Patrick Godron; (witness) Peter Conway [only one witness]; [no wit. oath mentioned]; book 11 p. 413.

3701. Sept. 15, 1763 Jacob Sheppard, John Williams, & John "Clithereal" (Craven Co) to John Williams, Joseph leech, John Clitheral, & Andrew Scott, justices of the peace & their survivors (same); a bond for £100 proclamation money; David Hall, orphan of Joseph Hall deceased is to "commit" to tuition of "aforesaid"; Jacob Sheppard is guardian of David Hall; bond void if Sheppard brings up David Hall "according to his degree", cares for his estate, render an inventory to Craven Co Inferior Court, & account to the court for the estate. (signed) Jacob Sheppard, John Clitheral, & John Williams; wit. oath William Good [only one witness]; [no wit. oath mentioned]; book 11 p. 414.

3702. Jul. 29, 1761 Richard Cogdell esq, high sheriff (Craven Co) to Andrew Scott esq (Newbern, Craven Co); for £75 proclamation money sold 0.5 ac in lot #108 in New Bern; border: begins at Water Street & Short Street; lots 108 & 109 (sic) are 13 by 13 poles; being one of 2 lots sold Feb. 16, 1749 by New Bern commissioners to Edward Griffith; & (b) 0.5 ac in front of water lot of #108; border: begins at farther side of Water or Front Street opposite upper corner of said lot; lot is 6.5 by 13 poles; sold Dec. 4, 1743 by New Bern commissioners to Edward Griffith; sold due to writ of fieri facias from New Bern Dist Superior Court of Pleas & Grand Sessions May 11 last & returnable to court Nov. 2 next due to suit by Andrew Scott against Peter Rutgnes, merchant (of Craven Co) for £25.9.3 proclamation money damages & £7.13.9½ costs; and sold due to act of Parliament of Great Britain passed in 5th year of reign of King George II concerning collection of debts in America. (signed) Richard Cogdell; (witness) Peter Conway; [note at end indicates Scott paid Cogdell £75 on Jul. 29, 1761]; Oct. 1761 (sic) acknowledged; book 11 p. 415.

3703. Feb. 2, 1758 Benjamin Griffin, planter (Craven Co) to Solomon Griffin, planter (same); for £27 proclamation money sold 150 ac on S side of Neuse R; border: begins at Joseph Trechett's [or Trochett] corner on W side of Half Moon Swamp; part of grant to C Loftin sr. (signed) Benjamin Griffin; (witness) Thomas Jackson [only one witness]; [no wit. oath mentioned]; book 11 p. 417.

3704. "Sr. Grovia Frederichstad" Dec. 28, 1763 I promise to pay George Nichols or his order 600 pieces of eight by Mar. 1 next being for value received [not signed]; pay contents to Samuel Cornell or order [for] value received] this Jun. 17, 1764 (signed) George Nichols; book 11 p. 419.

3705. Feb. 15, 1764 Abner Neale [or Neal] (Craven Co) to Stephen Mahnes; for £50 proclamation money sold [omitted] ac on head of Long Cr & on S side of Neuse R; border: begins at Bell's beginning corner, joins side of a pocosin at S end of Piny Ridge, Russell's beginning tree beside the marsh; "also" 7 ac bought of James Duke "being" part of patent bought of John Russell. (signed) Abner Neale; (witness) Peter Duke, Lazarus Thomas, & Winfield Thomas; wit. oath Jul. 1764 by Lazarus Thomas; book 11 p. 419.

3706. May 14, 1763 Richard Daves, carpenter (Craven Co) to Thomas Haslin esq (Newbern, Craven Co); for £0.5 proclamation money sold 0.5 ac in lot #255 in New Bern & house thereon; border: begins at corner of Broad Street & Handcocks Street; lot is 6.5 by 13 poles; sold Apr. 17, 1750 by New Bern commissioners to Thomas Andrews who sold Mar. 21, 1752 to Richard Daves who sold lot & house thereon Oct. 27, 1753 to John Fonville, planter (of Craven Co) who "after" resold to Richard Daves; Mary Moore, widow obtained a judgment in Superior Court for Craven, Carteret, Jones, Beaufort, & Hyde Counties at New Bern court house on third Tuesday in Mar. 1759 against Daves for £7.15 damages & £7.7.6½ costs and writ of fieri facias issued Mar. 30, 1759 & returnable to court third Tuesday in Sept. next to Craven Co sheriff and sheriff levied £4.2.6 (sic) and another writ of fieri facias issued against Richard Daves due to suit by Mary Moore Sept. 28, 1759 & returnable to court third Tuesday in Mar next so sheriff levied on house & lot which was sold to Thomas Haslin for £32 proclamation money, but Craven Co Sheriff Joseph "Carthers" failed to make a title to Haslin, an money from judgment was paid to Mary Moore "or" came to Haslin and there is £11.2.3½ due on the judgment, Haslin agreed to discharge Daves from payment of £11.5.3 (sic) & "cause" satisfaction to be rendered. (signed) Richard Daves & Thomas Haslin; (witness) Andrew Moyer & Richard Fenner; wit. oath Jul. 1764 by Richard Fenner; book 11 p. 420.

3707. Jun. 18, 1764 John Mackime, planter (Craven Co) to William Jones, carpenter (same); for £100 proclamation money sold 320 ac; border: begins at a white oak "parting it" from a tract surveyed for Thomas Spring & joins the river swamp; part of 640 ac granted Aug. 29, 1730 by Lords Proprietor to Jas Harris who sold to George Levingston who devised it to his daughter Christian and sold by James Abston & his "now" wife Christian to John Benson who sold to John Rice who sold to Margaret Mackime now wife of William Jones who gave it to said John Mackime. (signed) John Mackime; (witness) John "Couart" & Jeremiah Slade; wit. oath Jul. 1764 by Jeremiah Slade; book 11 p. 424.

3708. Jul. 4, 1764 John Lingfield (Craven Co) to John Molliston, yeoman (same); for £25 proclamation money sold [omitted] ac on S side of Bay R; border: begins at a pine on the river side being beginning tree of a dividing line of part of said tract formerly sold to Wm Dobe, joins mouth of a creek at beginning tree of the whole tract, dividing line of Wm Dawson's deed; part of grant Apr. 25, 1724 to Wm Bell. (signed) John Lingfield; (witness) John "Camelhus" & John Rice; wit. aoth Jul. 1764 by John "Camlhus"; book 11 p. 425.

3709. Nov. 13, 1763 John Fulker (Craven Co) to John Oliver (same); for £20 proclamation money sold 90 ac on N side of Neuse R; border: begins at a red oak at mouth of a gut on "the run" side between Dawson's Cr & where Vallentine Bowers deceased formerly lived, joins head of the creek, Bowers' back line, Samuel Grambring's Landing, & mouth of Dawson's Cr; except School house Point "which" is to be followed on each side various courses of the patent from the creek upwards for 6 acres and liberty to cut fire wood from the whole land forever. (signed) John Fulker; (witness) Christ. Dawson, John Berry, & Robert Allen; wit. oath Jul. 1764 by Christopher Dawson; book 11 p. 426.

3710. Apr. 3, 1762 William Isler, planter (Craven Co) to Frederick Becton, planter (same); for £20 proclamation money sold 100 ac on S side of Beaver Cr; border: begins at a pine, joins Jacob Ipock; granted Oct. 12, 1748 [72nd (sic) year of "our" reign] to [omitted]. (signed) William Isler; "Michiel" Koonce, George Becton, & Frederick Isler; Jul. 1764 acknowledged; book 11 p. 428.

3711. May 8, 1764 Charles Cogdell, gentleman (Craven Co) to Robert Reynolds, planter (same); for £100 proclamation money sold 170 ac on E side of Brices Cr; border: begins at mouth of Holstons Br of said creek, joins a dividing line made for Lewis Williams, "Rogdon" Brice, Brice's Cr, & includes an island in the creek; "except" the island in the creek which was formerly sold by John A Brice to Lewis Williams who resold it May 28, 1762 to John A Brice who sold Jun. 28, 1762 to me; 100 ac "joying" being at £0.0.6 per 100 ac quit rent bounded by straight line from Holstons Br to Rigdon Brice's line and 70 ac bounded by several courses of the creek as by patent May 5, 1743 to [omitted]. (signed) Charles Cogdell; (witness) Jno Rice & Wm Isler; wit. oath Jul. 1764 by William Isler; [note at end indicates Reynolds paid Cogdell £105 (sic) on May 8, 1764]; book 11 p. 429.

3712. Sept. 13, 1758 John Holloway, planter (Craven Co) to Longfield Cox; for £26 proclamation money sold 150 ac on S side of Neuse R & lower side of Half Moon Swamp; known as "the" Garden; border: begins at a red oak, joins Half Moon Swamp, & a given line; part of grant Jun. 30, 1735 to C Loftin sr. (signed) John Holloway; (witness) Isaac Tull & Thomas Jackson; Jul. 1764 acknowledged; book 11 p. 431.

3713. Nov. 29, 1763 Isaac Little, planter (Craven Co) to Edward Mashbun, planter (same); for £20 proclamation money sold 120 ac on N side of Trent R; border: begins at a pine near the river and joins Samuel Moses; part of 640 ac granted by Gov. "Gabrial" Johnston deceased to Martin Franks deceased & recorded in the

Secretary's office. (signed) Isaac Little; (witness) John Gilbert & John Franks; wit. oath Jul. 1764 by John Franks; book 11 p. 432.

3714. Apr. 17, 1764 Ernest Granade, gunsmith, & wife Rachael (Craven Co) to John Jones, planter (same); for £52 proclamation money sold 240 ac on S side of Neuse R below New Bern [no more description]; where Ernest Granade lives. (signed) Ernest Granade & Rachael's mark "X"; (witness) Wm S Foster & Jno Dunn; [note at end indicates Jones paid the Granades £55 (sic)]; Jul. 1764 acknowledged by Ernest & Rachael Granade; book 11 p. 434.

3715. Oct. 5, 1762 James Taylor, planter (Craven Co) to Joseph Bryan, merchant (same); for £70 proclamation money sold 100 ac in Palmetto Swamp on N side of Swift Cr; border: begins at a white oak on a branch, joins a dividing line, & "the" head line; part of a grant Oct. [blank], 1748 to said Joseph Bryan (sic). (signed) James Taylor's mark "X"; (witness) Thomas Bartlett & William Murphey; wit. oath Jul. 1764 by "Joseph Weasley"; book 11 p. 435.

3716. Sept. 26, 1761 Mary Kerney (Craven Co) to John Spicers (same); for £10 proclamation money sold 100 ac on Swift Cr; border: begins at a line on S side of a branch where said Solomon Griffin lived, joins a corner opposite head of a branch, a line concluded between Mary Kerney & Solomon Griffin, crosses a fork; being "plantation" where Mary Kerney formerly lived; part of grant Apr. 20, 1745 to Solomon Griffin. (signed) Mary Kerney's mark "X"; (witness) Joseph Bryan, George Bryan, & Thomas Bryan; wit. oath Jul. 1764 by Joseph Bryan; book 11 p. 437.

3717. Oct. 10, 1761 Charles Hollinsworth, planter (Craven Co) to Joseph Bryan (same); for £150 proclamation money sold 100 ac on N side of Neuse R; border: begins at a white oak 73 yards above "the ferry landing called Hollinsworth Ferry, joins John Short, & the river; being "plantation" & ferry where said Hollinsworth dwells. (signed) Charles Hollinsworth; (witness) John Hackburn, Joshua Hill, & Joseph Mosley; wit. oath Jul. 1764 by Joseph Mosley; book 11 p. 438.

3718. Apr. 20, 1764 "Fornifold" Green (Craven Co) to Frederick Becton (same); for £30 proclamation money sold 250 ac; border: begins at Wm Kitche's corner hickory in Becton's line & near Mary Kitche; part of grant Jun. 30, 1758 to said Fornifold Green. (signed) Fornifold Green; (witness) Frederick Isler & William Bryan; [note at end indicates Becton paid Green £30 on Apr. 24, 1764 (sic)]; Jul. 1764 acknowledged; book 11 p. 439.

3719. Jun. 14, 1764 Elihue Hall (Craven Co) to George P Lovick (same); for £100 proclamation money sold 300 ac on S side of Neuse R; border: begins at lower bounds of the patent at mouth of "Damm" Cr, joins George P Lovick, the woods, "the" back line "in proportion" to 640 ac; said land belonged to my father and after his death came to my brother Joseph Hall by heirship who sold to me; part of 640 ac granted in 1706 [written above 1760] to Chas Worthgloves [probably

Charlesworth Glover]. (signed) Elihue Hall; (witness) "Bazell" Smith & Arthur Johnston; wit. oath Jul. 1764 by Bazill Smith; book 11 p. 441.

3720. May 21, 1764 James Whiting (Craven Co) to Thomas Cuthril (same); for £4 proclamation money sold 50 ac on N side of Neuse R & runs on S side of a small swamp running out of Upper Broad Cr; border: begins at a pine near John Marshell's, joins Great Br, & "the" head line; except 1 poles (sic) for use of George Graham. (signed) James Whiting; (witness) David Lewis & Lawrence Blakely; Jul. 1764 acknowledged; book 11 p. 443.

3721. Jun. 29, 1764 Solomon Beasley [or Beesley] (Craven Co) to my loving son Abraham Beasley (same); for natural affection & fatherly love gave 160 ac on N side of Core Cr; border: begins at Samuel Pope's corner white oak; part of 310 ac granted to John Turner who sold Aug. 11, 1759 to me. (signed) Solomon Beasley; (witness) James Little & John Fenner; Jul. 1764 acknowledged; book 11 p. 444.

3722. Mar. 9, 1764 (Quaker style date) inventory of estate of Levi Bush deceased near Clubfoots Cr in Craven Co by the subscribers with assistance of John Phiscoe & John Tomlonson: money in the house $1,514 (sic), a hand mill, 10 gammons, 12 shoulders, 6 jowles, 5 pieces smoked beef, kitchen items, household items, earthen pot with some hogs fat, 2 power horns with some powder, shot bag with some shot, farming utensils, 272 yards home spun cloth, 95 yards oznabriges, 75 yards scotch cheeks, 12 vest buttons, a ram, 2 horses, a mare, 2 cows & calves, a cow & yearling, 2 heifers with calf, a bull, yarling heifer, parcel of hogs in the woods, horse bell, & some dunghill fowles; [note at end] part of provisions in inventory expended in maintaining the children of the deceased since his death until vendue & part of cloth was made up for the children who were almost "necked". (signed) Parmenas Horton; book 11 p. 445.

3723. Jun. 28, 1764 will of John Mill, mariner (Craven Co): in name of God amen; soul to God & body to be buried in Christian like manner; (a) 3 of my Negro wenches Nancy, Lucy, & Sabrina to be sold by my executors to "return" my son William's Negro & pay my debts; (b) to my son William Mill: a "plantation" on E side of Smiths Cr known as "Jones" which I bought of Wm Norwood with my Negro boy; (c) to my daughter Mary Graham: "plantation" where I live & for want of heirs of her body to my son John Mill; and to daughter Mary half of my household goods, a feather bed excepted, and half of my cattle, half of my sheep, my Negro Abigia & her child Flora, my horse with 2 plows & 3 wedges; (d) to my daughter Susannah Mill 300 ac bounded by Benjamin Hall's land & new patented land that I gave my son John being a new survey for which I paid Christopher Neale for patenting containing 300 ac; and to daughter Susannah a Negro wench Visbett, Negro girl Nanan, other half of my household goods, half of my cattle, half of my sheep, a black mare, my new saddle, & a desk; (e) to my son John Mill 100 ac at head of NW branch of Smiths Cr, joins Thomas Nelson & Benjamin Hall; and to son John 150 ac on Core Banks that I bought of James Johnson deceased and 2 Negro men Cats & Lendon, a yearling horse that came of my "black", a feather bed, & a gun; (f) other items such as hoes, "acres", crops, & cut saw go my children in common; Joseph Edmondson sr, my son William Mill, & my daughter Mary Graham are executors & executrix. (signed) John Mill; (witness) John West, Benjamin Hall, & John Bryan; wit. oath Jul. 1764 by John Bryan; book 11 p. 446.

3724. Apr. 14, 1764 (Quaker style date) account of sales of sundry goods of estate of Levi Bush deceased by Parmenas Horton, administrator: total accounts of Levi Bush £102.2.8 [minus] sheriff's 2% commission £2.11 [equals] £99.11.8 (signed) Parmenas Horton & Richard Cogdell, sheriff; book 11 p. 448.

3725. Apr. 27, 1764 account of sales of estate of Stephen Brice deceased: total accounts £84.5.2 [minus] sheriff's 2% commission £2.2 [equals] £82.3.2. (signed) Richard Cogdell, sheriff; book 11 p. 449.

3726. Oct. 20, 176 account of sales of estate of Elizabeth Mason deceased: total account £73.14.2 [minus] sherif's 2% commission £1.16.10 [equals] £71.18.4. (signed) Richard Cogdell, sheriff; book 11 p. 449.

books 12 & 13 (1764-1766)
3727. Apr. 8, 1766 Peter Conway, gentleman (New Bern, NC) to Robert Orme & Thomas Webber; for £79.11 proclamation money sold 10 mahogany hair bottomed chairs, 18 rush bottomed chairs, 6 leather bottomed chairs, an elbow chair, black walnut desk & book case, 3 large looking glasses, 5 small looking glasses, 8 feather beds with bed cloths bolsters & pillows, 4 pair "hand" irons, 48 puter plates, Negro wench Rose, 4 mahogany tables, & sundry household furniture; sale void if Conway pays Orme £47.15 by Nov. 10 next; Orme & Webber obtained bond from Conway for that amount today. (signed) Peter Conway; (witness) Amb C Bagley [only one witness]; wit. oath Jul. 1766 by Ambrose C Bagley; books 12 & 13 p. 1.

3728. Sept. 4, 1765 William Herritage, gentleman (Craven Co) to Stephen Lee, gentleman (Onslow Co, NC); for £0.5 proclamation money sold Negro woman Rachel & her child Ralph, Negro girl Francis, Negro boy & girl (twins) Peter & Hannah, & Negro boy Junus. (signed) Wm Herritage; (witness) John Williams & Robt Orme; [note at end indicates Lee paid Herritage consideration money Sept. 4, 1765]; wit. oath Jul. 1766 by Robt Orme; books 12 & 13 p. 2.

3729. Jun. 20, 1766 Thomas Persons [or Perssons] jr (Craven Co) to John Persons (same); for £10 proclamation money sold 200 ac [no more description]; where John Persons lives; being land that descended to Thomas Persons by death of his father Jeremiah Persons. (signed) Thomas "Perrsons"; (witness) Thomas Rue & Southey Rew; wit. oath Jul. 1766 by "Charles Rue"; books 12 & 13 p. 3.

3730. Feb. 8, 1763 Joseph Pittman (Craven Co) to John Pittman (same); for £212 proclamation money sold 175 ac; border: begins at Sandy Point on E side of

Adams Cr, joins Bashshabor Cr, a branch, Francis Hill's head line, land formerly owned by "his" brother "Obedience" Pittman, land owned by Joseph Pittman jr; given to me by [my] father Joseph Pittman deceased & being where Joseph Pittman deceased lived when he died. (signed) Joseph Pittman; (witness) Silvenius Walesbury, Charles Rew, & Thomas Cullen; wit. oath Jul. 1766 by Charles Rew; books 12 & 13 p. 4.

3731. Jun. 30, 1766 Longfield Cox, planter (Craven Co) to John Hollaway, planter; for £150 proclamation money sold 76 ac on S side of Neuse R & on Half moon Swamp; border: begins at Loflin's corner white oak, joins a branch, Williams, & Griffin; granted Apr. 24, 1764 to Longfield Cox. (signed) Longfield Cox; (witness) Benjamin Newport & Samuel West; wit. oath Jul. 1766 to Samuel West; books 12 & 13 p. 6.

3732. Mar. 2, 1765 John Baker, planter (Craven Co) to John Roe, planter (same); for £20 proclamation money sold 150 ac on N side of Neuse R & on Buckleberry Swamp; includes an island; border: begins at a chesnut oak. (signed) John Baker's mark "X"; (witness) Carson Scott & Peter Harper; wit. oath Jul. 1766 by Carson Scott; books 12 & 13 p. 8.

3733. Aug. 11, 1766 John Bryan, planter (Craven Co) to Samuel Cornell esq (New Bern, Craven Co); for £500 proclamation money sold 2 tracts: 571 ac on S side of Trent R; (a) sold Dec. 17, 1742 by Martin Franks & Edward Franks to Edward Bryan father of John; & (b) [omitted] ac on S side of Trent R & E side of Cypress Cr; border: sold Dec. 12, 1745 by Edward Frank to Edward Bryan father of John; [reference to both previous deeds for metes & bounds]; & (c) for £500 proclamation money sold Negro man Caesar, Negro man Tom, Negro man Peter, Negro man Isaac, Negro man Francks, Negro man Jack, Negro boy little Tom, Negro boy Quash, Negro boy little Caesar, Negro woman Tiner, Negro woman Nancy, Negro girl little Nancy, Negro girl Hagar, Negro girl Peg, Negro girl Phillis, Negro girl little Tina, Negro girl Sal, all the cattle, horses, sheep, & household furniture on "said several" tracts that are now are property of John Bryan as in a schedule prepared by John Bryan; sale void if Bryan pays Cornell £500 proclamation money with lawful interest within next 2 years; if there is a default, Cornell can sell the land & other property & use proceeds to pay debt. (signed) Jon. Bryan & Samuel Cornell; (witness) Stephen Dewey & Chrisr. Neale; [memo at end] Aug. 11, 1766 quiet possession of property was given by Bryan giving Cornell a Negro boy Tom in name of all Negroes & other property (signed) Jon Bryan [same witnesses]; [another note indicates Cornell paid Bryan £500 on Aug. 11, 1766]; wit. oath Aug. 23, 1766 by Christopher Neale before Jas Harrell, CJ; books 12 & 13 p. 9.

3734. Jun. [blank], 1764 Peter Conway, gentleman (Craven Co) to my beloved son William Conway; for love, good will, & affection and for £0.10 sterling Great Britain money sold lot #257 in New Bern on Broad Street; border: joins lot where Peter Conway dwells; sold Sept. 8, 1751 by Francis Maclewain to Peter Conway recorded in Craven Co book N p. 395; (b) Negro girl Rose & her increase; sold by Thomas Clifford Howe esq to Peter Conway. (signed) Peter Oonway; William Erven & Isaac Partridge; wit. oath Mar. 19, 1767 by Isaac Partridge before M Howard, chief justice; books 12 & 13 p. 15.

3735. Oct. 30, 1765 Peter Steel (Craven Co) to Stephen Golver, planter (same); for £20 proclamation sold 60 ac near Steels Run; border: begins at a white oak; part of tract Peter Steel sold to said Stephen Glover on Sept. 28, 1756, but when Peter Steel resurveyed his land it left out part of said land sold to Stephen Glover. (signed) Peter Steel's mark "X"; (witness) Jas Donald, Edmund Hatch jr, & Edmund Hatch; wit. oath Apr. 1766 by "Edmond" Hatch; [Christopher Neale is clerk of court now]; books 12 & 13 p. 16.

3736. Aug. 2, 1765 James Steel, planter (Onslow Co, NC) to John Eubanks, planter (Craven Co); for £85 proclamation money sold 200 ac on S side of Trent R & joins Lemuel Hatch's mill Pond; border: begins at a willow oak on side of said pond. (signed) James Steel; (witness) Lemuel Hatch & Edmond Hatch; wit. oath Apr. 1766 by Edmond Hatch; books 12 & 13 p. 18.

3737. Aug. 2, 1765 Lemuel Hatch (Craven Co) to Peter "Steele" (Craven Co) & James Steel (Onslow Co, NC); for £15 proclamation money sold 52 ac; border: begins at edge of Steel's old field where Lemuel Hatch's line "goes through" & joins the mill pond. (signed) Lemuel Hatch; (witness) Benj Hatch & Edmond Hatch; wit. oath Apr. 1766 by Edmond Hatch; books 12 & 13 p. 20.

3738. Aug. 2, 1765 James Steel, planter (Onslow Co, NC) to Peter Steel, planter (Craven Co); for £15 proclamation money sold 46 ac; border: joins land where Peter Steel lives and land where John Eubanks lives that I sold him on "other" side; part of land left to me by my deceased father Alexander Steel. (signed) James Steel; (witness) Lemuel Hatch & Edmond Hatch; wit. oath Apr. 1766 by Edmond Hatch; books 12 & 13 p. 22.

3739. Apr. 4, 1766 Richard Reynolds, planter (Craven Co) to Moses Almond, carpenter (same); for £175 proclamation money sold 170 ac "exclusive" of the island on E side of Brices Cr; border: begins at mouth of Holstons Br on the creek, joins a dividing line made for Lewis Williams, Rigdon Brice, & includes an island; sold by John Acton Brice to Lewis Williams who sold it back to J A Brice on May 20, 1762 who sold Jun. 28, 1762 to Charles Cogdell who sold May 8, 1764 to me; 100 ac of the land has quit rent of £0.0.6 per 100 acres and joins a straight line from Holstons Br to Rigdon Brice's line and 70 ac joins courses of the branch as by patent May 5, 1713 to [omitted]. (signed) Robert Reynolds; (witness) Elihu Hall & Sarah Hall; [note at end indicates Almond paid Reynolds £175]; wit. oath Oct. 1766 by Elihu Hall; books 12 & 13 p. 23.

3740. May 7, 1765 Solomon Cox & Jeremiah Cox (Craven Co) to John Conway (same); for £5 proclamation money sold 200 ac on S side of Swift Cr; border:

begins at upper end of said land [no more description]; part of Daniel Cox's patent dated Oct. 7, 1749; Conway to pay yearly quit rent of £0.4 proclamation money per 100 ac. (signed) Solomon Cox & Jeremiah Cox's mark "X"; (witness) Azariah Mackape & "Tabilha" Cox; wit. oath "Oct." by Azariah "Mackapee"; books 12 & 13 p. 26.

3741. Oct. 4, 1766 Thomas Moor (Craven Co) to Benjamin Hickman (same); for £50 NC money sold 182 ac; border: begins at a hickory near Benjamin Hickman's, joins John Barker, & near George Churlton; granted Oct. 20, 1762 [2nd year of reign of King George II] to [omitted]. (signed) Thomas Moor's mark "X"; (witness) William Bryan & Lewis Bryan; Oct. 1766 acknowledged; books 12 & 13 p. 27.

3742. Mar. 13, 1766 Thomas Sitgreaves & "his wife" John Cady Bryan to Joseph Hall; Thomas Smith died owning land on E side of S fork of Coor Cr; land descended to Nathan Smith as heir at law who sold to John Cady Bryan wife of Thomas Sitgreaves and Thomas & wife have "contracted" to sell the land to Joseph Hall; SO for £24 proclamation money sold 100 ac on E side of S fork of Coor Cr; border: begins at a white oak; Hall to pay yearly quit rent of £0.4 proclamation money per 100 ac to the king. (signed) Thomas Sitgreaves & John Cady "Sitgreaves'" mark "X"; (witness) Chrisr. Neale & Ann Cady Bryan; [note at end indicates Hall paid Thos Sitgreaves £24 Mar. 13, 1766]; Oct. 1766 acknowledged by Thomas & John Cady Sitgreaves and John C Sitgreaves renounced dower before Frederick Becton esq (signed) Chrisr Neale, CIC; books 12 & 13 p. 29.

3743. Nov. 12, 1766 Richard Bleckledge, high sheriff (Craven Co) to Samuel Crowell esq (Newbern, Craven Co); for £61 sold 300 ac on N side of Neuse R & E side of Beards Cr; border: begins at mouth of Beards Cr, joins a small gut, & "the" back line; part of 640 ac granted Jun. 10, 1706 to James Beard and David Smith claims an "interest in residue" of said grant or 340 (sic) ac; sold due to writ of fieri facias from New Bern Dist Superior Court on May [blank], 1766 & returnable to court Nov. 2 next for £79.19.4 proclamation money damages & £7.14.4 costs against David Smith due to suit by Samuel Crowell; and sold due to act of Parliament of Great Britain & Assembly passed in 5th year of reign of King George II concerning collection of debts in America. (signed) Richard Blackledge; (witness) William Green & William Green jr; [note at end indicated Crowell paid Blackledge £61 on Nov. 12, 1766]; Jan. 1767 acknowledged; books 12 & 13 p. 31.

3744. Sept. 20, 1766 John Edmindson (Craven Co) to James Barranton (same); for £60 proclamation money sold 100 ac on N side of Neuse R & on W side of Upper Broad Cr; border: begins at mouth of a branch, joins head of a branch, & "the" back line; part of 200 ac granted Feb. 27, 1735 to [omitted]. (signed) John Edmindson's mark "o"; (witness) Isaac Barranton & William Barranton; wit. oath Oct. 1766 by Isaac Barranton; books 12 & 13 p. 34.

3745. Jul. 1, 1766 Susannah Mackichen (Craven Co) to Peter Anderson jr (same); for £15 proclamation money sold 100 ac; known as Pulen Paincer's Landing "or Diping hole"; border: begins at a white oak on the river; part of 300 ac granted Apr. 20, 1745 to [omitted]. (signed) Susannah Mackichen's mark "S M"; (witness) Edward Frank & Harriet Hannah; wit. oath Oct. 1766 by Edward Frank; books 12 & 13 p. 35.

3746. Jan. 4, 1766 Stephen Glare (Craven Co) to Joseph Reasonover (same); for £60 proclamation money sold 75 ac; border: begins at Edmond Hatch's corner pine & joins "the" patent line; part of grant May 6, 1760 to Edmond Hatch. (signed) Stephen Glare's mark "X"; (witness) Edmond Hatch, Benjamin Hatch, & Jonathan Ray; wit. oath Oct. 1766 by Edmd Hatch; books 12 & 13 p. 37.

3747. Sept. 20, 1766 William Clark (Craven Co) to William Lewis (same); for £30 proclamation money sold on N side of Swift Cr & E side of Creeping Swamp; border: begins at corner pine of division line between William Clark & William Lewis; Lewis to pay yearly quit rent of £0.4 proclamation money per 100 ac to the king. (signed) William Clark's mark "M" & Winifred Clark's mark "M" (sic); (witness) John Hill, Joseph Letchworth, & Kezia Hill; Oct. 1766 by William Clark & wife Winifred and Winifred renounced dower before Frederick Becton; books 12 & 13 p. 39.

3748. Apr. 30, 1764 Robert Hall (Craven Co) to Thomas Hall, planter (same); for £65 proclamation money sold 500 ac on N side of Nuce R & E side of "Broad Creek Upper Broad Creek"; border: begins on Deep Run above Shine's Landing at a pine, joins a patent line, & a road; sold by Francis Davison to me. (signed) Robert Hall; (witness) Cason Bryan jr & Wm Spight; Oct. 1766 acknowledged; books 12 & 13 p. 41.

3749. Jan. 21, 1766 Eliza Martin (Craven Co), widow of Thomas Martin gentleman (late of Craven Co) to Joseph Pitman (same); for £12 proclamation money sold £50 on W side of South R & N side of Southwest Cr; border: begins at Richard Hill's corner pine, joins Mr. Mills, & "the" back line; sold by Joseph Royal to Thomas Martin. (signed) Eliza Martin; (witness) John West & Slocumb Ferguson; wit. oath Oct. 1766 by John West; books 12 & 13 p. 42.

3750. Aug. 18, 1766 (witness) John Blake, planter (Cohookie Cr, Craven Co) to John Bishop jr (Clubfoots Cr, Craven Co); for £30 proclamation money sold 200 ac on S side of Nuse R, E side of Handcocks Cr, & joins Cohookie Cr "or Branch"; border: begins at a pine on said Handcock's former line and joins Cohookie Cr & Branch; granted Sept. 1, 1759 by Gov. Arthur Dobbs to James Handcock who sold to said John Blake. (signed) John Blake; (witness) John Thomlinson & Daniel Frazier; wit. oath "Oct." by John Thomlinson; books 12 & 13 p. 44.

3751. Oct. 4, 1766 Elizabeth Martin, widow (South R, Craven Co) to my little grandson Richard Martin Wallis, "infant" (Craven Co); for love & good will gave, at my death, (a) {omitted] ac on S side of Nuce R & W side of South R; being "plantation" where I live; granted to me; & (b) gold ring, pair of gold sleeve buttons, pair of silver shoe buckles, 4 cows & calves, a hand mill, pair shoe buckles set with stone, Negro girl Lucretia, & silver spoon; all to de delivered at my death; if Richard dies in his minority, Negro goes to "its" mother Angelina; Richard to pay yearly quit rent on land of £0.0.6 per 100 ac to the king. (signed) Elizabeth Martin's mark "E"; (witness) Jno Jones, John Nelson, & Thos Nelson; wit. oath Oct. 1766 by John Nelson; books 12 & 13 p. 46.

3752. Oct. 16, 1766 Ruben Phillips (Craven Co) to John Williams, rosliner(?) (same); for £21 NC money sold 100 ac; border: begins at a pine on N side of Little Contentney Cr, joins "a child" of Christian "Ceel" called Lewis Williams, Thomas Blount's former line, & corner made between Peter Low & Thomas Phillips; part of tract sold by Joseph Jackson to Thomas Phillips. (signed) Reuben Phillips; (witness) Edward Cannon, Shadrach Allen & Samuel Smith; wit. oath Jan. 1767 by Edward Cannon; books 12 & 13 p. 48.

3753. Feb. 12, 1767 Rev. Henry Addison, rector of St. John's called King George's Parish (Prince Georges Co, Maryland) age 48 or thereabouts before John Beale Birdley; swears he knows Doctor Andrew Scott (formerly of said county) having been his parishiner; about 14 years ago, he moved from said province and "understood settled" in New Bern, NC, wher he resided and it is said died sometime last summer; Addison is well acquainted with George Scott, brother of the deceased, who has ben for many years & now is his parishiner. (signed) H Addison, "M A" rector of St. Johns Parish, before John Beale Birdley; [no wintess]; books 12 & 13 p. 49;

Feb. 16, 1767 Walter Derlang esq (Annapolis, Maryland) age 42 or thereabouts before Jno B Birdley; swears he was well acquainted with Doctor Andrew Scott (formerly of Prince George's Co, Maryland) for many years; several years ago, he moved to North Carolina, as Delang understood, & it is said died sometime last Summer; he is also well acquainted with George Scott, brother of the deceased, who is inhabitant of Prince George Co, Maryland. (signed) Walter Derlang before Jno B Birdley; [no witness]; books 12 & 13 p. 50;

Feb. 16, 1767 (Maryland Secretary's office) Daniel "Darlang" esq, Secretary of Maryland certifies John Beale Birdley esq is one of Right Honorable Lord Propriety of Maryland and justice of Provincial Court. [not signed]; "see p. 53 for instrument which should follow this"; books 12 & 13 p. 50;

Feb. 16, 1767 George Scott, gentleman (Prince George's Co, Maryland), brother & heir of Doctor Andrew Scott deceased (late of New Bern, NC), to Ebenezer Fisher, gentleman ("said" county); power of attorney to take possession of real & personal estate and anything else in North Carolina of said deceased; attorney can sell the property & sign deeds for me and send money to me. (signed) G Scott; (witness) Walter Derlang [only one witness]; books 12 & 13 p. 51;

(Maryland) Feb. 19, 1767 Horatio Sharpe, Lieutenant General & "chief" Governor of Maryland, certifies Daniel Derlang esq is Secretary of Maryland.

(signed) Horo. Sharpe;

May 2, 1767 Robert Bail, merchant (Philadelphia) recognized with handwriting of George Scott before M Howard, chief justice, and Martin Howard compared handwriting of Daniel Derling with official certificate under handwriting of Daniel Derlang & find they compare (signed) M Howard, chief justice; books 12 & 13 p. 53.

3754. Apr. 10, 1765 Peter Conway (Craven Co) to Richard Cogdell (same); for £45 proclamation money sold 0.5 ac in lot #81 in New Bern [no more description]; sold Jun. 29, 1759 by William Heritage to "Honoro Doncan" [female] who sold Oct. 18, 1763 to Peter Conway. (signed) Peter Conway & Mary Conway (sic); (witness) Robt Orme & Geo Ormsbee [or Ormsby]; [note at end indicates Cogdell paid Conway £45 on Apr. 10, 1765; wit. oath Jan. 1767 by Robt Orme; books 12 & 13 p. 54.

3755. Jan. 2, 1767 Christopher Shelling to Robert Orme; for £76 proclamation money leased for 60 years Shelling's interest in 2 tracts: (a) 114 ac on E side of Mill Cr; border: begins at corner pine between said Shelling & "Gordins Richetson", & joins a swamp "of" eastermost branch of Mill Cr; leased by Thomas Pollock to said Christopher Shelling; & (b) 6 ac on NW corner of "said land" sold Nov. 25, 1755 to Thomas Pollock to Christopher Shelling; yearly quit rent is £0.15 sterling per 100 ac to be paid to Pollock. (signed) Christopher Shelling; (witness) John Granade, John Mace, & James McConnell; [note at end indicates Orme paid Shelling £67 on Jan. 3, 1767]; wit. oath "Jan." by James McConnell; books 12 & 13 p. 56.

3756. Oct. 18, 1766 Edward Cannon (Craven Co) to Shadrach Allen (same); for £50 proclamation money sold 50 ac on N side of Swift Cr; border: begins at a white oak "all" below first branch made by Edward Cannon & Shadrach Allen; part of grant to Henry Smith; (b) 100 ac on N side of Swift Cr & NW side of Jespers Swamp; border: begins at said Cannon's corner formerly Henry Smith's corner on side of Swift Creek Swamp & joins Thomas Tartten; granted Apr. 21, 1764 by Gov. Arthur Dobbs to Edward Cannon; Allen to pay yearly quit rent of £0.4 proclamation money per 100 ac to the king. (signed) Edward Cannon; (witness) Josias Hardie, Samuel Smith, & John Grainger; wit. oath "Jan." by Samuel Smith; books 12 & 13 p. 58.

3757. Dec. 7, 1765 Gideon Tingle (Craven Co) to John Bedscot; for £40 proclamation money sold 136 ac on N side of Nuce R & W side of Upper Broad Cr; border: begins at a pine, joins a branch, & "the" back line; granted to George "Tuler". (signed) Gideon Tingle; (witness) Wm West, William Tyer, & Solom. Smith; wit. oath Jan. 1767 by Wm West; books 12 & 13 p. 60.

3758. Oct. 2, 1765 Samuel Collins & Joseph Collins, planters (Craven Co) to Jacob Taylor, carpenter (same); for £33 proclamation money sold 250 ac on S side of Nuce R & on Slocumbs Cr; border: begins at mouth of Colmans Cr, joins Glovers Cr, George Lovick, head of Broad Cr, & mouth of Broad Cr; granted

Sept. 10, 1707 to Robert Colman and granted [date blank] to Samuel Sullins. (signed) Joseph Collins & Samuel Collins; (witness) John Granade & Joseph Granade; wit. oath Jan. 1767 by John Granade; books 12 & 13 p. 61.

3759. Dec. 9, 1765 Thomas Robinson, taylor (Craven Co) to Thomas Smart, merchant (same); for £30 proclamation money sold 100 ac on S side of Trent R & "in" Deep Neck; border: begins at a white oak on the river side and joins Michel Shelfer's fence; being upper part of grant to Matthew Whilk [or Whick]. (signed) Thomas Robinson; (witness) John Parrey jr & William Jones; wit. oath Jan. 1767 by John Parrey jr; books 12 & 13 p. 63.

3760. Oct. 28, 1765 Jacob Tayler, planter (Craven Co) to Thomas Moss, "carbenter" (same); for £60 sold 150 ac on S side of Nuce R & on Slocumbs Cr; border: begins at "Collmans" Cr, joins mouth of a small branch by Riggs Landing, head of the branch, Lovick, head of Broad Cr, & mouth of Broad Cr; granted Sept. 10, 1707 by Lords Proprietor to Robert Coleman; Moss to pay yearly quit rent of £0.0.6 per 100 ac to the king. (signed) Jacob Tayler; (witness) Benjamin Riggs & Susana Riggs; wit. oath Jan. 1767 by Benjamin Riggs; books 12 & 13 p. 65.

3761. Apr. 13, 1767 [7th year of reign of King George III] Thomas McLin, merchant (Craven Co) to Samuel Cornell, merchant (same); for £250 proclamation money sold part of lot #15 in New Bern; border: begins at corner of Front Street & Craven Street, runs N 40 feet on Craven Street to Jacob Sheppard's house occupied by Mrs. Richardson, W 40 feet at right angle, S 40 feet with line of "the tenement" occupied by Charles Johnston cord winder due to lease from Arthur Johnston to Front Street, & E on Front Street to first station; where stands late dwelling house & store of McLin & Borroughs now occupied by Jacob Sheppard. (signed) Thomas McLin; (witness) John Pittman & Thomas James Emery; May 7, 1767 acknowledged before M Howard, chief justice; books 12 & 13 p. 67.

3762. Apr. 26, 1767 Edward Brice Dobbs esq, captain of his Majesty's 7th Regiment of Foot or Royal Fusiliers by his attorney Frederick Gregg, to Samuel Cornell, merchant (Newbern, Craven Co); for £600 proclamation money sold 2 tracts: (a) 600 ac on S side of Neuse R; granted May 13, 1714 by John Lord Carteret & other Lords Proprietor to Captain Frederick Jones deceased; & (b) 260 ac on S side of Neuse R; being E part of 460 ac granted Mar. 15, 1745 to Katherine Hannis [reference to grant for metes & bounds of both tracts]. (signed) Edward Brice Dobbs, by Frederick Gregg his attorney; (witness) Robert Bail & Chris Neale; [note at end indicates Cornell paid Gregg £600 on Apr. 26, 1767; wit. oath May 7, 1767 by Christopher Neale before M Howard, chief justice; books 12 & 13 p. 69.

3763. May 4, 1767 Joseph Leech, merchant, & wife Mary (Newbern, Craven Co) to Gabriel Cathcart, gentleman (New Bern, NC); for £400 NC money sold 350 ac on S side of Neuse R & on Batchelors Cr; called Williams' Neck; border: begins at a white oak on side of the creek & joins a branch. (signed) Joseph Leech & Mary Leech; (witness) Thos Hoslen [or Huslen]; [note at end indicates Cathcart paid Leech £400 on May 4, 1767]; May 14, 1767 acknowledged by Joseph Leech and Mary Leech renounced dower before Mar. Howard, chief justice; books 12 & 13 p. 73.

3764. Oct. 29, 1762 Richard Blackledge, sheriff (Craven Co) to William Heritage, gentleman (same); for £26 proclamation money sold house & 0.5 ac in lot #221 in New Bern; sold first Tuesday in Oct. 1762 due to writ of fieri facias issued Jul. 6, 1765 "after" Sept. 29, 1732 (sic) from Craven Co Pleas & Quarter Sessions Court & returnable to court first Tuesday in Oct. next against personal estate of Mary Dove deceased in hands of George Hays administrator if sufficient but it not sufficient then against personal estate & land of Mary Dove for £23.0.7½ due to suit by William Heritage; and sold due to act of Parliament of Great Britain passed in 5th year of reign of King George III (sic) concerning collection of debts in America and act of General Assembly. (signed) Richd Blackledge, sheriff; (witness) Eliza. Bayley & Amb Cox Bayley; [note at end indicates Heritage paid Blackledge £26 on Oct. 29, 1765; Jan. 1767 acknowledged; books 12 & 13 p. 74.

3765. Dec. 23, 1756 Christopher Shilling & Michael Brener; "memorandum": on Nov. 25, 1755 Shilling & Benner leased for 60 years from Thomas Pollock 214 ac on E side of Mill Cr; border: begins at a hickory on the creek side, joins Slilius Rhiner, & swamp of eastermost branch of Mill Cr; yearly rent is £0.15 per 100 ac; Shilling & Benner divided the land: 100 ac to Benner begins at a shrubby red oak on line "already marked" N40W 60 poles to a lightwood stake, S70W 60 poles to pine, S50@ to the creek, up the creek to Jno Frederick Sherbert's corner hickory, & along his line to first station; lower part or 114 ac to Shilling; Shilling to pay rent for 114 ac; SO Shilling & Brener agree to bond of £50 sterling to abide by this agreement. (signed) Christopher Shilling & Michael "M" Brener; (witness) John Granade & Jno Frederick Merkin [or Muscot]; wit. oath Jan. 1767 by John Granade; books 12 & 13 p. 78.

3766. Jan. 5, 1765 George Becton, planter (Craven Co) to Samuel Slade, planter (same); for £100 proclamation money leased for 20 years "mansion" house and 322 ac on W side of Moselys Cr; known as "Jucobs" Wells; "lately" occupied by said George Becton [no more description]; yearly rent is a pepper corn to be paid Dec. 1 if demanded. (signed) George Becton; (witness) Samul. Slade jr & Ebenezer Slade; wit. oath Oct. 1766 by Samuel Slade jr; books 12 & 13 p. 79.

3767. Sept. 1, 1766 Rd Ellis, merchant (New Bern, NC) to Eleanor Cox; for yearly rent leased for 18 years beginning May 1 last part of front lot #13 in New Bern; where said Ellis lives; border: begins at a store now kept by Bartholomew Rooke, runs 50 feet in front towards said Ellis' stable & chair house, back as far as the lot runs, & opposite John Clitherall esq's house where he lives; yearly rent is £5 proclamation money to be paid Nov. 1 & May 1 in 2 installments; Ellis can take the land back if rent isn't pai. (signed) Richd Ellis & Eleanor Cox's mark "X"; (witness) Chrisr. Neale & James Stevenson; wit. oath Oct. 1766 by Chrisr. Neale; books 12 & 13 p. 82.

3768. May 6, 1767 [7th year of reign of King George III] Francis Brice & wife Abigail (Duplin Co, NC) to Timothy Clear (Newbern, Craven Co); for £800 proclamation money sold 400 ac on E side of Brice's Cr; includes land, low grounds, & marsh between William Wilson deceased, Richard Spaight deceased, Francis Brice jr; border: joined on N by William Wilson, on [W--lined out] by Richard Spaight deceased, on E by Francis Brice jr, on S by Holstons Br, & W by Brice's Cr; part of 2 grants: (a) 1,280 ac on May 12, 1713 to Col. William Brice and (b) 187 ac on May 5, 1742 to Francis & William Brice and 283 ac is within line of first grant at quit rent of £0.0.66 per 100 ac and residue or 117 ac within lines of said new patent & front land at quit rent of £0.4 per 100 ac. (signed) Fran. Brice & Abigail's mark "X"; (witness) Jno Smith & Will Green jr; May 6, 1767 acknowledged by Francis Brice and Abigail Brice renounced dower before Mar. Howard, chief justice; [note at end indicates Clear paid Brice £800 on May 6, 1767]; books 12 & 13 p. 84.

3769. at Craven Co court first Tuesday in Apr. 1763 John Rice, gentleman swore: about 1746 he "happened" at house of William Heritage gentleman (of Craven Co); at same time William Hancock (of Craven Co) was present, whose business there was to include sale of land near New Bern known as Green Springs; on same day Heritage sold said land to Hancock with Rice as evidence; Rice understood all of Green Springs was sold. (signed) Jno Rice; deposition agreeable to court minutes on same day it was taken was ordered recorded (signed) Chrisr. Neale, CIC; books 12 & 13 p. 86.

3770. May 10, 1766 Thomas Smart, merchant (Craven Co) to "Michel" Koonce, planter (same); for £40 proclamation money sold 150 ac on S side of Trent R & on mouth of Deep Neck; border: begins at corner pine of "the" survey and middle of upper line being first line of the survey; being E end of said survey; part of land "taken up" by Thomas Robinson and sold to Thomas Smart. (signed) Thomas Smart; (witness) John Parrey jr & Arthur Barrons; wit. oath Oct. 1766 by Arthur "Barons"; books 12 & 13 p. 86.

3771. Oct. 9, 1765 William Jones, planter (Dobbs Co, NC) to Elizabeth McKeney [or McKinney] & Anne [or Anna] McKeney, 2 orphans of Garrat McKeney deceased (late of Craven Co); for £200 proclamation due to Elizabeth & Anna from their father's estate & for "good causes" sold following Negroes: (a) Cloe to Elizabeth McKinney; (b) Rachel to Anne McKinney; & (c) Rose & her increase to be hired out for raising of above children while they come of age & then she and her increase "if any" to be sold and equally divided among 6 children of "Garret" McKinney deceased: Mary, John, Rachel, Joseph, Elizabeth, & Anne. (signed) Wm Jones; (witness) Wm Bryan & Lewis Bryan jr; wit. oath Oct. 1766 by Wm Bryan; books 12 & 13 p. 88.

3772. May 14, 1767 [7th year of reign of King George III] Arthur Johnston, planter, & wife Susannah (Craven Co) to Robert Williams, merchant (New Bern, NC); for £160 proclamation money sold part of lot [no number] in New Bern on N side of Front Street in New Bern; border: joined on E by house of Charles Johnston shoemaker, on N by garden in possession of Mrs. Sarah Richardson, on W by "poles" of a tenement in occupation of Richard Cogdell, 40 feet long, & 40 feet wide; with store house & cellar thereon which was "lately" in possession of Joseph Jones. (signed) Arthur Johnston & Susannah Johnston; wit. oath M Howard & Amblen Bugley, CIC; note at end indicates Williams paid the Johnstons £160 May 14, 1767]; May 14, 1767 acknowledged by Arthur Johnston and Susannah Johnston renounced dower before M Howard, chief justice; books 12 & 13 p. 89.

3773. Jan. 4, 1765 [5th year of "our" reign] Thomas Dick, carpenter (Craven Co) to Ephraim Lane, planter (same); for £40 proclamation money sold 564 ac in 2 tracts; 100 ac; border: joins Thomas Pollock; granted Mar. 13, 1756 to Thomas Dick; & (b) 464 ac; border: joins Thomas Pollock & Mr. Graves; granted Sept. 29, 1756 to Thomas Dick [reference to grant for metes & bounds for both tracts. (signed) Thos Dick; (witness) Samuel Lane & Arthur Mackey; [note at end: (Brunswick, NC) Jan. 23, 1765 Lane paid Dick £40 on Jan. 23, 1765 (sic)]; wit. oath Nov. 5, 1766 by Samuel Lane before Jas Hasell, CJ; books 12 & 13 p. 91.

3774. May 4, 1764 Andrew Guerry, planter (Craven Co) to Richard Blackledge, merchant (same); a bond for £300 sterling Great Britain money; bond void if, by Jan. 1 next, Guerry makes Blackledge a good deed for (a) 400 ac in a grant that's "mine or my wife Anne's"; known as Cooper's old place; land was granted Jun. 17, 1736 to Caleb "Mattcalf" who gave it to his daughter Anne, my present wife; & (b) 100 ac; border: joins said patent on N side of Nuse [R]; granted to William Handcock; deed to be made when Blackledge pays Guerry £0.20 South Carolina money per acre for the land allowing a dollar at £0.31. (signed) Andw. Guerry; (witness) Benjn. Blackledge, Thos Hixson [or Hexon], & Wm Morris; wit. oath Oct. 1766 by Benjamin Blackledge; books 12 & 13 p. 93.

3775. Oct. 9, 1766 John McKinney (Craven Co) to Furnifold Green (same); for £5 proclamation money sold on S side of Neuse R; border: begins at a white oak & cypress in the thorofare about 50 yards below upper Tarr Landing, & joins Sprigs' or Powell's corner on side of a hill near a swamp. (signed) John McKinney; (witness) William Heath & John Lane; wit. oath Oct. 1766 by William Heath; books 12 & 13 p. 95.

3776. Oct. 21, 1766 Absalom Taylor, black smith (Craven Co) to Moses Taylor, planter (same); for £100 proclamation money sold 10 ac on S side of Neuse R & E side of Flat Swamp; border: begins in the run of Flat Swamp at George Lewis' upper corner red oak and joins fork of a small drain; part of grant Sept. 29, 1756 to Robert & James Green jr. (signed) Absalom Taylor; (witness) Robert Taylor &

Aaron Taylor; Apr. 1767 acknowledged; books 12 & 13 p. 96.

3777. Feb. 8, 1767 Elisha Blackshare, planter (Craven Co) to John Fillyaw, wheel wright (same); for £80 proclamation money sold 100 ac on S side of Tackahoe Cr; border: begins at a large white oak in an angle of a small branch of Tuckahoe [Cr] near Johnson's line and joins a swamp. (signed) Elisha Blackshare; (witness) Jno Bryan & "Fredeck" Harget; wit. oath Apr. 1767 by Jno Bryan; books 12 & 13 p. 97.

3778. Oct. 10, 1756 Robert Taylor, planter (Craven Co) to my loving son Absalom Taylor, black smith (same); for love, good will, & affection gave 100 ac on S side of Neuse R & E side of Flat Swamp; border: begins at George Lane's upper corner red oak on the run of Flat Swamp and joins fork of a small drain; part of grant Sept. 29, 1756 to Robert Taylor & Robert Green jr. (signed) Robert Taylor; (witness) Moses Taylor & Aaron Taylor; wit. oath Apr. 1767 by Moses Taylor books 12 & 13 p. 99.

3779. assignment of lease from John Acton Brice to Elihu Hall which lease is recorded in book P p. 299: Oct. 31, 1765 Elihu Hall (Craven Co) to Rigdon Brice (same); Hall is one of parties in a lease, by John Action Brice to Elihu Hall, and for £65 proclamation money paid by Rigdon Brice sold land & Negroes mentioned in the lease for the term of the lease; Rigdon Brice to pay annual rent to J A Brice. (signed) Elihu Hall & Rigdon Brice; Robt Reynolds & Beniam Trowbridg; Oct. 1766 acknowledged by both parties; books 12 & 13 p. 101.

3780. May 21, 1745 William Heritage, attorney at law (Craven Co) to William Handcock, gentleman (same); George Roberts esq (late of Craven Co) signed his will giving William Heritage land called Green Spring where said Roberts lived; SO for 800 barrels of tar sold 300 ac on S side of Neuse R; border: begins at Williams Cr "or" Green Spring Cr, joins Richmond Gut, & westermost branch of said gut to head thereof. (signed) Willm. Heritage; (witness) Jno Rice & Daniel Dupree; [note at end indicates Handcock paid Heritage 800 bls. of tar "judged" at £03 sterling per barrel on May 2, 1745]; Jul. 1767 acknowledged; books 12 & 13 p. 102.

3781. Apr. 3, 1764 William Powell, gentleman (Newbern, Craven Co) to Penelope Rice, daughter of John Rice gentleman (same); for £0.5 proclamation money sold Negro wench Flora. (signed) Wm Powell; (witness) James Handcock & Chas Cawford; wit. oath Apr. 1767 by Chas Crawford; books 12 & 13 p. 103.

3782. Apr. 3, 1764 William Powell, gentleman (Newbern, Craven Co) to Elizabeth Rice, daughter to John Rice gentleman (same); for £0.5 sold Negro girl Warsaw, daughter of Negro woman Flora. (signed) Wm Powell; (witness) James Handcock & Chas Crawford; wit. oath Apr. 1767 to Chas Crawford; books 12 & 13 p. 104.

Craven County, NC Deed Books 11-13

3783. Apr. 1, 1767 [7th year of reign of King George III] Robert Palmer esq (Beaufort Co, NC) to David Kennedy; for a bay horse & "circumstances" of David Kennedy as he settled on a small piece of land or 95 ac granted to me "somewhere near" Swifts Cr sold said 95 ac; [reference to grant Palmer delivered to Kennedy]; Kennedy to pay quit rents to the king. (signed) Robert Palmer; (witness) Samuel Thompson & Absalom Tuten; wit. oath Apr. 1767 by Absalom Tuten; books 12 & 13 p. 105.

3784. Feb. 23, 1767 John Moore (Newbern, Craven Co) to my beloved son Jessee Moore (same); for love, good will, & affection & for £0.10 proclamation money sold (a) lot 212 in New Bern; where I dwell; & (b) a feather bed & furniture, a case & bottles, pair of scales & weights, a chest, 3 iron wedges, 2 large "puter" dishes, 2 pewter plates, a tankard, 12 spoons, 2 "gunns", an axe, a hatchet, a drawing knife, set of shoe maker's tools, & 12 [blank]. (signed) John Moore; (witness) Chrisr Neale, Will Green jr, & Jno Gray Blount; wit. oath Apr. 1767 by Will Green jr; books 12 & 13 p. 106.

3785. Oct. 11, 1766 Thomas Moor (Craven Co) to Lewis Bryan (same); for £50 proclamation money sold 73 ac in bent of Clayroot [Swamp] on N side; border: begins at a white oak in fork of said swamp & Creeping Swamp. (signed) Thomas Moor; (witness) William Bryan & Simion Bryan; wit. oath Apr. 1767 by William Bryan; books 12 & 13 p. 107.

3786. Feb. 25, 1767 [7th year of reign of King George III] David Fonville ("late" inhabitant of Craven Co now dwelling in Craven Co, NC (sic)) to Umphrey Wilks, planter (Craven Co); for £40 proclamation money sold 100 ac on S side of Neuse R & on Mill Br; border: begins at a white oak on head of the branch; granted Apr. 20, 1745 [18th year of reign of King George II] by Gov. Gabriel "Johnson" to James Durham. (signed) David Fonville; (witness) John Fonville jr & Isaac Fonville; wit. oath Apr. 1767 by Joh Fonville jr; books 12 & 13 p. 108.

3787. Aug. 25, 1764 Amos Small, planter (Craven Co) to John Granade jr, planter (same); for £20.1 proclamation money sold 28 ac on S side of Trent R; border: begins at a white oak on Mr. Thomas Pollock's line, joins Daniel Simmons' patent line, & "his" old corner; granted Oct. 4, 1747 to Daniel Simmons. (signed) Amos Small; (witness) Edwd Hatch & Daniel Simmons; wit. oath Oct. 1766 by Daniel Simmons; books 12 & 13 p. 110.

3788. Sept. 20, 1766 John Hatch (Craven Co) to James Busick (same); for £150 proclamation money sold 300 ac on S side of Trent R & on Crooked Meadows; border: begins at a red oak at head of Batchelors Br & the river; granted Jun. 8, 1739 to John Richards who sold to "said" Humphrey Wilks who sold to John Hatch. (signed) John Hatch; (witness) Mary Hatch & Lemuel Hatch; wit. oath Apr. 1767 by Lemuel Hatch; books 12 & 13 p. 112.

3789. Apr. 3, 1767 Jos Reasonover, planter (Craven Co) to Jeremiah Watson, planter (same); for £75 proclamation money sold 75 ac; border: begins at Edmd. Hatch's corner pine and joins "the" patent line; part of grant May 6, 1760 to Edmd Hatch. (signed) Joseph Reasonover's mark "X"; (witness) Edmund Hatch, Lemuel Hatch, & Jas "Monald"; wit. oath Apr. 1767 by Lemuel Hatch; books 12 & 13 p. 114.

3790. Jan. 11, 1767 John Green & Peter Knight, merchants & partners, to Richard Ellis, merchant (New Bern, NC); for £90 with interest, secured to be paid by Richard Ellis, sold lots #257 & 285 in New Bern; mortgaged Aug. 13, 1766 Peter Conway gentleman deceased (late of New Bern) to Peter Knight & John Green for £90 proclamation money; mortgage was to be void if Conway paid Knight & Green £90 with interest by Dec. 25 next, but the money wasn't paid; so Knight & Green now sell the lots. (signed) John Green for Peter Knight, John Green, & Richd Ellis; (witness) Bernard Parkinson & Rd Cogdell; [note at end indicates Knight & Green received principal, interest, & £2.8 for drawing the deed]; wit. oath Jul. 1767 by Richard Cogdell; books 12 & 13 p. 115.

3791. Nov. 5, 1766 Joseph Hall (Craven Co) to George Phenney Lovick (same); for £300 proclamation money sold 640 [or 340, after exception] ac on S side of Neuse R; border: begins at mouth of Otter Cr, runs "into the woods", joins mouth of Damin Cr, & the river; except 300 ac sold by me to my brother Elihu Hall; Lovick to pay yearly quit rent of £0.0.6 per 100 ac to the king. (signed) Joseph Hall; (witness) William Wilton & Hen J Heritage; Nov. 5, 1766 acknowledged before Jas Hasell, CJ; books 12 & 13 p. 118.

3792. Oct. 12, 1765 Jacob Taylor & Benjamin Riggs (Craven Co) to George Phenney Lovick (same); for l20 proclamation money sold 120 ac on S side of Neuse R & W side of Slocumbs Cr; border: begins at mouth of a small branch between Thomas Moss & said Benjamin Riggs, joins above Lovick, & a large cove than makes out of Glover's Cr; being 70 ac old purchase at £0.0.6 per 100 [acres] & 50 ac new purchase at £0.4 per 100 ac [yearly quit rent rates]. (signed) Jacob Taylor & Benjn Riggs; (witness) Thomas Moss & Samuel Collins; wit. oath Apr. 1767 by Thomas Moss; books 12 & 13 p. 120.

3793. Dec. 24, 1764 John Stanaland [or Spinaland], planter (Craven Co) to William Bastin Whitford (same); for £20 proclamation money sold 200 ac on N side of Trent R; border: begins at a white oak on W side of N prong of Batchelors Cr and joins "said" branch; granted Nov. 16, 1764 by John Stanaland. (signed) John Stanaland; (witness) Thomas Lovett, Thomas Stanaland, & John Stanaland (sic); wit. oath Apr. 1767 by Thomas Stanaland; books 12 & 13 p. 122.

3794. Dec. 30, 1766 [7th year of reign of King George III] Timothy Cleur (Newbern, Craven Co) to James Stevenson (same); for £105 proclamation money sold 0.5 ac in lot #73 in New Bern on W side of Middle Street; border: joined on N by lot #75 and on S by said Stevenson's lot #70 [(sic) 71]. (signed) Timo. Cleur & James Stevenson; (witness) James Green jr & Chrisr Neale; [note at end indicates Stevenson paid Cleur £105 on Dec. 30, 1766]; Apr. 1767 acknowledged; books 12 & 13 p. 123.

3795. Nov. 11, 1766 John Berry (Amherst Co, Virginia) to Thomas McLin, merchant (Craven Co); for £215 proclamation money sold Negro man Primus, Negro man Luke, Negro woman Sarah, Negro boy Samuel; formerly owned by John Curmey deceased (late of Craven Co) and "recovered" by said John Berry in action of detinue against Thomas McLin & wife Mary, administrator of John "Curney", in New Bern Dist Superior Court; [note at end"] on same day Jacob Blount esq, due to power of attorney from John Berry, signed this deed. (signed) John Berry, by Jacob Blount; (witness) Saml Spencer & Rd Caswell; wit. oath Apr. 1767 by Richard Caswell; books 12 & 13 p. 125.

3796. Jan. 16, 1767 [6th year of reign of King George III] John Taylor, planter (Craven Co) to my loving son Absalom Taylor, planter (same); for love, good will, & affection gave 50 ac [no more description]; part of tract given by James Davis printer, out of Peter Smith's "paten", to [omitted]; property given to Absalom & heirs of his body lawfully begotten & if Absalom dies without heirs then to his wife as long as she remains a widow to live on the "plantation" but if she marries then land goes to "the heir". (signed) John Taylor; (witness) John James, John How, & John Wright; Apr. 1767 acknowledged; books 12 & 13 p. 126.

3797. Jan. 30, 1767 Richard Graves, gentleman (Craven Co) to my loving mother Sarah Graves, widow (same); for natural love & affection gave for her natural life 320 ac; part of tract on S side of Neuse R & upper side of Batchelors Cr; border: begins at a small spanish oak on the pecosin side & upper end of the new cleared ground, joins "the" back line; Sarah to have the lower part next to mouth of Batchelor's Cr from said spanish oak & in before mentioned land (sic); where Sarah Graves lives; Sarah to pay Richard a pepper corn per year if demanded. (signed) Richd Graves; (witness) Joseph Hill, Richard Nixon, & W Grice Fonville; wit. oath pr. 1768 by Richd Nixon; books 12 & 13 p. 127.

3798. Dec. 14, 1764 Elizabeth Martin, widow (Craven Co) to my grandson Adam Wallis, planter (same); for love & good will gave all my cattle & increase of whatever kind ranges on land on S side of Southwest Cr "whose" mark is crop in left ear. (signed) Elizabeth E Martin's mark "X"; (witness) Robert Wallis & Saml Martin; wit. oath Apr. 1767 by Robert Wallis; books 12 & 13 p. 129.

3799. Feb. 12, 1767 William Heath sr, planter (Craven Co) to Longfield Cox, planter (same); for £20 proclamation money sold 200 ac on S side of Neuse R; border: begins at a white oak near the river, joins Henry Smith, John Williams, & the river pecosin; known as Heath Island; granted Oct. 23, 1761 to said Heath. (signed) William Heath sr's mark "X"; (witness) Christopher Beckman & James Bradbury; Apr. 1767 acknowledged; books 12 & 13 p. 130.

3800. Feb. 14, 1767 John Francks, gentleman (Craven Co) to George Koonce, planter (same); for £31 proclamation money sold 85 ac on N side of Trent R; border: begins at George Koonce's upper corner red oak on N side of Chinquapin Cr, joins Martin Francks' old patent, & a branch. (signed) John Francks; (witness) Levin Lane & Jacob Rhem; wit. oath Apr. 1767 by Jacob Rhem; books 12 & 13 p. 132.

3801. Oct. 15, 1766 Isaac Barrenton jr, planter (Craven Co) to John Edmonson, planter (same); for £35 proclamation money sold 150 ac on N side of Neuse R & N side of Upper Broad Cr; border: begins at a red oak at main run of said creek and joins Daniel Shingle. (signed) Isaac "Barrunton" jr; (witness) John Barrenton & James Barrenton; wit. oath Apr. 1767 by James Barrenton; books 12 & 13 p. 133.

3802. Jul. 20, 1765 Arthur Carriway (Craven Co) to William Burk (same); for £80 proclamation money sold 62 ac on both sides of Chinquepin Cr; border: begins at Lewis Conner's corner in James Stevenson's line and joins William Davis; granted Apr. 24, 1762 to Arthur Carriway. (signed) Arthur Carriway; (witness) Thomas Carriway, William Meeks, & Jacob Hill; wit. oath Apr. 1767 by Thomas Carriway; books 12 & 13 p. 135.

3803. Jul. 16, 1766 Jacob Blount, planter (Craven Co) to William "Millinder" jr (same); for 150 proclamation money sold 200 ac; border: begins at an ash on mouth of Cabbin Br and joins "Samuell" Wingate; where Rowly Williams formerly lived; being lower part of grant Sept. 29, 1756 to said Samuell Wingate. (signed) Jacob Blount; (witness) Wm Guttery, Richard Bell, & William Milner; Apr. 1767 acknowledged; books 12 & 13 p. 136.

3804. Mar. 31, 1767 Benjamin Messor, planter (Craven Co) to Elisha Blackshear, planter (same); for £10 proclamation money sold 100 ac on N side of Trent R; border: begins at an elm on N side of the river and joins Edward Brown; granted Sept. 26, 1766 to said Benjn Messor. (signed) Benjamin "Mesor's" mark R M (sic); (witness) James Blackshear & Alexander Blackshear; wit. oath Apr. 1767 by Alexander Blackshear; books 12 & 13 p. 138.

3805. Jan. 4, 1767 Beverly Rew to James Godfrey; for £10 proclamation money sold 100 ac on S side of Neuse R and between Browns Cr & Turnagain Bay [no more description]; part 200 ac granted Dec. 3, 1750 to Mark Ferguson & Solomon Rew. (signed) Beverly Rew; (witness) Thomas McLin & John Carney; [unsigned note at end indicates Godfrey paid £10 on Jan. 4, 1767]; wit. oath Apr. 1767 by Thomas McLin; books 12 & 13 p. 140.

3806. Apr. 4, 1767 George Koonce, planter (Craven Co) to Jacob Koonce (same); for £100 proclamation money sold 100 ac on N side of Trent R & E side of Chinkapin Cr; between "Mical" Koonce & George Koonce jr [no more description]; where George Koonce lives. (signed) George Koonce; (witness)

John "Franck" & John Koonce; wit. oath Apr. 1767 by John Franck; books 12 & 13 p. 141.

3807. Apr. 4, 1767 James Jones, planter (Craven Co) to Thomas McLin, merchant (same); for £140 proclamation money sold 100 ac on [blank] side of Neuse R & W side of Nelsons Cr; border: begins at mouth of a small gulf, joins Nelson's "plantation", joins a head of a branch of the gulf, head line of Nelson's land, & Nelson's back line; part of a grant sold by said John Nelson to Richard Heill [or Hill] and now occupied by said James Jones. (signed) Jas Jones; (witness) Samuel Masters, Thomas Pittman, & Chas McLin; [note at end indicates McLin paid Jones £140 on Apr. 11, 1767]; Apr. 1767 acknowledged; books 12 & 13 p. 142.

3808. Jun. 22, 1760 Thomas Fulsher (Craven Co) to Robert Burney (same); for £13.6 sold 125 ac on N side of Neuse [R] & head of Pearces Cr; border: begins at a beach on a ridge at head of run of Pearces Cr, joins back line of head of Cedar Br, & joins Maxe Fulsher's "plantation". (signed) Thomas Fulsher's mark "E" (sic) & Winnifred Fulsher (sic); (witness) John Tolson & William Fulsher; wit. oath Apr. 1767 by William Fulsher; books 12 & 13 p. 145.

3809. Jan. 16, 1767 Robert Reynolds (Craven Co) to George Mallard (same); for £30 sold 50 ac on S side of Trent R; border: begins at George Mallard's corner pine and joins John Saulsbury; part of 640 ac granted Jun. 30, 1758 to Samuel Hatch. (signed) Robt Reynolds; (witness) Campbell Miller & William "Hoakes"; [note at end indicates Reynolds received "within contents" on Jan. 16, 1767]; Apr. 1767 acknowledged; books 12 & 13 p. 147.

3810. Oct. 16, 1765 Valentine King, planter (Craven Co) to Thomas Gray, planter (same); for £60 proclamation money sold [omitted] ac on S side of Swift Cr; border: begins at an oak on side of the creek swamp; granted in 1759 to John Gallar. (signed) Valentine King; (witness) Jacob Blount, Leavin Ross, & George Browning; wit. oath Apr. 1767 by Jacob Blount; books 12 & 13 p. 148.

3811. Feb. 23, 1767 Robert Reynolds, planter (Craven Co) to Thomas Kent, planter (same); for £210 proclamation money sold 340 [also called 320 once] ac on both sides of Gum Swamp; border: begins at a pine near Flatt Swamp, joins an old survey, a dividing line between Geo Stringer & his brother Jno Stringer, runs through "Gumb" Swamp to mouth of Bee Tree Br, & joins "the" patent line; known as [blank]; granted to Col. Francis Stringer who sold to George Stringer sr who sold to Geo Stringer jr & William Stringer and "other part" was granted Nov. 16, 1764 to Geo Stringer and Geo Stringer & William Stringer sold to Robert Reynolds. (signed) Robt Reynolds; (witness) Fred Harget & Christopher Reynolds; Apr. 1767 acknowledged; books 12 & 13 p. 150.

3812. Feb. 14, 1767 George Koonce, planter (Craven Co) to my son Geo Koonce; for love, good will, & affection gave 60 ac; border: begins at a "seder" tree on N side of Chinkapin Cr at mouth of a small branch and joins my upper line; includes "plantation" where said George Koonce jr lives. (signed) George Koonce; (witness) John Franck & Michael Koonce; wit. oath Apr. 1767 by John Franck; books 12 & 13 p. 153.

3813. Mar. 14, 1767 John Booth, waterman (Carteret Co, NC) to John Sherman, inn holder at Beaufort (same); for £30 proclamation money sold 100 ac on E side of South R; border: begins at a small black gum beside the marsh, joins the river, line that parts John Tomlinson's land from land of late Stephen Wallace deceased, a pecoson, & land where widow Wallace lived; part of Mulberry Point land & presently known as Mezick's place. (signed) John Booth; (witness) David Gordon & Thomas Rees; [note at end indicates Sherman paid Booth consideration money]; wit. oath Apr. 1767 by David Gordon; books 12 & 13 p. 155.

3814. [date along with bottom part of deed missing] Beverly Rew (Craven Co) to Thomas Hawk, tavern keeper (same); for £70 proclamation money sold lots #92 & 97 in New Bern on Pollock Street & Metcalf Street. [signature & witness blank]; books 12 & 13 p. 157.

3815. Sept. 26, 1767 [top part of deed blank] David Fonville, planter, & wife Anne to John Cliterall; for £600 proclamation money sold 500 ac on S side of Neuse R; border: begins on side of a small creek between John Fonville sr & Peter Handy; presently possessed by said David Fonville; granted Aug. 2, 1726 by deputies of Lords Proprietor to said John Fonvielle sr who willed on Aug. 14, 1741: 250 ac to John Fonville his eldest son and 250 ac to Peter Fonville his second son and 250 ac to David Fonville his third son and 250 ac to "Isaack" Fonville his fourth & youngest son and Peter Fonville died without issue so his 250 ac descended to David "immediate younger brother as heir" of Peter which means David owned 500 ac of his father's land which is now sold. (signed) David "Fonvielle" & Anne Fonvielle; (witness) James Coor & John Stanaland; [note at end indicates Clitherall paid Fonville £600 on Sept. 26, 1767]; wit. oath Oct. 1767 by James Coor and Anne Fonville renounced dower before James Davis; books 12 & 13 p. 159.

3816. Oct. 9, 1767 [7th year of reign of King George III] William Barran (Craven Co) to John Green, merchant (Newbern, Craven Co); for £20 proclamation money sold 100 ac on E side of "Batchellors" Cr; border: begins at a red oak on the patent line of said tract & runs across the land to the "other" line of said patent; part of grant Oct. 30, 1765 to said William Barran. (signed) Willm Barran & John Green (sic); (witness) Jas Jones & Chrisr. Neale; [note at end indicates Green paid Barran £20 on Oct. 9, 1767]; Oct. 1767 acknowledged; books 12 & 13 p. 162.

3817. Aug. 27, 1767 [7th year of reign of King George III] John Council Bryan (Newbern, Craven Co) to John Green, merchant (same); for £75 proclamation money sold eastermost part of front of lot #16 in New Bern on S side of Front Street; border: 30 feet on Front Street and runs S parallel with W side of front of lot #16 to channel of Trent R. (signed) Jno C Bryan; (witness) Arthur Blackman

& Pald Hynes; Oct. 1767 acknowledged; books 12 & 13 p. 164 or 166 [pages 164 & 166 contain same information and pages 165 & 167 contain same information].

3818. Aug. 27, 1767 [7th year of reign of King George III] John Council Bryan (Newbern, Craven Co) to Thomas Sitgreaves, merchant (New Bern, NC); for £75 proclamation money sold his undivided third of front of lot #16 in New Bern on S side of Trent Street; sold by John Bryan to Richard Cogdell who sold to said John Council Bryan, Sarah Bryan, & Mary Bryan. (signed) Jno C Bryan & Thos Sitgreaves (sic); (witness) Chrisr. Neale & Will Green jr; [note at end indicates Sitgreaves paid "John C Green" (sic) £75 on Aug. 27, 1767]; Oct. 1767 acknowledged; books 12 & 13 p. 168.

3819. Oct. 11, 1766 Smith Fields (Craven Co) to William Heath jr (same); for £80 proclamation money sold 160 ac on E side of Half Moon Swamp; border: begins at mouth of Mill Br, joins Half Moon Swamp, & Benjamin Griffin's line of another patent. (signed) Smith Fields; (witness) John Heath jr & Samuel "Peirson"; wit. oath Oct. 1767 by John Heath jr; books 12 & 13 p. 170.

3820. Sept. 22, 1767 [7th year of reign of King George III] John Carruthers, planter (Craven Co) to John Paul, carpenter (same); for £20 proclamation money sold 50 ac on S side of Bay R & S side of Wanes Cr; border: begins at a pine on E side of mouth of a small creek called Bryans Cr, joins a pine "a little" below head of said creek, a marsh, & a gut that makes out of the creek. (signed) John Carruthers; (witness) Joshua Fulsher & George Carruthers; Oct. 1767 acknowledged; books 12 & 13 p. 172.

3821. Feb. 22, 1766 Hugh Rigby, planter (Craven Co) to John Thomas, planter (same); for £20 proclamation money sold on E side of Swifts Cr; border: begins a white oak that was Jacob Robertson's lower corner, joins said Robertson's patent, "the" back line, & a spring branch; where John Berry formerly lived; part of grant Jul. 13, 1736 to said Robertson. (signed) Hugh Rigby's "O"; (witness) James Pearce & Peter Reel; wit. oath Oct. 1767 by James Pearce; books 12 & 13 p. 174.

3822. Jul. 2, 1766 Ann Bright (Craven Co) to Ezekiel Everton (same); for £6 proclamation money sold 20 ac; border: begins at chincapin on "the" pecoson and joins Edward Gatlin near "the" thorofare; granted Apr. 20(?), 1745 by King George II to John Gatlin. (signed) "An bright's" mark "X"; (witness) Peter Ipoch & James Arthur; wit. oath Oct. 1767 by James Arthur; books 12 & 13 p. 176.

3823. Jul. 16, 1764 Richard Cogdell, sheriff (Craven Co) to Alexander Adair, merchant (New Bern, NC); for £100 proclamation money sold 0.25 ac in front of lot #18 in New Bern; sold Mar. 6, 1746 by Cullen Pollock to John Bryan who with wife Ann Cady Bryan sold Jan. 10, 1748 to John Parkinson; sold due to (a) writ of fieri facias from New Bern Superior Court Nov. 12, 4th year of reign of King George III & returnable to court May 2 next against James Parkinson merchant (late of Craven Co) & Peter Conway (late of Craven Co) for £553 proclamation money debt & £5.15.5 costs due to suit by Alexander Adair, (b) writ of fieri facias from New Bern Dist Superior Court on same day & returnable May 2 next against James Parkinson merchant (late of Craven Co) for £36.13 proclamation money damages & £5.11 costs due to suit by William Henry, & (c) writ of fieri facias from New Bern Superior Court on same day & returnable to court May 2 next against James Parkinson merchant (late of Craven Co) for £106.2 proclamation money damages & £2.11 costs due to suit by William Henry; and sold due to act of Parliament of Great Britain passed in 5th year of reign of King George II concerning collection of debts in America & due to veniditioni exponas from said court May 2, 4th year of reign of King Geoge III because no bidders wanted to pay amount of court suits. (signed) Richard Cogdell; (witness) Richd Fenner & Stephen Yorke; [note at end indicates Adair paid Cogdell £100 Jul. 16, 1764]; Nov. 6, 1767 acknowledged before M Howard, chief justice; books 12 & 13 p. 178.

3824. Jul. 17, 1764 Richard Cogdell, sheriff (Craven Co) to Alexander Adair, merchant (same); for £13 sold 0.5 ac in lot #70 in New Bern; sold [date blank] by New Bern commissioners to [blank] and lot "came to hands" of James Parkinson; sold due to writ of fieri facias from New Bern Superior Court Nov. 12, 4th year of reign of King George III & returnable to court May 2 next against James Parkinson merchant (of Craven Co) for £553 proclamation money damages & £5.15.5 costs due to suit by Alexander Adair, (b) writ on same day & returnable on same date against John Parkinson merchant (of Craven Co) for £6.13 proclamation money damages & £5.11 costs due to suit by William King, & (c) writ on same day & returnable on same date against James Parkinson merchant (late of Craven Co) for £106.11 proclamation money due to suit by [omitted]; and sold due to act of Parliament of Great Britain passed in 5th year of reign of King George II concerning collection of debts in America and due to writ of venidictioni exponas from said court May 2 because no bidders wanted to pay amount of court suits. (signed) Rd Cogdell; (witness) Richd Fenner & Stephen Clark; [note at end indicates Adair paid Cogdell £13 on Jul. 17, 1764]; Nov. 6, 1767 acknowledged before M Howard, CJ; books 12 & 13 p. 184.

3825. Sept. 29, 1767 [7th year of reign of King George III] Rigdon Brice, merchant (New Bern, NC) to Alexander Gaston (same); for £275 proclamation money sold 200 ac; border: begins at corner pine of dividing line between said land & Rigdon Brice's other land on Brices Cr, joins land of late Robert Reynolds, Thomas Brice jr, & "the" back line; sold Jan. 10, 1727 by John Acton Brice eldest son & heir of William Brice deceased to said Rigdon Brice. (signed) Rigdon Brice & Alexr Gaston (sic); (witness) Richd Blackledge & Jas "Macarbury"; [note at end indicates "Doct" Alexander Gston paid Brice l200 on Sept. 29, 1767]; Oct. 1767 acknowledged; books 12 & 13 p. 189.

3826. Sept. 2, 1767 Samuel Vines, planter (Craven Co) to James Coor (Newbern, Craven Co); for £30 proclamation money sold 0.4 of lot #266 (sic) in Newbern on corner of Craven Street & New Street; border: begins at said corner, runs 96 feet on Craven Street, crosses the lot parallel with the street to back line, along back line to New Street, & on New Street to beginning. (signed) Samuel Vines; (witness) Cornelius "Groenendeyle" & Mathew Arthur; [note at end indicates Coor paid Vines £30 on Sept. 23, 1767 (sic)]; wit. oath Oct. 1767 by Cornelius Groenendeyle; books 12 & 13 p. 191.

3827. Jul. 24, 1767 John James, planter (Craven Co) to James Coor, trader (Newbern, Craven Co); for £25 proclamation money sold 100 ac [maybe] on N side of Neuse R & on Little Swifts Cr; [following description confusing] half of 200 ac granted Nov. 24, 1738 by Gov. Gabriel Johnston to John James & recorded in Secretary's office by John Rice, Depty. Secretary; border: begins at a cypress on James Swamp, joins a branch, near George Fisher, & between John Hill & George Fisher; "other" half of said land was granted May 6, 1764 to John James & Dennis Perdue; and "other half or residue" of above land or all of said 200 ac except 100 ac was granted to Dennis Perdue and 100 ac begins at said cypress in James Swamp, joins Dennis Perdue, & "the" patent line. (signed) John James; (witness) Cornelius Groenendeyle & William Wain; wit. oath Oct. 1767 by Cornelius Groenendeyle; books 12 & 13 p. 193.

3828. [blank] 23, 1767 Richard Blackledge, high sheriff (Craven Co) to James Coor, trader (New Bern, NC); for £40.1 proclamation money sold 0.5 ac in lot #277 in New Bern; sold due to writ of vend. exponas from New Bern Dist Superior Court May 13, 7th year of reign of "his Majesty" & returnable to court Nov. 2 next against William Evild, heir of Charles Evild deceased (late of Craven Co), for £26.2.10 proclamation money damages & £7.16.4 costs due to suit by John Clitherall esq (of Craven Co); and sold due to act of Parliament of Great Britain passed in 5th year of reign of King George II concerning collection of debts in America and act of General Assembly passed in 4th year of reign of King George III. (signed) Richard Blackledge; (witness) James Reed & Geo "Rayre"; [note at end indicates Coor paid Blackledge consideration money on Sept. 24, 1767 (sic)]; "Oct." acknowledged; books 12 & 13 p. 196.

3829. Oct. 2, 1766 Richard Blackledge, high sheriff (Craven Co) to James Coor, trader (New Bern, NC); for £17.1 proclamation money sold 100 ac on E side of Brice's Cr; border: begins at Thomas Smith's corner gum on side of a swamp and joins William Wilson; granted to Mary Stevens present wife of John Norwood; sold due to writ of venditioinus exponas from Craven Co court Apr. 3, 1766 & returnable to court first Tuesday in July next against John Norwood (late of Craven Co) for £13.12 proclamation money damages & £2.4.2 costs due to suit by John Clitherall esq; and sold due to act of Parliament of Great Britain passed in 5th year of reign of King George II concerning collection of debts in America and act of General Assembly passed in 4th year of reign of King George III. (signed) Richard Blackledge; (witness) James Reed & Geo Rayre; [note at end indicates Coor paid Blackledge £17.1 on Sept. 24, 1766 (sic)]; Oct. 1767 acknowledged; acknowledged; books 12 & 13 p. 199.

3830. May 13, 1763 John Starkey esq (Onslow Co, NC) & Mary Crawford formerly Mary Carruthers, widow (New Bern, NC), executor & executrix of will of Joseph Carruthers deceased (late of New Bern, NC), to Charles Crawford (New Bern, NC); for £1.2 proclamation money sold 0.5 ac in lot #295 in New Bern; border: begins at Muddy Street & New Street [no more description]; during his lifetime Joseph Carruthers owned "sundry" lots in New Bern including above lot; in his will in 1759 Carruthers appointed John Starkey & Mary Crawford formerly Mary Carruthers as executor & executrix and ordered lots to be sold to pay his debts. (signed) John Starkey & Mary Crawford; (witness) Jno Burroughs & Phil Ambrose; wit. oath Oct. 1767 by John Burroughs; books 12 & 13 p. 202.

3831. Sept. 10, 1767 George Kernegy, planter (Craven Co) to Joseph Kernegy, planter (same); for £200 proclamation money sold 640 ac on N side of Trent R; border: begins at a pine on E side of Beverdam Br below Chincapin Road. (signed) George Kernegy's mark "E K" (sic); (witness) Simon Foscue & Samuel Simmons; wit. oath Oct. 1767 by Samuel Simmons; books 12 & 13 p. 204.

3832. Feb. 21, 1767 [7th year of reign of King George III] Richard Ellis esq (Newbern, NC) & wife Mary, widow of Harding Jones esq deceased (late of Craven Co) and mother & guardian of Mary Jones, minor & only daughter and heir of Harding Jones, to Isham Andrews, William Hill Andrews, & Micajah Andrews (of Halifax Co, NC); Richard & Mary, as guardians, for rents mentioned leased for 12 years 1,000 ac on S side of Trent R, on E side of Island Cr, W side of "Rachoon" Cr, & runs "back" as far as the patent; lease begins Feb. 1 instant; yearly rent is £20 in 2 installments to be paid Aug. 1 and Feb. 1 each year with first payment on Aug. 1 next; grantees to pay yearly quit rent to the king & the taxes; grantors can retake the land if rent payment is more than 21 days late. (signed) Richd Ellis, Mary Ellis, & Isham Andrews, Wm Hill Andrews, & Micajah Andrews (sic); (witness) Will Green jr & "Antihas" Tisdale; wit. oath Oct. 1767 by William Green jr; books 12 & 13 p. 206.

3833. Sept. 5, 1767 Christopher Reynolds, planter (Craven Co) to Robert Reynolds, planter (same); for £200 proclamation money sold 320 ac on N side of Trent R & N side of Beaver Cr; border: begins at a maple & joins Beaver Cr. (signed) Christopher Reynolds; (witness) Fredk. Harget & Simon Spright; [note at end indicates Robert paid Christopher £200 on Sept. 5, 1767]; wit. oath Oct. 1767 by Simon Spright; books 12 & 13 p. 209.

3834. Oct. 5, 1767 John Whitehead, planter (Craven Co) to Joseph Luck (Newbern, Craven Co); for £30 proclamation money sold 196 ac on S side of Trent R & on Racoon Cr; border: begins at a small red oak by a branch "thereof", joins a savanna, & Mr. Pollock; granted Sept. 1, 1759 to William Whitehead, father of John Whitehead, & recorded in Secretary's office book 11 p. 303 [book 16 p. 305 (sic)] & recorded in Auditor General's office Sept. 29, 1759 and at death of William land went to his son John. (signed) John Whitehead; (witness) John Holland & David Ramsey; [note at end indicates Luck paid Whitehead £20 on

Oct. 30, 1767 (sic)]; wit. oath Oct. 1767 by John Holland; books 12 & 13 p. 211.

3835. Sept. 28, 1767 Alexander Macquillan, planter (Craven Co) to Phillip Macquillan, planter (same); for £20 proclamation money sold 100 ac on N of Trent [R] in fork of Roman Br; border: begins at a popler beside the branch; half of grant Nov. 26, 1757 to David Palmer. (signed) Alexr Macquillan's mark "A"; (witness) Fredk Harget & Simon "Spight"; [note at end indicates Phillip paid Alexander "the contents" on Sept. 20, 1767 (sic)]; wit. oath Oct. 1767 by Simon Spight; books 12 & 13 p. 213.

3836. Sept. 28, 1767 Alexander Macquillan, planter (Craven Co) to Walter Macquillan (same); for £20 proclamation money sold 10 ac on N side of Trent R & in the fork of Roman Br; border: begins at Phillip Macquillan's lower corner pine, joins "the" patent line, & Briery Br, a prong of said brach; half of grant Nov. 26, 1757 to David Palmer. (signed) Alexr Macquillan's mark "A"; (witness) Fredk Harget & Simon Spight; [note at end indicates Walter paid Alexander £20 on Sept. 28, 1767]; wit. oath Oct. 1767 by Simon Spight; books 12 & 13 p. 215.

3837. Aug. 26, 1767 Samuel Box to Peter Gilstrap; for £25 proclamation money sold 125 ac on S side of Southwest Marsh & on Cabin Br; border: begins at Christopher Neale's corner hickory & joins Ruly Br; "N B the original not legible" [written sideways on p. 218]. (signed) Samuel Box; (witness) William Easterling & John "Gillstrap"; wit. oath Oct. 1767 by William Easterling; books 12 & 13 p. 218.

3838. Jan. 7, 1765 [1st (sic) year of reign of King George III] Thomas Box, yeoman (Dobbs Co, NC) to Samuel Box; for £20 proclamation money sold 125 ac on Southwest Cr & on Cabin Br; border: begins at Christopher Neale's corner hickory & joins Ruly Br. (signed) Thomas Box's mark "R" (sic); (witness) Wm Easterling & Samuel Dailey; wit. oath Oct. 1767 by William Easterling; books 12 & 13 p. 219.

3839. Dec. 23, 1766 Nicholas Swilla, black smith (Craven Co) to Christopher Reynolds (same); for £30 proclamation money sold half of [omitted] ac on N side of Beaver Cr [no more description]; being upper half of grant oct. 1, 1750 to Patrick Stanaland; includes "plantation" Stephen Swilla bought of said Stanaland. (signed) Nicholas Swilla; (witness) Fredk Harget & Robt Reynolds; wit. oath Oct. 1767 by Robt Reynolds; books 12 & 13 p. 221.

3840. Sept. 19, 1765 George Stringer, planter (Dobbs Co, NC) to Robert Reynolds, planter (Craven Co); for £50 proclamation money sold 200 ac on Flat Swamp "in Dover"; border: begins at a pine near said swamp, joins "Gumb" Swamp, beginning of his former survey, straight line through Gum Swamp, mouth of Bcc tree Br, & "the" patent line; part of 250 ac granted Nov. 16, 1764 to said George Stringer. (signed) George Stringer; (witness) Jeremiah Slade & Waddell Cade; [unsigned note at end indicates £50 was paid Sept. 19, 1765]; wit. oath Oct.

1767 by Waddell Cade; books 12 & 13 p. 223.

3841. Nov. 30, 1767 Sarah Richardson, widow (New Bern, NC) to my loving daughter Dorothy Richardson (same); for natural love, good will, & affection and for £0.10 proclamation money sold following Negroes: Daniel, Grace, Jenny, & their increase; Sarah reserves "use & benefit" of Daniel for her natural life. (signed) Sarah Richardson; (witness) Isaac Patridge & John Richardson; [unsigned note at end indicates Negro "boy" Daniel was delivered in name of all the Negroes (sic)]; wit. oath Dec. 10, 1767 by Isaac Patridge before M Howard, CJ; books 12 & 13 p. 226.

3842. Oct. 16, 1765 John Fulcher, planter (Craven Co) to Francis Dawson, planter (same); for £25 proclamation money sold 60 ac on N side of Neuse R & on S side of Lower Broad Cr; border: begins at a sweet gum at first gut below the "plantation" formerly owned by Samuel Harvey, joins Francis Dawson, Harvey's Pecoson, Thomas Simmons, head of Giddones Cr, & "the" main line; part of grant Nov. 11, 1719 to Rice Price. (signed) John Fulcher's mark "Ŧ"; (witness) William Carraway & Thomas Delamar; wit. oath Oct. 1767 by William Carraway; books 12 & 13 p. 227.

3843. Oct. 4, 1766 Thomas Moore (Craven Co) to Isaac Chance (same); for £50 proclamation money sold 100 ac on N side of Neuse R; includes the islands in Lewis Bryan's mill Swamp; border: begins at a pine above Ezekiah Smith's improvements; "held by" grant Apr. 21, 1764 [4th year of his Majesty's reign] to said Thomas Moore. (signed) Thomas Moore's mark "T"; (witness) William Bryan & Lewis Bryan; Oct. 1767 acknowledged; books 12 & 13 p. 229.

3844. Aug. 1, 1767 John Pendar, mariner (Craven Co) to James Fulcher, planter (same); for £10 proclamation money sold 50 ac on W side of Beards Cr; known as James Fulcher's "plantation" (sic); border: begins at Hoover's corner white oak on the creek, joins a gut below Hoover's "plantation", & a dividing line between Hoover & said Fulcher. (signed) "James" Pendar; (witness) William Carraway & Susanah Morris; wit. oath Oct. 1767 by William Carraway; books 12 & 13 p. 231.

3845. Feb. 14, 1767 George Koonce, planter (Craven Co) to my son Michael Koonce; for love, good will, & affection gave 80 ac; border: begins at my lower corner white oak on N side of Chincapin Cr and joins a "branch or bottom". (signed) George Koonce; (witness) john Franck & Jacob Koonce; wit. oath Oct. 1767 by Jacob Koonce; books 12 & 13 p. 233.

3846. May 1, 1764 Richard Cogdell, high sheriff (Craven Co) to Phillip Ambrose, merchant (same); for £4.5 proclamation money sold 0.5 ac in lot #43 in New Bern at corner of Jones Street, "otherwise" called St. Johns Street, & Front St; border: 6.5 poles on Front Street and 13 poles on Jones Street; sold Aug. 13, 1724 by New Bern commissioners to Thomas Folliwood and sold Sept. 21, 1725 by his attorney [blank] Metcalf to Thomas Martin "by assignment on back of the deed" who sold

Craven County, NC Deed Books 11-13

Aug. 21, 1726 to Frederick Jones deceased and sold Feb. 10, 1759 by his eldest son & devisee Harding Jones to Nathaniel Richardson who sold Jun. 28, 1760 to James Parkinson; sold due to writ of fieri facias from New Bern Dist Superior Court Nov. 1, 1763 & returnable to court May 2 next due to (a) suit by William Henry against James Parkinson for £96.13 proclamation money damages & £5.11 costs, (b) suit by William Henry against James Parkinson for £106.10 proclamation damages & £5.11 costs, and (c) suit by Alexander Adair against James Parkinson & Peter Conway for £253 proclamation money debt & £5.15.5 costs; and sold due to act of Parliament of Great Britain passed in 5th year of reign of King George II concerning collection of debts in America. (signed) Rd Cogdell; (witness) John Tomlinson & Richd Fenner; [unsigned note at end indicates Ambrose paid £4.5 on May 1, 1764]; Jul. 1765 acknowledged; books 12 & 13 p. 234.

3847. Jun. 6, 1765 "Philip" Ambrose, merchant (Newbern, Craven Co) to Richard Cogdell esq (same); for £4.5 proclamation money sold 0.5 ac in lot #43 in New Bern on corner of Jones street, "otherwise or formerly" called St. Johns Street, & Front Street; border: 6.5 poles on Front Street & 13 poles on Jones Street. (signed) Phil Ambrose; (witness) Alexr Gaston & Richd Fenner; [note at end indicates Cogdell paid Ambrose £4.2 (sic) proclamation money Jun. 6, 1765]; wit. oath Jul. 1765 by Richd Fenner; books 12 & 13 p. 238.

3848. May 1, 1764 Richard Cogdell, high sheriff (Craven Co) to Alexander Gaston, "chineryeon" (Newbern, Craven Co); for £2 proclamation money sold 100 ac on E side of Pamplico Road; includes part of Juniper Swamp; border: begins at a gum on the swamp side near Chinkapin Ridge and joins John Nelson; being upper part of 300 ac granted Dec. 8, 1757 to Ruben Parker & William Carraway and 100 ac was sold Sept. 8, 1760 by William Carraway to John "Pindar"; sold due to writ of fieri facias from New Bern Dist Superior Court Nov. 12, 1763 & returnable May 2 next against John Pindar sr mariner (late of Craven Co) for £42.6 proclamation money damages & £0.7 costs due to suit by James Green jr; and sold due to act of Parlaiament passed in 5th year of reign of King George II concerning collection of debts in America. (signed) Rd Cogdell; (witness) John Tomlinson & Richd Fenner; [note at end indicates Gaston paid Cogdell £2 on May 1, 1765 (sic)]; Jul. 1765 acknowledged; books 12 & 13 p. 241.

3849. May 31, 1762 George Pollock esq gentleman (Bertie Co, NC) to Edward Griffith, son of Edward Griffith esq merchant (Craven Co); for £10 proclamation money sold 28 ac; border: begins at a stake on boundary line of town of New Bern 70 poles from Neuse R, joins Thomas Luck's upper corner, & Neuse R; part of [blank] hundred acre grant Jan. 22, 1713 to Daniel Richards esq who sold Apr. 14, 1714 to Honble. Thomas Pollock esq who bequeathed it to Cullen Pollock esq who bequeathed it to his son George Pollock. (signed) George Pollock; (witness) Rd Cogdell & Joseph Luck; wit. oath Jul. 1765 by Richard Cogdell; books 12 & 13 p. 244.

3850. May 26, 1764 [4th year of reign of King George III] Thomas Clifford Howe gentleman & wife Elizabeth (Christ Church Parish, Craven Co) to George Hays (or Hay), carpenter (Paris Creek, Craven Co); for £121 proclamation money leased for 21 years lots #47, 49, & 300 in New Bern on Pollock Street (sic); yearly rent is a pepper corn to be paid on last day "of said term". (signed) Thos C Howe & Elizabeth Howe; (witness) Timo "Clrod" & "Banta" Brice; "turn over for probate of this deed (signed) George Hays; books 12 & 13 p. 247;

Sept. 18, 1765 George Hays (New Bern, NC) to James Coor; for £50 proclamation money quit claim my interest in within 3 lots to Coor. (signed) George Hays; (witness) James Falconar [only one witness]; wit. oath Jul. 1765 by Banta Brice; books 12 & 13 p. 249.

3851. May 3, 1765 John Pendar jr, mariner (Craven Co) to James Hollis, planter (same); for £30 proclamation money "in pace of 8 at £0.8.8 piece of eight" sold 200 ac on N side of Nuce R; border: begins at a Richard Spaight's lower corner small pine of his "plantation" called Tilson's in an old cedar swamp at mouth of Cedar Gut and joins mouth of a gut above Thomas Little's house. (signed) John Pender jr; (witness) Rigdon Brice, Henry "Bylus", & Jeremiah Pritchard; wit. oath Jul. 1765 by Jeremiah Pritchard; [note at end indicates Hollis paid Pendar £38 (sic) on May 3, 1765]; books 12 & 13 p. 250.

3852. Jun. 5, 1765 Christian Free (Craven Co) to Jonathan Ray; for £25 proclamation money sold 30 ac on W side of Mill Cr; border: begins at an ash, joins dividing line between Thomas Pollock & said Simmons, William Wickliffe, & Bunch [or Punch] Boll Br; part of 100 ac granted to Thomas Simmons. (signed) Christian Free; (witness) Simon Foscue & Sarah Foscue; wit. oath Jul. 1765 by Simon Foscue; books 12 & 13 p. 252.

3853. Feb. 19, 1764 Edward Frost to Thomas Bose; for £35 proclamation money sold 325 ac on N side of Neuse R & E side of Southwest Cr; border: begins at a pine in James Cogdell's line, joins mouth of Cabbage Br opposite Lane's corner, Lane's upper corner, Mott, Morris, & Christopher Neale. (signed) Edward Frost; (witness) Kittrell Mundine, Samuel Bose, & Alexander Skeen; wit. oath Jul. 1765 by Samuel Bose; books 12 & 13 p. 254.

3854. May 21, 1764 Joseph Wright (Craven Co) to Joseph Crispin, mariner (same); for £15 proclamation money sold 150 ac on N side of main branch of Dawsons Cr; between Whitly & Brice [no more description]; granted Nov. 27, 1762 to said Joseph Wright. (signed) Joseph Wright; (witness) Chris Neale & John Dawson; [note at end indicates Crispin paid Wright £15 May 21, 1764]; wit. oath Jul. 1765 Christopher Neale; books 12 & 13 p. 256.

3855. May 23, 1765 Robert Orme, merchant (Craven Co) to William Gibson (Onslow Co, NC); for £0.5 proclamation money sold 150 ac on S side of Trent R and on "E & W side" of Island Cr; border: begins at a stake on W side of Island Cr 15 yards S of Kingey's Path in a savannah and a stake 15 yards S of the "maine" road; part of 400 ac granted Oct. 3, 1765 to Robert Orme. (signed) Robt Orme; (witness) Edmd Holland & John Fowlan [or Fowlun]; Jul. 1765 acknowledged; books 12 & 13 p. 258.

3856. Feb. 12, 1762 Thomas Robinson, taylor (Craven Co) to Thomas Smart, dealler(?) & shop man (same); for £50 proclamation money sold 300 ac on S side of Trent R; begins at John Perry's corner hickory, & Richard Perry, & the river. (signed) Thomas Robinson; (witness) John Perry sr & John "Oiffer"; wit. oath Jul. 1765 by John Perry sr; books 12 & 13 p. 260.

3857. Jul. 28, 1764 (Quaker style date) Charles Jones, planter (Clubfoots Cr, Craven Co) to John Crosby (near Clubfoots Cr, Craven Co); for £30 proclamation money sold 200 ac on N side of Nuce R & W side of Cowhookie Swamp that runs into Hancocks Cr; border: begins at a red oak on Cowhookie Swamp; granted Sept. 27, 1745 by Gov. Gabriel Johnston to Evan Jones. (signed) Charles Jones; (witness) John Tomlinson & Martha Tomlinson; Jul. 1765 acknowledged; books 12 & 13 p. 263.

3858. Oct. 26, 1764 Henry Vanpelt (Craven Co) to Robert Hutchins (same); for £20 proclamation money sold 75 ac [no more description]; part 150 ac granted Nov. 16, 1758 by Anthony Vanpelt; land is divided by a line of marked trees and Hutchins to hae land on W side of the line; where Henry Vanpelt lived. (signed) Henry Vanpelt; (witness) Jacob Blount & Anthony Vanpelt; Jul. 1765 proved; books 12 & 13 p. 265.

3859. Aug. 22, 1764 (Quaker style date) Robert Orme, merchant (Craven Co) to David Rose; for £25 proclamation money sold [omitted] ac on S side of Trent R; border: begins at a red oak, Steele, & Emmanuel Simmons; where "Anm" Ireland lives; except 1 acre where the chappel stands. (signed) Robt Orme; (witness) Redmond Lyons & Thomas Hopkins; Jul. 1765 acknowledged; books 12 & 13 p. 268.

3860. Jul. 2, 1765 Richard Blackledge, John Smith, John Green, & John Carruthers (Craven Co) to the king; a bond for £1,000 sterling; Blackledge was appointed Craven Co sheriff to serve at pleasure of & due to commission dated Apr. 8, 1765 from Lt. Governor William Tryon; bond void if Blackledge returns all processes & receipts and performs duties of the office. (signed) Richard Blackledge, Jno Smith, John Green, & John Carruthers; (witness) Patr. Conway [only one witness]; [no wit. oath mentioned]; books 12 & 13 p. 270.

3861. Jul. 2, 1765 [6th year of reign of King George III] Richard Blackledge, John Smith, John Green, & John Carruthers (Craven Co) to Lt. Governor William Tryon; a bond for £1,000 sterling; Blackledge was appointed Craven Co sheriff to serve at pleasure of & due to commission dated Apr. 8, 1765 from Lt. Governor William Tryon; bond void if Blackledge collects & returns all taxes & dues as "appointed" by the General Assembly. (signed) Richard Blackledge, Jno Smith,

John Green, & John Carruthers; (witness) Patr. Conway [only one witness]; [no wit. oath mentioned]; books 12 & 13 p. 271.

3862. Apr. 21, 1764 William Morris, planter (Craven Co) to Samuel Payn, planter (same); for £38 proclamation money sold 75 ac on N side of Little Cr; border: begins at mouth of Little Cr on N side, join "the" patent line, & a branch; part of 150 ac granted Jun. 30, 1768 (sic) to William Carruthers. (signed) William Morris; (witness) Thomas Willis, George Pugh, & Sarah "Nelles"; wit. oath Jul. 1765 by George Pugh; books 12 & 13 p. 272.

3863. Oct. 31, 1764 Joshua Stafford, planter (Craven Co) to Francis Buck, planter (Pitt Co, NC); for £40 NC money sold 200 ac [no more description]; granted in 1738 to [omitted]; where William Clark lived "some years". (signed) Joshua Stafford's mark "I" & Martha Stafford's mark "mar" (sic); (witness) Edmd Stafford, Thos "Fomes", & Mary Butler; wit. oath Jul. 1765 by Thomas Fonnes; books 12 & 13 p. 273.

3864. May 31, 1763 John Ives (Craven Co) to Bazill Smith, planter (same); for £20 sold 150 ac on N side of Nuse R & in fork of Brices Cr; border: begins at a cypress on South Br or prong of said creek. (signed) John Ives; (witness) Lavin Lane & Elizabeth Smith; wit. oath Jul. 1765 by Lavin Lane; [note at end indicates Smith paid Ives £20 on May 31, 1763]; books 12 & 13 p. 275.
3865. Jan. 13, 1764 John Slade, planter (Craven Co) to Ignatius Wadsworth, planter (same); for £20 proclamation money sold 100 ac in Dover on S side of Nuce R; border: begins at a white oak in Colonel Francis Stringer's line; granted Mar. 29, 1764 to John Slade. (signed) John Slade; (witness) Saml Slade jr & George Becton; Jul. 1765 acknowledged; books 12 & 13 p. 276.

3866. Nov. 17, 1764 Matthew Willets, planter (Craven Co) to Henry Green (same); for £30 proclamation money sold 50 ac on N side of Trent R; border: begins at a pine at said "Mathew" Willets' upper corner on upper fork on N side of main prong of Resolution Br, joins a dreen, & "the" back line. (signed) Matthew Willets' mark "M"; (witness) Fredk Hargett & Humphrey Wilkes; wit. oath Jul. 1766 by Frederick "Hargit"; books 12 & 13 p. 278.

3867. May 16, 1765 John Rice, gentleman (Craven Co) to Peter Starkey jr (Onslow Co, NC), who married Catherine Wickliffe daughter of William Wickliffe merchant deceased (late of Craven Co); on Mar. 8, 1752 John Rice mortgaged to William Wickliffe, merchant deceased, 2 tracts for £340 Great Britain money: (a) 220 ac on S side of Neuse R; border: begins at a white oak by mouth of a branch that parts said land from Allen's land, joins land of Eleazer Allen esq deceased, & a laurell line [or mase]; known as Doctors [or Dutors] Folly; where John Rice lived; sold Mar. 8, 1752 by John Rice to William Wickliffe merchant deceased; & (b) house & lot #62 in New Bern on Broad Street; sale to Wickliffe was to be void if Rice paid £150 Great Britain money by Jun. 9, 1754; SO now for £150 Great Britain money secured to William Wickliffe Mar. 8, 1752 sold above 2 tracts due to Wickliffe's will & division of his estate with Peter Starkey jr as executor. (signed) Jno Rice; (witness) Frederick Jones, Willoughby Bartlett, & Chrisr. Neale; Jul. 1765 acknowledged; books 12 & 13 p. 280.

3868. [no date] deposition of John Taylor: sometime in Nov. 1745 he was requested by Thomas & James Smith (of Brices Creek) to see a division of land by Thomas; they marked a pine "T" on S side and "I" on N side beside a little pond, runs on a line of marked trees nearly West to a hickory marked by Thomas "T" on S side & "I" on N side which tree Taylor showed the surveyor & free holders appointed to procession the bounds of land of Thomas & James Smith agree that division they made should extend to back line; Taylor says afterward Thomas insisted that Taylor draw a memorandum of the division which he did and Thomas wanted to keep it; sometime in Dec. 1746 Thomas came to Taylor's house and urged him to go to New Bern court to prove the division; but Taylor was prevented by bad weather, so proving was neglected. (signed) John Taylor; Jul. 1765 acknowledged; books 12 & 13 p. 287.

3869. Aug. 15, 1761 will of Edmond Mitchell (Craven Co); in name of God amen; all debts to be paid; to son Thomas Mitchell £0.1 sterling; to my daughter Martha Tomlinson my dark(?) horse called Prince; my loving wife Levinah Mitchell to have use of rest of my estate for remainder of her natural life provided she remains my widow and at her death this part of estate goes to son-in-law & daughter John & Martha Tomlinson; if my wife marries, she gets a third of residue of estate and other two thirds goes to Martha Tomlinson; executor is son-in-law John Tomlinson. (signed) Edmond Mitchell's mark "X"; (witness) Chrisr. Neale & Daniel Smith jr; wit. oath Jul. 1765 by Christopher Neale; books 12 & 13 p. 288.

3870. Feb. 20, 1765 William "Hearbird", planter (Craven Co) to Tobias Koonce, planter (same); for £20 proclamation money sold 100 ac; border: begins at a white oak on Trent R at mouth of Joshua's Resolution Br, head of a small bottom making into the river, & mouth of a gut at "Herbead's" Landing. (signed) William Herbird's mark "X"; (witness) Matthew Rhem & Jacob Rhem; wit. oath Jul. 1765 by Jacob Rhem; books 12 & 13 p. 289.

3871. Nov. 19, 1764 will of Thomas Roe (Craven Co): in name of God amen; soul to God & body to be buried; to son Mathew Roe a "madlen cow(?) Pott, a cow & calf, lower end of land where I live from beginning to head of the great cove; to son Luke Roe rest of my land and if Luke dies without issue, land goes to son Mathew Roe; to beloved wife [no name] rest of my goods during her life & at her death it goes to son Luke; to daughter Sarah Read £0.1 sterling; to daughter Ann Stevens £0.1 sterling; to daughter Affy Fowler £0.1; to son Thomas Roe £0.1; executors are sons Mathew & Luke Roe. (signed) Thomas Roe; (witness) Jacob Taylor, James Read, & William "Reed"; wit. oath Jul. 1765 by Jacob Taylor; books 12 & 13 p. 291.

3872. Oct. 25, 1763 will of John Williams, planter (Craven Co): in name of God amen; soul to God & body to be buried by executor; to my brother Solomon

Williams all my wearing clothes and brinnsit(?) musle gunn; rest of real & personal estate, after debts are paid, to wife Mary Williams for her natural life and at her death half goes to my brother Solomon Williams & rest my wife can do what she will with it; executrix is wife Mary. (signed) John Williams' mark "I"; (witness) Peter Dicks, Edmund Millen, & James Duke; wit. oath Jul. 1765 by James Duke "proved at April court"; books 12 & 13 p. 292.

3873. Feb. 16, 1765 will of Francis Searles (Craven Co): in name of God amen; soul to God & body to be buried in Christian like manner; to dearly beloved wife "Juda" Searles all my real & personal estate for her widowhood except sorrel mare I give to my loving son Coventon Searles at my wife's marriage or death; to loving son Edward Searles 74 ac where my house & "plantation" is; to my beloved son Coventon Searles 50 ac joins my plantaion on N end; to well beloved daughter Winiford Searles 2 cows & yearlings and cow & calf and 2 ewes and 2 sows on day of her marriage or when she is 21; rest of estate to be equally divided among my sons & daughters, son Edward & daughter Winniford excepted at my wife's marriage or death (sic); executors are my wife Judah Searles & beloved friend John Hartley. (signed) Francis Searles' mark "F"; (witness) Martin Whitford, John Thomas, & Mary Whitford; wit. oath Jul. 1765 by Martin Whitford; books 12 & 13 p. 294.

3874. Jun. 4, 1765 account of sales of part of estate of Stephen York deceased (late of New Bern, NC): buyers are John Carruthers, John Rinnik, Mary York, William Good, Thomas Nelson, Davd. Smith Kelley, Thomas Dawson, Thomas Dollamare, Robt Runney, Joseph Brooks, Francis Dellamare, James Ball, Elizabeth "Physcock", Nathaniel Phipps, John Paul, John Moleston, Joseph Brooks, & Thomas Willis. (signed) John Carruthers, admr; books 12 & 13 p. 295.

3875. Jul. 3, 1765 inventory of estate of John Guiss by Thomas McLin, admr: cash £13.19.6, Jno Mason & Solomon Northam bond £0.19.8, Jno Pittman & James Godfrey bond £3.19.10, Joseph Pittman bond £1.1.4, Jeremiah Taylor bond £1.14.8, Abner Neal jr bond £4.8.7, Charles Rew bond £1.1.6 [total] £26.18.1. (signed) Thomas McLin, admr; books 12 & 13 p. 297.

3876. inventory of Stephen York deceased (of New Bern, NC): household items, wearing apparel, kitchen items, & farming utensils. (signed) John Carruthers, administrator; books 12 & 13 p. 298.

3877. account of estate of John Miller: May 16, 1761 funeral expenses £5; Mar. 1765 sale £3.17.4½; "May 24" paid Eunice Carruthers £2 [total] £16.16.2½. [not signed]; books 12 & 13 p. 299.

3878. inventory of estate of Jno Williams deceased: carpenter tools, cooper tools, farming items, household items, & kitchen items. (signed) Mary Williams' mark "X", executrix; books 12 & 13 p. 299.

3879. Apr. 1765 court John Turner, John Fonvielle, & James Green examined return of George Pope, executor of George Pope who was executor of Samuel Pope, in account of estate of Samuel Pope & account of settlement to next court (signed) Peter Conway, CIC; books 12 & 13 p. 300.

3880. account of Sarah Mill admx: Feb. 5, 1765 sale of part of estate £8, Apr. 6 sale of part of estate £2.17.6, received of John Smith £2, yearling sold to John Moore £1.10, [total] £13.7.6, tools sold John Dailey £1.10, [new total] £14.17.6. [not signed]; books 12 & 13 p. 300.

3881. May 5, 1766 [account of] surviving executor George Pope who was executor of Samuel Pope, estate of Samuel Pope: paid Robt Taylor & Clements, proving will £0.6, recording will £0.5.4, Secretary's fee £0.2.8, sheriff's fees for vendue £2, boarding & clothing Samuel Pope son of "Do" & small Negro wench 4 years & 1 month £49, 1 year schooling £1.12, boarding & clothing Mary Pope daughter of Do & 2 small Negroes 4 years 1 month £73.10, [total] £126.12.8. (signed) George Pope; books 12 & 13 p. 300;
        May 20, 1765 John Turner, John Fonville, & James Green appointed by Craven Co court to inspect return of George Pope, executor of George Pope who was executor of Samuel Pope; we find there is £95.9.4 (sic) proclamation money due to George Pope. books 12 & 13 p. 301.

3882. Jul. 4, 1765 Willoughby Bartlett, Thomas McLin, William Willis (Craven Co) to justices of Craven Co; a bond for £500; bond void if Bartlett to carefully & honestly bring up Southey Rew during his minority & nonage with necessary meat, drink, washing, lodgings, apparel, "seaming" according to his degree, tutor him, & accounts for money spent. (signed) Willoughby Bartlett, Thomas McLin, & William Willis; (witness) Isaac Partridge [only one witness]; [no wit. oath mentioned]; books 12 & 13 p. 301.

3883. Jul. 16, 1765 (Quaker style date) "Parmonas" Horton & John Bishop (both of Clubfoots Cr, Craven Co) purchased in partnership from Col. Thomas Lovick land on W side of Clubfoots Cr; on Mar. 10, 1757 (Quaker style date) "the parties" divided the land; mention was made of a gut between "their his" dwelling house being dividing line from mouth to a pine on S side of the gut; but there is a problem; Horton & Bishop agree today to divide land again: begin at a gut, runs up to a stake or post at head of the gut, & N84½W to a marked pine on S side of a branch. (signed) John Bishop & Parmenus Horton; (witness) John Tomlinson & John Shepard;
        Mar. 10, 1757 laid out 217 ac 20 perches for Parmenus Horton; begins at mouth of a small gut that parts him & Bishop, runs up gut to a pine above Bishop's house, then into the woods, joins a pine opposite a small island in the creek, & mouth of Clubfoots Cr; this is Horton's part of land purchased by Horton & Bishop from Col. Lovick. (signed) John Bishop; (witness) John Ellerdridge & George Yarborough; [no wit. oath mentioned]; books 12 & 13 p. 302.

3884. Sept. 3, 1765 James Cunningham, taylor (Craven Co) to my beloved daughter-in-law Biddey Connesty (same); for love, good will, & affection and for £0.10 proclamation money sold a feather bed & furniture, tea chest, 6 "brown china" & tea pot, pair of brass candle sticks, 6 silver tea spoons, a chest, & "clothes". (signed) James Carruthers; (witness) James Davis & Jonathan Feldon; Oct. 1765 acknowledged; books 12 & 13 p. 304.

3885. Oct. 4, 1763 William Jones (Dobbs Co, NC) to William Jones (Onslow Co, NC); a bond for £300 proclamation; grantor was appointed guardian for children of Garrell McKinney deceased; bond void if grantor gives Elizabeth McKinney, daughter of Garrell McKinney, her share of the estate and Ann McKinney her share of the estate, & Joseph McKinney, son of Garrell, his share of the estate including Negroes Rose & Basson & Rachael; grantor to divide estate among Garrell McKinney's children: Mary Hollinsworth, John McKinney, Rachel Blackleddge, Joseph McKinney, Elizabeth McKinney, & Ann McKinney. (signed) Wm Jones; (witness) Jeremiah Slade & James Little; Oct. 1765 acknowledged; books 12 & 13 p. 305.

3886. Oct. 11, 1765 Peter Conway (Newbern, Craven Co) to Gabriel Cathcart esq collector of port of Beaufort, NC; for £434.15 proclamation money sold house & 0.5 ac in lot #258 on Broad Street in New Bern; includes office, kitchen, & all other buildings on the lot; border: joins lot #286; where Peter Conway lately dwelt but now in occupation of Hon. Charles Berry who rented the place for 3 years from Aug. 16 last at yearly rent of £50 proclamation money. [not signed, no witness, & no wit. oath]; [unsigned note at end indicates Cathcart paid £434.15 on Oct. 11, 1765]; books 12 & 13 p. 307.

3887. Jul. 4, 1765 William Mill, mariner (Craven Co) to Benjamin Whitaker, merchant (Newbern, Craven Co); for £40 proclamation money sold 43 ac on N side of Nuce R & E side of Smiths Cr; border: joined on E by Cason Brinson, on S by Anne Bryan, & on W & NW by the creek [no more description]; granted to said William Mill. (signed) William Mill; (witness) John Whitherall & Saml(?) Crawford; wit. oath Oct. 1765 by John Whitherall; books 12 & 13 p. 311.

3888. May 20, 1765 will of William Powell (Craven Co): to wife Jane Powell & her heirs all my real estate and my personal estate in North Carolina; to my mother Alice Powell, widow (of "Clytha") all my personal estate in Great Britain and if she dies property goes to Ciely Vaughn wife of Rev. Thomas Vaughn (of Clytha) independent of her husband; my wife is executrix for North Carolina part of estate and Ciely Vaughn is executrix of part in Great Britain. (signed) Wm Powell; (witness) Mary Conway, Andrew Cord(?), & Phil Ambrose; wit. oath Oct. 1765 by Andrew Cord esq; books 12 & 13 p. 313.

3889. Jul. 30, 1765 Edward Brice Dobbs, captain in his Majesty's 7th Regiment of Foot or Royal Fusiliers, to Frederick "Greg" esq (Wilmington, NC) & William Powell esq (Newbern, NC); power of attorney to take possession of all my land

and rent any of the land. (signed) Edward Brice Dobbs; (witness) Richard Quince & Josiah Loving; wit. oath Oct. 20, 1765 by Richard Quince; books 12 & 13 p. 314.

3890. Aug. 20, 1755 (sic) 433 ac laid out for John Bishop & Parmenas [Horton] on W side of Clubfoots Cr; border: begins at Mugreth's corner red oak by a small gut, joins a great pond, a branch, Blake's pasture fence, & Blakes Cr [plat on p. 319. (signed) Gregg Yarbrough; books 12 & 13 p. 319;

    Mar. 10, 1757 laid out for Parmanas Horton 217 ac 80 perches; border: begins at "A" mouth of a small gut that parts him & Bishop, runs up the gut to a pine above Mr. Bishop's house, "into the woods", joins side of marsh of Blakes Cr, a small pine opposite a small island of said creek; [plat on p. 320]. (signed) John Bishop; (witness) John "Worgridge" & Gregg Yarbrough; books 12 & 13 p. 320;

    Jul. 6, 1763 (Quaker style date) Parmenas Horton & John Bishop (both of Clubfoots Cr, Craven Co) purchased in partnership from Col. Thomas Lovick land on W side of Clubfoots Cr; on Mar. 10, 1757 (Quaker style date) "the parties" divided the land; mention was made of a gut between "their his" dwelling house being dividing line from mouth to a pine on S side of the gut; but there is a problem; Horton & Bishop agree today to divide land again: begin at a gut, runs up to a stake or post at head of the gut, & N84½W to a marked pine on S side of a branch. (signed) John Bishop & Parmenus Horton; (witness) John Tomlinson & John Hupard; [some of this same as on p. 302]; purchased in partnership from Col. Thomas Lovick land on W side of Clubfoots Cr; on Mar. 10, 1757 (Quaker style date) "the parties" divided the land; mention was made of a gut between "their his" dwelling house being dividing line from mouth to a pine on S side of the gut; but there is a problem; Horton & Bishop agree today to divide land again: begin at a gut, runs up to a stake or post at head of the gut, & NW(?) to a marked pine on S side of a branch. (signed) John Bishop & Parmenas Horton; (witness) John Tomlinson & John Shepard; wit. oath Jul. 1765 by John Tomlinson; books 12 & 13 p. 321

3891. Feb. 27, 1765 Benjamin Keith, plu[blank] (SC) to Richard Blackledge, merchant; for £68 proclamation money sold 120 ac on N side of Nuse R; border: begins at a white oak near mouth of a beaver dam on W side of it, joins corners in deed by James Keith to Benjamin Keith, & Bass; part of 394 ac granted Feb. 16, 1736 to James Keith remainder of land was taken away by "law from the patents" [blank] by prior patent to Andrew Bass and "said" land was sold Feb. 27, 1763 by William Keith to James Keith (sic) who sold Apr. 14, 1763 to BenjaminKeith. (signed) Benjn. Keith; (witness) Benja Blackledge, Thomas Cradick, & Benja Blackledge jr; [note at end indicates Blackledge paid Keith £68 on Feb. 27, 1765; wit. oath Oct. 1765 by Benjamin Blackledge sr (sic); books 12 & 13 p. 322.

3892. May 5, 1764 Joseph Crispin, mariner (Craven Co) to Richard Blackledge, trader (same); in a deed dated Sept. 14, 1768 (sic) Richard Blackledge agreed, at his own cost, to sell the land mentioned, but some of the description was incorrect, according to Joseph Crispin; SO for £0.5 sold 331 ac on N side of Nuce R; border: begins at a water oak beside the river "a little" below mouth of Stony town Cr; part of a tract called Hemleh; granted by Lords Proprietor to William Handcock who sold Sept. 1, 1743 to Walter Lane who willed it to his son George Lane who sold to said Joseph Crispin. (signed) Joseph Crispin; (witness) Jacob Blount & Chrisr. Neale; [note at end indicates Blackledge paid Crispin £0.5]; wit. oath Oct. 1765 by Jacob Blount; books 12 & 13 p. 325; [most of p. 328 is blank; end of first part of books 12 & 13].

[second half of books 12 & 13]
3893. Aug. 5, 1765 Andrew Bass sr, planter (Dobbs Co, NC) to Richard Blackledge, merchant (Craven Co); for £150 proclamation money sold 2 tracts: (a) 100 ac on N side of Neuse R; border: begins at Caleb Metcalf's corner pine and joins Thomas Branton; granted Mar. 7, 1736 by Andrew Bass; & (b) 225 ac on N side of Neuse R; border: begins at corner black oak or black jack between Andrew Bass sr & Richard Blackledge; part of 450 ac granted Sept. 10, 1737 to Andrew Bass sr. (signed) Andrew Bass sr's mark "X"; (witness) Benjamin Blackledge & John "Kennedey"; [note at end:] it is agreed "what" land is in said Blackledge's line in his deed from Joseph Crispin the he take only said Bass' right "but" all the rest is warranted by said Bass agreeable to body of foregoing deeds (signed) Andrew Bass' mark "A" (sic) (witness) Benjamin Blackledge & John "Kenneday"; wit. oath Oct. 1765 by Benjamin Blackledge; books 12 & 13 p. 329.

3894. Jul. 27, 1765 [5th year of reign of King George III] William Sitgreaves, merchant, & wife "Susaanah" (Philadelphia, Pennsylvania) to our trusty & loving friend Richard Blackledge, merchant (Craven Co); power attorney to receive money & goods owed to us. (signed) Wm Sitgreaves & Susana Sitgreaves; (witness) Samuel "Cornel" & William Rhea; wit. oath Oct. 1765 by Samuel Corwell; books 12 & 13 p. 332.

3895. Oct. 3, 1765 William Green (late of Wilmington, Pennsylvania (sic)), & now of Craven Co) to Richard Blackledge; a bond for £500 proclamation money; today Richard Blackledge, as attorney for William & "Susanah" Sitgreaves, sold to William Green lot #17 in New Bern; bond void if Green keeps Blackledge harmless on any charges about sale of the lot. (signed) William Green; (witness) Willm. Herritage & Rd Caswell; wit. oath Oct. 1765 by Richard Caswell; books 12 & 13 p. 333.

3896. Oct. 3, 1765 William Green, merchant (late of Wilmington, Pennsylvania, & now of Craven Co) to William Sitgreaves, merchant (Philadelphia, Pennsylvania); a bond for £500 proclamation money Richard Blackledge, as attorney for William & Susanah Sitgreaves, sold to William Green 0.5 ac in lot #17 in New Bern; leased for 20 years on Apr. 11, 1755 by John Bryan to Richard Cogdell and leased Jul. 2, 1756 by Richard Cogdell to John Campbell for "said term then not expired"; bond void if Green doesn't claim title to the lot due to above lease. (signed) William Green; (witness) Wm Herritage & Rd Caswell;

"Oct." acknowledged; books 12 & 13 p. 335.

3897. Oct. 3, 1765 Richard Blackledge, attorney of William Sitgreaves, merchant, & wife Susannah (Philadelphia, Pennsylvania) to William Green, merchant (late of Wilmington, Pennsylvania, & now of Craven Co); in 1765 William & Susannah Sitgreaves agreed with William Green "for the purchase" of lot #17 in New Bern for £200 Philadelphia currency; SO due to power of attorney by William & Susannah Sitgreaves and for £260 sold 0.5 ac lot #17 in New Bern; between lots formerly known as John Campbell's lot & James Parkinson's lot; sold by Cornelius Fowler, attorney of Ambrose Steel, to John Bryan esq (of Craven Co) and sold Sept. 19, 1759 by John Bryan planter ("late" of Craven Co) & wife Ann Cady Bryan to Thomas Sitgreaves inn keeper (of New Bern) and sold Feb. 7, 1763 John Cady Sitgreaves to William Sitgreaves merchant (of Philadelphia). (signed) Richard Blackledge; (witness) Wm Herritage & Rd Caswell; Oct. 1765 acknowledged; books 12 & 13 p. 337.

3898. Oct. 20, 1765 Peter Conway, gentleman (Newbern, Craven Co) to John Smith, planter (Craven Co); for £25 proclamation money sold 250 ac on S side of Neuse R; border: begins at a red oak in John Fonvielle's line. (signed) pet. Conway; (witness) Isam Patridge & John Smith; Oct. 1765 acknowledged; books 12 & 13 p. 341.

3899. Sept. 30, 1765 John Fonvielle, planter (Craven Co) to William Brice Fonvielle, planter (same); for £20 proclamation money sold 206 ac on E side of Coor Cr between Green Pond Br & Handy Br; border: begins at a gum, joins a branch, & Green Pond Br. (signed) John Fonvielle; (witness) Frederick Fonvielle, Samuel Taylor, & Mood Streadle; Oct. 1765 acknowledged; books 12 & 13 p. 343.

3900. Oct. 4, 1765 Richard Blackledge, high sheriff (Craven Co) to Christopher Neale, gentleman (same); for £0.5 proclamation money sold 100 ac; border: joins "plantation" called Jacobs Wells; known as horse pastures; sold due to writ of fieri facias from Craven Co Inferior Court Jul. 5, 1760 & returnable to court first Tuesday in Oct. next against G Gilyard planter (late of Craven Co) for £4.17 proclamation money damages & £2.4.3 costs due to suit by "Christoper" Neale; and sold due to act of Parliament of Great Britain passed in 5th year of reign of King George II concerning collection of debts in America & act of Assembly passed in 4th year of reign of King George III; land sold by Joseph Carruthers "then" Craven Co high sheriff for £6 but he failed to make a deed to Neal, so Blackledge now makes deed for [additional] £0.5. (signed) Richard Blackledge; (witness) Thos Sitgreaves & Isam Patridge; [note at end indicates Neale paid Blackledge £0.5 on Oct. 4, 1765]; wit. oath Oct. 1765 by Isam "Potridge"; books 12 & 13 p. 344.

3901. Oct. 5, 1765 Christopher Neale, gentleman (Craven Co) to Joseph Carruthers, infant son of Joseph Carruthers esq deceased (same); for love, good will, & affection and for £0.10 proclamation money sold 100 ac; border: joins "plantation" called Jacobs Wells; known as the horse pasture. (signed) Christr. Neale; (witness) Pet Conway & Ja Jones; Oct. 1765 acknowledged; books 12 & 13 p. 347.

3902. Dec. 24, 1764 John Stanaland, planter (Craven Co) to William Bastin Whitford (same); for [remainder of deed blank]; books 12 & 13 p. 349.

3903. Jul. 2, 1765 Abner Neale, planter (Craven Co) to my much beloved son Christopher Neale; for natural love & affection gave 200 ac; border: begins at a live oak in the water at mouth of Coates Cr, joins mouth of Two polled Bridge Gut "or Branch", a cypress marked "F N" on E side, my back line, & "the" river; where I dwell. (signed) Abner Neale; (witness) James Seaman jr, James Godfrey, & Abner Neal jr; wit. oath Apr. 1766 by James "Seamen" jr; books 12 & 13 p. 349.

3904. Aug. 2, 1765 William "Makey" (Currituck Co, NC), only son of John Mackey deceased (of South R, Craven Co), to Christopher Neale (Craven Co); for £60 proclamation money sold 60 ac on W side of South R & N side of Kettings Cr; border: begins at an old corner pine at the Indian Landing & joins a swamp; granted May 19, 1713 to John "Makey". (signed) William Mackey; (witness) John Caney & Beverly Rue; wit. oath Apr. 1766 by Beverly Rue; books 12 & 13 p. 351.

3905. Oct. 25, 1765 [4th (sic) year of reign of King George III] Rawly Williams, planter (Craven Co) to Jacob Blount (same); for £70 proclamation money sold 200 ac; border: begins at an ash in mouth of Cabbin Br and joins Samuel Wingate's back line; where said "Rawny" Williams lives; being lower part of grant Sept. 29, 1756 to Samuel Wingate. (signed) "Raly" Williams; [no witness]; wit. oath Apr. 1766 by Wm Blamnt [or Blamert]; books 12 & 13 p. 253.

3906. Aug. 10, 1765 George Pope, planter, & wife Jane (Craven Co) to John Daley, gentleman (same); £150 proclamation money sold 222 ac sold on S side of Neuse R & each [or East] side of Stoney Br; border: begins at a red oak in Mr. Harris' line and joins Mr. F Green; sold May 28, 1745 Thomas Greaves gentleman (of Craven Co) for £210 NC money to George Pope, father of grantor of this deed, who died but willed land May 26, 1761 to his loving wife Elisabeth Pope for her widowhood and when Elisabeth dies or marries land was to go to son George Pope and on Aug. 1, 1765 Elisabeth Pope sold (or gave) land to her son George for consideration mentioned; lease by grantor to grantee mentioned [see next item]. (signed) George Pope & Jane's mark "X"; (witness) Richard Scott, John Pope, & Eliz Pope; [note at end indicates Daley paid the Popes £100 (sic) on Aug. 4, 1765]; wit. oath Oct. 2, 1765 by Richard Scott before Chas Berry; books 12 & 13 p. 354.

3907. Aug. 9, 1765 George Pope, planter (Craven Co) to John "Daly", gentleman (same); for £0.5 great Britain money leased for a year 222 ac on S side of Neuse

R & each side of Stony Br; border: begins at a red oak in Mr. Harris' line and joins F Green; rent is a pepper corn if demanded to be paid next Easter. (signed) George Pope; (witness) Richd Scott & John Pope; wit. oath Oct. 2, 1765 by Richard Scott before Chas Berry; books 12 & 13 p. 360.

3908. Aug. 1, 1765 Elizabeth Pope, widow of George Pope planter deceased (late of Craven Co) to her son George Pope, eldest son & heir of George Pope deceased; for natural love & affection and for £15 proclamation money sold 222 ac on S side of Neuse R & each side of Stony Br; border: begins at a red oak in Mr. Harris' line and joins F Green; sold May 28, 1745 by Thomas Graves gentleman (of Craven Co) to George Pope deceased for £210 NC money; about May 26, 1761 George Pope signed his will giving the land to his loving wife Elizabeth Pope, being land where he lived, for her widowhood and land to go to son George when Elizabeth marries or dies. (signed) Elizabeth Pope's mark "X"; (witness) Richd Scott & John Pope; [note at end indicates George paid Elizabeth £15 on Aug. 1, 1765]; wit. oath Oct. 12, 1765 (sic) by Richard Scott before Chas Berry; books 12 & 13 p. 362.

3909. Aug. 21, 1765 George Pope, planter (Craven Co) to John Daly, gentleman (same); for £90 proclamation money sold all cattle, sheep, hogs, goods, household stuff, implements, & furniture as in annexed schedule and at land on S side of Neuse [R] & both sides of Stony Br lately in occupation of [blank]; Pope put Daly in possession of a feather bed in name of other items. (signed) George Pope; (witness) Richd Scott & John Pope; [note at end indicates Daly paid Pope £90 on Aug. 21, 1765]; books 12 & 13 p. 365;

    inventory of items sold to John Daly: 63 three year old hogs at 1.57 £15.15; 25 sows at 12/6 £15.12.6; 5 year old hogs 20.5; yoke of oxen £9 £52.01.10 (sic); 2 steers, 3 heifers, a cow, yearling £11, a sheep at 10 £3.10 (sic), bee hives 10 £15.20.50; a grindstone 10/6, a hand mill 61, a feather bed £6 £11.8; [total] £90. [not signed]; (witness) Richd Scott & John Pope; wit. oath Oct. 12, 1765 by Richd Scott before Chas Berry; books 12 & 13 p. 367.

3910. Sept. 16, 1765 William Trapnall, planter (Johnston Co, NC) to William Holloway, joiner (Craven Co); for £30 proclamation money sold 150 ac on "the" main road near Fort Barnwell about 0.5 miles from John Tulan's place; border: begins at a red oak by a branch, joins Cooper, & Russells Br. [not signed]; (witness) Benjamin Griffin & Jesse Griffin; wit. oath Apr. 1766 by Benjamin Griffin; books 12 & 13 p. 368.

3911. Oct. 5, 1765 Longfield Cox, "joyner" (Craven Co) to Thomas Loftin; for £40 proclamation money sold 150 ac on S side of Nuce R & lower side of Half Moon Swamp; border: begins at a red oak, joins Half Moon Swamp, & "the" given line; known as "the" garden; granted Jun. 30, 1728 to Cornelius Loftin sr. (signed) Longfield Cox; (witness) John Clements & John "Hollaway"; wit. oath Apr. 1766 by John Halloway; books 12 & 13 p. 370.

3912. Oct. 5, 1765 Longfield Cox, joyner (Craven Co) to Thomas Loftin; for £10 proclamation money sold 200 ac on S side of Nuce R; border: begins at a red oak in Benj Griffin's line of land granted to Cornelius Loftin near Mill Br and joins Griffin's "or now" Loftin's line; granted Apr. 24, 1764 to said Longfield Cox. (signed) Longfield Cox; (witness) John Clements & John Halloway; wit. oath Apr. 1766 by John Halloway; books 12 & 13 p. 372.

3913. Oct. 28, 1765 Richsrd Blackledge, high sheriff (Craven Co) to Alexander Mackguillin, planter (same); for £6 proclamation money sold 200 ac on N side of Trent R & in forks of Roman Br; border: begins at a poplar at side of the branch and joins Briery Br; [granted ?] Nov. 26, 1757 to [omitted]; sold due to writ of fieri facias from New Bern Superior Court May 1765 & returnable to court Nov. 2, 1765 due to suit by John Suiter against David Palmer deceased for £88.10.6 proclamation money damages with interest from May 2 past and "716" his costs; and sold due to act of Parliament of Great Britain passed in 5th year of reign of King George II concerning collection of debts in America and act of Assembly passed in 4th year of reign of King George III. (signed) Richd Blackledge; (witness) Wm Bryan & Daniel Shine; Apr. 1766 acknowledged; books 12 & 13 p. 374.

3914. Dec. 7, 1765 John Bedscott, planter (Craven Co) to Gideon Tingle, planter (same); for £100 proclamation money sold 235 ac on N side of Nuce R; border: begins at Hog's upper corner pine, joins a large gut at the river, & Franklin. (signed) John "Bedscot's" mark ["F" laying on its side]; (witness) Wm West & William Tyer; wit. oath Apr. 1766 by William Tyer; books 12 & 13 p. 376.

3915. Mar. 26, 1765 Rigdon Brice, merchant (Craven Co) to Moses Allamand, carpenter (same); for £25 proclamation money sold 25 ac near Brices Cr; border: begins at a corner small white oak & joins the creek swamp; part of land sold Feb. 12, 1755 by John Acton Brice to said Rigdon Brice. (signed) Rigdon Brice; (witness) Elihu Hall, John Kennedy, & Acton Brice; [note at end indicates Allamand paid Brice £25 on Mar. 26, 1766 (sic)]; wit. oath Apr. 1766 by Acton Brice; books 12 & 13 p. 378.

3916. Jan. 29, 1766 Solomon Griffin, planter (Craven Co) to William Halloway (same); for £65 proclamation money sold 150 ac on S side of Nuce R; border: begins at Joseph Trewhitt's corner on W side of Half Moon Swamp; part of grant to Cornelious Loftin sr & Solomon Griffin; (witness) William Carraway & Levi Dawson; wit. oath Apr. 1766 by William Carraway. (signed) books 12 & 13 p. 380.

3917. Oct. 10, 1765 Cornelius Groenendeyke [or Grunnindike] (Craven Co) to Henry Vanpelt [or Nanpelt] (same); for £50 proclamation money sold 100 ac on S side of Little Contentna Cr; border: begins at a red oak on the creek; granted Oct. 2, 1750 to "said" John Bradly. (signed) Cornelius Groenendeyke; (witness) John Turner & John Carruthers; wit. oath Apr. 1766 by John Carruthers; books

Craven County, NC Deed Books 11-13

12 & 13 p. 382.

3918. Jul. 11, 1765 Nathaniel Draper (Craven Co) to James Tingle; for £25 NC money sold 153 ac on S side of Bay R; border: begins at a marked cypress at mouth of a small branch above Solomon Tingle's, joins head line of "the insueing" patent, & includes half of 306 ac that said Draper purchased of John Linkfield and half of front land on the river; granted Nov. 14, 1730 to Daniel "Shnies". (signed) Nathl. Draper; (witness) Amos Squirs, Esaw Tingle, & John Tillman; wit. oath Apr. 1766 by "Easaw" Tingle; books 12 & 13 p. 384.

3919. Oct. 19, 1765 Martin Worsley, cooper (Craven Co) to Samuel Nines, planter (same); for £120 proclamation money sold 0.5 ac in lot #276 in New Bern; border: begins at corner of Craven Street & New Street, runs 13 poles on Craven Street, & 6.5 poles on New Street; sold Jul. 8, 1746 by New Bern commissioners to John Arthur who willed it to Matthew Arthur & William Arthur who sold Dec. 1, 1755 to James Stephenson who sold Apr. 12, 170 to said Martin Worsley. (signed) Martin Worsley; (witness) Isaac Patridge & Samuel Cole; Apr. 1766 acknowledged; books 12 & 13 p. 386.

3920. May 8, 1761 Benjamin West (Craven Co) to Gideon Tingle; for £6 proclamation money sold 70 ac on N side of Nuce R & W side of Upper Broad R; border: begins at a pine, joins a branch, & "the" back line; granted to George Taylor. (signed) Benjamin West; (witness) David Lewis & Hugh Ward; wit. oath Apr. 1766 by David Lewis; books 12 & 13 p. 389.

3921. Feb. 18, 1765 John Mill, planter (Craven Co) to James Stephenson, planter (same); for £10 proclamation money sold 1,050 ac on N side of Nuce R; border: begins at a white oak at head of a gutt; granted Jun. 26, 1746 by Gov. Gabriel Johnston to John Mill deceased. (signed) John Mill; (witness) Charles Rew, Thomas Putman, & William Mill; wit. oath Apr. 1766 by Charles Rew; books 12 & 13 p. 390.

3922. Sept. 23, 1765 Joseph Carmach, planter (Craven Co) to James Carmach, planter (same); for £45 NC money sold 100 ac on S side of Nuce R; border: begins at a white oak in "the" meadow, joins Joseph "Treuwhit", & Solomon Daughity; part of a grant in Nov. 1744 to Levi Treuwhitt. (signed) John Carmach's mark "Ŧ"; (witness) Jonathan Mackfarson & Daniel Mackfarson; wit. oath Apr. 1766 by Jonathan Mackfarson; books 12 & 13 p. 392.

3923. Sept. 2, 1765 Simon Clark to James Carmack; for £26 sold 50 ac on S side of Nuce R; border: begins at a willow oak in Aligator Br and joins a great glade. (signed) Simon Clark; (witness) Jonathan Mackfarson & Jonathan "McFerson" (sic); wit. oath Apr. 1766 by Jonathan McFerson; books 12 & 13 p. 394.

3924. Jul. 15, 1765 Leonard Loftin, cooper to my loving son-in-law Henry Alway & my daughter Sarah his wife; for love, good will, & affection gave 640 ac; part or 450 ac begins at a great cypress at Pledgere's Landing on E side of Handcocks Cr & crosses a neck [remaining 190 ac not described]; granted Oct. 10, 1707 by Lords Proprietor to William Handcock sr who sold to William Handcock jr who sold to me; given for their lives & at their deaths to heirs of said Henry lawfully begotten of body of his wife but if no heirs then land returns to Conrad Loftin or his heirs. (signed) Len. Loftin; (witness) John Parkinson & Thos Moss; Apr. 1766 acknowledged; books 12 & 13 p. 396.

3925. Sept. 28, 1765 John Bryan (Craven Co) to William Bryan (same); for £150 proclamation money sold 125 ac on N side of Nuce R & W side of Island Cr; border: begins at mouth of Citts Gut & joins Island Cr; known as Citts Neck; being land left to me by my father's will [no name]. (signed) John Bryan; (witness) Ann Bryan & Jesse Bryan; Oct. 1765 acknowledged; books 12 & 13 p. 399.

3926. May 25, 1765 Abner Neale, planter (Craven Co) to Joseph Bryan (same); for £50 proclamation money sold 250 ac on N side of Nuce R & W side of Orchard Cr; border: begins at Hog Point, joins a cove, Fulcher, joins land sold to John Williams now in possession of William Fulcher, Fulcher's old patent, 100 ac sold to Thomas Martin, mouth of Dennis' Gut, & Orchard Cr. (signed) Abner Neale; (witness) Chrisr. Neale & Etheldred Piles; [note at end indicates Bryan paid Neale £50 on May 25, 1765]; wit. oath Oct. 1765 by Chrisr. Neale; books 12 & 13 p. 400.

3927. Oct. 1, 1765 Isaac Eselick {"Cartrite" Co, NC) to Ann Bryan (Craven Co); for £11 proclamation money sold 100 ac on N side of Nuce R & head of Orchard Cr; border: begins at a gum marked by Francis Bond, Samuel "Easlick", & Thomas Martin beside a small branch, joins "the" back line, & runs through a swamp; sold out of Wilkey's patent. (signed) Isaac "Eslick"; (witness) Hardy Bryan & John Bryan; wit. oath Oct. 1765 by John Bryan; books 12 & 13 p. 402.

3928. Apr. 6, 1765 Samuel West, planter (Craven Co) to William West, cooper (same); for £15 proclamation money sold 150 ac joins Hammonds Pecosin & Wild catt [Cr]; border: begins at or near John Carlton's corner on Hammonds Pecosin & joins Wild catt [Cr]; where William West lives. (signed) Samuel West; (witness) James West & John Clements; wit. oath Oct. 1765 by John Clements; books 12 & 13 p. 404.

3929. May 25, 1765 William Jones, carpenter (Dobbs Co, NC) to John Slade, planter (Craven Co); for £1,002.3 proclamation money sold 320 ac; border: begins at a white oak parting it from land sold for Thomas Sprigg & joins "the" river swamp; part of 640 ac granted Aug. 29, 1730 to Jos Hannis who "acknowledged" it to George Linnington who willed it to his daughter Christian and sold by James Alston & wife Christian to John Benson who sold to Jno Rice who sold to Margaret McKinne now wife of said William Jones. (signed) Wm Jones; (witness) John Wallin & Absalom Daughiy wit. oath Oct. 1765 by Absalom Daughity; books 12 & 13 p. 406.

3930. Mar. 16, 1764 Thomas Dias (Craven Co) to Eleazer Nelson (same); for £100 proclamation sold 200 ac on Permeto [or Pumeto] Swamp on Swifts Cr; border: begins at beginning pine of the patent, joins Gum Br, Permeto Swamp, "the" lower corner, & Hardy Bryan; part of grant Apr. 20, 1745 to Edward Bryan. (signed) Thomas Dias' mark "/"; (witness) Joseph Bryan, John Hill, & Elizabeth Lewis; wit. oath Oct. 1765 by Joseph Bryan; books 12 & 13 p. 408.

3931. Jul. 25, 1765 Beverly Rew, planter (Craven Co) to John Salmon, planter (same); for £25 proclamation money sold 50 ac on S side of Nuce R between Adams Cr & South R; border: begins at John Carney's corner gum at Bustery Point & joins a marsh; part of grant [date blank] to Thomas Lipper. (signed) Beverly Rew; (witness) Jas Jones, David Wallace, & John Nelson; wit. oath Oct. 1765 by Jas Jones; books 12 & 13 p. 410.

3932. Mar. [blank], 1765 Christopher Dawson, planter (Craven Co) to Antipass Tisdale, hatter (same); for £90 proclamation money sold 0.5 ac lot #302 in New Bern on corner of Short Street & Graves Street; sold Feb. 16, 1749 by New Bern commissioners to Philip Smith who sold to said Christopher Dawson as written on back on the deed. (signed) Christopher Dawson; (witness) James Coor & Thomas Skinner; [note at end indicates Dawson received £90 on Mar. 16, 1765]; wit. oath Oct. 1765 by James Coor; books 12 & 13 p. 412.

3933. Jan. 31, 1765 Thomas Clifford Howe esq (Craven Co) & wife Elizabeth, daughter & heiress of William Wilson deceased (late of Craven Co) to Richard Ellis (Newbern, Craven Co); for £0.5 proclamation money & due to an agreement leased for 21 years (a) 0.5 ac house & lot #13 and kitchen & other edificies in New Bern at corner of Front Street & Pollock Street; where Richard Ellis lives; & (b) "proper" front of lot #13 & stores built thereon; where Thomas Clifford Howe & wife Elizabeth agreed to rent to Richard Ellis (sic); Elizabeth owns the "sundry tracts" due to will of William Wilson in North Carolina and sundry lots & houses in New Bern; Ellis to make any necessary repairs; yearly quit rent is £40 proclamation money. (signed) Richd Ellis (sic); (witness) John Williams & James Stephenson; [note at end:] Thos C Howe & wife Elizabeth signed in error and that is corrected Feb. 12, 1765; Oct. 1765 acknowledged by Richd Ellis; books 12 & 13 p. 414.

3934. Sept. 14, 1764 Richard Ellis, merchant (Newbern, Craven Co) and Mary Ellis "otherwise" Jones widow of Harding Jones esq (late of Craven Co) to Thomas Clifford Howe esq (Craven Co); for £60 proclamation money lease for 14 years 413 ac on S side of Trent R; being surplus of 4,560 ac grant to Frederick Jones, father of Harding Jones who devised it to Mary his widow; yearly rent is £0.5 proclamation money per year to be paid in 2 installments on Nov. 1 and May 1. (signed) Richd Ellis & Mary Ellis; (witness) John Williams & James "Stevenson"; wit. oath Oct. 1765 by Richard & Mary Ellis and Mary Ellis renounced dower before John Benners esq; books 12 & 13 p. 418.

3935. (Beaufort Co, NC) Jun. 18, 1765 Richard Cortis to Jacob Tingle (Craven Co); for £5 proclamation money sold 100 ac; border: begins at Richard Cortis' N corner pine on W side of White houses Cr, joins Clubfoots Cr, a little gut, a pond, & head line of Richard Cortis' survey; part of a grant Mar. 17, 1765 to said Richard Cortis. (signed) Richard Cortis' mark "R"; (witness) Ja Wilcox & Amos Saucers [or Samers]; wit. oath Oct. 1765 by James Wilcox; books 12 & 13 p. 421.

3936. Dec. 20, 1765 Jacob Miller (Craven Co) to William Wilson (same); for £13.6.8 proclamation money sold 300 ac on Permeter Swamp in Swifts Cr; border: begins at a pine on William Nelson's line, joins Eleazer Nelson, & "Patgeto" corner; reserving 20 ac that begins at a pine on S side of the swamp, then to run of the swamp, up the swamp to upper line and reserving "that" part of the swamp & a point that comes into the swamp leaving 280 ac now sold; granted Feb. 22, 1764 to Jacob Miller "No. 76". (signed) Jacob Miller; (witness) Elias Nelson, Christian Ipock, & Jacob Nelson; Oct. 1766 acknowledged; books 12 & 13 p. 423.

3937. Aug. 6, 1764 Amos Small, planter (Craven Co) to Abrm Bussett Simmons, planter (Dobbs Co, NC); for £100 proclamation money sold 120 ac on S side of Trent R; border: begins at a black gum on E side of Crooked Run in Abraham Bussett's line, joins Peter Andrews, a branch, & "the" main swamp; part of 200 ac granted Oct. 3, 1755 to Benjamin Simmons. (signed) Amos Small; (witness) James "Macdaniel" & James Harper; wit. oath Oct 1765 by James McDaniel; books 12 & 13 p. 425.

3938. Jul. 19, 1765 William Gallagher, gentleman (Philadelphia, Pennsylvania), due to power of attorney from Lawrence Coffee, gentleman (Dublin Co, Ireland) eldest son & heir of Barnard Coffee gentleman "or" trader lately deceased (late of New Bern, NC) who died intestate, to my trusty & esteemed friend Robert Orme, trader (New Bern); power of attorney to receive money owned to Coffee by Richard Cogdell esq who lately took on administration of goods & chattels of Barnard Coffee and from Joseph Leech gentleman and anyone else who owes said estate. (signed) Wm Gallagher; (witness) Bernard Parkinson & Paul Ambrose; wit. oath Oct. 1765 by "Barnard" Parkinson; books 12 & 13 p. 428.

3939. Sept. 26, 1765 Thomas Fish (Craven Co) to James Jorden (same); for £8 proclamation money sold 100 ac on Nuce [R], Cotininy [Cr], & on a branch that makes out of Bare Pecosin; border: begins at 3 pines being second bound tree of said tract and near Ester Kilpatrick; granted to him. (signed) Thomas Fish; (witness) Edward Fitspatrick & William Jorden; wit. oath Oct. 1765 by William Jorden; books 12 & 13 p. 430.

3940. Mar. 29, 1765 William Lewis (Craven Co) to Ezekiel Adams (same); for £25 proclamation money sold 150 ac on N side of Swifts Cr & E side of Creeping Swamp; border: begins at a pine on side of a run or branch made by said Lewis as a corner tree, joins William Charles, division line between William Lewis &

William Charles, Chapman, & a small branch; granted Mar. 13, 1756 to John Chapman. (signed) William Lewis' mark "W"; (witness) Joseph Bryan, Thomas Bonner, William Clark, & Elizabeth Lewis; wit. oath Oct. 1765 by William Clark; books 12 & 13 p. 433.

3941. May 2, 1764 John "Yeats" to Alexander Skeen; for £16 NC money sold 100 ac on E side of Southwest Cr & N side of Nuce R; border: begins at pine on Juniper Swamp and joins Daniel "Mckforson". (signed) John Yeates' mark "V"; (witness) Jonathan Mckfarson & Jonathan Mckfarson (sic); Oct. 1765 acknowledged; books 12 & 13 p. 435.

3942. Jan. 30, 1764 Miriam Harkel & Margaret Harkel, sisters (Craven Co) to James Brinson (same); for £2.10.8 proclamation money paid to each sister sold 37.5 ac on N side of Neuse R & E side of "Goos" Cr [no more description]; being our share or half of 75 ac that was owned by our father George Harkel deceased; part of grant Feb. 28, 1739 to Simon Molpus. (signed) Miriam Harkel's mark "M" & Margaret Harkel's mark "M" (sic); (witness) John Boyd & John Bacon; wit. oath Oct. 1765 by John Boyd; books 12 & 13 p. 437.

3943. Sept. 29, 1765 John Bryan (Craven Co) to William Gatlin (same); for £2.10 sold 160 ac on N side of Nuce R, E side of Swifts Cr, & on E & W sides of Bare Br; border: joins Joseph Norton on upper side, James Gatlin on lower side; being middle part of grant to Edward Bryan & part of land sold to Mr. Norton. (signed) John Bryan; (witness) Joseph Norton & Tobis Mott; wit. oath Oct. 1765 by Joseph Norton; books 12 & 13 p. 438.

3944. Sept. 2, 1765 Christopher Neale (Craven Co) to John Benners esq (same); for £20 proclamation money sold 193 ac on head of Long Cr; called "Russels" old field [no more description]; part of 200 ac granted to John Russell who sold to John Simcock who died intestate and land was taken by execution by the sheriff & sold to John Duke who sold to said Christopher Neale. (signed) Chrisr. Neale; (witness) Joseph Atherly & Benjn Blackledge jr; [note at end indicates Benners paid Neale £20 on Sept. 2, 1765]; Oct. 1765 acknowledged; books 12 & 13 p. 440.

3945. Jul. 21, 1764 George Becton, planter (Craven Co) to Frederick Islar, merchant (same); for £50 proclamation money sold all my interest in Negroes & their future increase: Rachel, "Kenus", Vilet, Sam, Ellott, Bett, George, Sam (sic); being part of estate of John Becton deceased or Rachel & Venus left by his will to Ann his wife for her life and wenches & future increase to return to his children and others were born since children of Rachel & Venus. (signed) George Becton; (witness) Sim. Spight & Jacob Rehm; Aug. 22, 1764 I assign my interest in above mentioned to Frederick Becton esq (sic) (signed) Frederick "Isler's" mark "F" (witness) Michael Becton & Mary Becton; wit. oath Oct. 1765 by Simon Spight for first sale & acknowledged by Frederick Isler for second sale; books 12 & 13 p. 442.

3946. Oct. 25, 1764 Thomas Stevens, planter (Craven Co) to John Smith, planter (same); for £5 proclamation money sold 10 ac; border: begins at end of Cherry Pond, joins a division line, & John Smith; part of land where said Thomas Stevens lives. (signed) Thomas Stevens; (witness) John dunn & Jacob Shepard; Oct. 1765 acknowledged; books 12 & 13 p. 443.

3947. Sept. 30, 1765 Jacob Taylor (Craven Co) to my well beloved son Joshua Taylor; for love & affection gave 75 ac on S side of Nuce R & W side of Auther Cr; border: begins at the creek side, joins mouth of a branch, & a small pond. (signed) Jacob Taylor; (witness) John Ives & Benenman Tolson; wit. oath Oct. 1765 by John Ives; books 12 & 13 p. 445.

3948. Apr. 17, 1765 Francis Dawson, planter (Craven Co) to Benjamin Price, silver smith (same); for £40 proclamation money sold 300 ac on N side of main road from Broad Cr to Goose Cr; border: begins at a white oak on S side of Woolf field Ridge on Coohoons Pecosin in John Lingfield's line and joins "the" great savannah; all of a grant May 10, 1760 to Francis Dawson. (signed) Francis Dawson; (witness) John Green, John Turner, & James Coor; [note at end indicates Dawson received £40 on Apr. 17, 1765]; wit. oath Oct. 1765 by James Coor; books 12 & 13 p. 446.

3949. Sept. 24, 1765 William Rutledge (Craven Co) to Thomas Bradcher (same) for 60 barrels of turpentine sold 100 ac; border: begins at a pine in Wickliffe's line on eastermost prong of Slocumbs Cr. (signed) William Rutledge's mark "V R" (sic); (witness) Roger Jones & Thomas Martin; wit. oath Oct. 1765 by Thomas Martin; books 12 & 13 p. 448.

3950. Feb. 2, 1765 [5th year of reign of King George III] Joseph Leech, merchant (Newbern, Craven Co) to Frederick Isler (Craven Co); for £90 proclamation money sold part of lot [no number, maybe 111] in New Bern; border: begins at corner of lot sold by Leech to Isler "sometime" now in occupation of Antipass Tisdale, runs 120 feet to line parallel to Union Street, then parallel to Front Street to Union Street, along Union Street to Front Street, & along Front Street to beginning. (signed) Joseph Leech; (witness) Thos Lucas & James "Seears"; [note at end indicates Isler paid Leech £90 on Feb. 1765]; wit. oath Oct. 1765 by James Seears; books 12 & 13 p. 450.

3951. (Duplin Co, NC) Jul. 9, 1765 Francis Brice, planter (Duplin Co, NC) to Robert Reynolds, planter (Craven Co); for £10 proclamation money sold 70 ac on E side of Brices Cr; border: joins John Acton Brice's front line, joins dividing line between said J A Brice & Francis Brice, & dividing line between said J A Brice & Rigdon Brice; part of grant May 5, 1742 to William Brice. (signed) Fran. Brice; (witness) N Gillespie & Rigdon Brice; [note at end: (Duplin Co) indicates Reynolds paid Brice £10 on Jul. 9, 1765]; Oct. 1765 acknowledged; books 12 & 13 p. 452.

3952. Aug. 3, 1765 James Tyre, planter (Pitt Co, NC) to William Jones, joyner (Craven Co); for £140 proclamation money sold 211 ac on N side of Nuce R; border: begins at a white oak on the river and joins a great branch; granted in 1737 to Henry Shore; Jones to pay yearly quit rent of £0.4 proclamation money per 100 ac to the king. (signed) James Tyre; (witness) Joseph Bryan, George Bryan, & William Casedy; wit. oath Oct. 1765 by Joseph Bryan; books 12 & 13 p. 454.

3953. Sept. 27, 1765 William Routledge, cooper (Craven Co) to Thomas Martin, planter (same); for £6 sold 140 ac on E side of Slocumbs Cr; border: begins at a red oak near Thomas Smith's corner, near a branch, & joins Wickliff. (signed) William Routledge's mark "W R"; (witness) Roger Jones, Thomas Bradclur, & Mary Thompson; wit. oath Oct. 1765 by Thomas Bradclur; books 12 & 13 p. 456.

3954. Jul. 31, 1764 Benjamin Griffin (Craven Co) to Smith Fields (same); for £65 proclamation money sold 80 ac; border: begins at mouth of Mill Br and joins Half moon Br; part of 100 ac sold Jan. 22, 1753 by Cornelious Loftin to me and 80 ac "more" being part of 150 ac granted May 23, 1757 to me. (signed) Benjamin Griffin's mark "B"; (witness) John Turner & John Turner jr; wit. oath Oct. 1765 by "John Turner"; books 12 & 13 p. 458.

3955. Mar. 26, 1764 Benjamin Griffin sr, cooper (Craven Co) to Thomas Loftin (same); for £12.10 proclamation money sold 50 ac; border: begins at line of land where Thomas Loftin lives on S side of a spring branch and joins Benjamin Griffin's head line; part of grant May 3, 1757 [30th year of "our" reign] to Benjamin Griffin. (signed) Benjamin Griffin's mark "B"; (witness) Samuel West & Jesse Griffin; wit. oath Oct. 1765 by Samuel West; books 12 & 13 p. 459.

3956. Feb. [blank], 1765 Roger Hodges (Craven Co) to Thomas Pollard (Pitt Co, NC); for £30 proclamation money sold 100 ac on head of Checod Cr; border: begins at a gum in Permeto Br "as runs" out of Checod [Cr]; formerly owned by Col. Robert West who sold to Stephen Lee (of Tyrrell Co). (signed) Roger Hodges; (witness) Benj Pollard, John Speir, & Hardy Brown; Apr. 1765 acknowledged; books 12 & 13 p. 461.

3957. Apr. 5, 1764 [5th year of reign of King George III] Peter Dubose (Bladen Co, NC) to my beloved friend Mr. Vincent Amiet, planter (Craven Co); power of attorney to receive from anyone any money or goods owed to me. (signed) Peter Dubose; (witness) Peter Amiet & Vincent Amiet (sic); wit. oath Oct. 1765 by Vincent Amiet; books 12 & 13 p. 463.

3958. Apr. 7, 1760 Richard Blackledge, merchant, & wife Ann (Craven Co) to John Smith, gentleman (same); for £155 proclamation money sold northermost half of lot #7 in New Bern; sold Dec. 23, 1757 by John Rutherford esq & wife Frances to John "Snedd" and "afterward" sold Oct. 1, 1756 (sic) by John Starkey, executor of will of John Snead, to Peter Knight who with wife Elizabeth sold May

11, 1759 to Richard Blackledge. (signed) Richard Blackledge & Ann Blackledge; (witness) Fulder Powell, Mary Hannis, John Allen, & Benj Kutts; [note at end indicates on Apr. 10, 1761 (sic) Smith paid Blackledge £55 and bond for £100 payable Oct. 30 next]; wit. oath May 1, 1761 acknowledged before Marmaduke Jones; books 12 & 13 p. 464.

3959. Aug. 13, 1766 Peter Conway, gentleman (New Bern, NC) to Peter Knight & John Green, merchants & partners; for £90 proclamation money sold 2 lots #257 & 285 in New Bern; title warranted except for judgment & interest in case by John Simpson against him obtained at Edenton Dist Superior Court and judgment against him by "Rumsey" & Willon at New Bern Superior Court; sale void if Conway pays Knight & Green [amount blank] by Dec. 25 next. (signed) Peter Conway, John Green for Peter Knight, & John Green; (witness) Rd Cogdell & William Creehmore [or Cruhmore]; wit. oath Aug. 22, 1766 by Richard Cogdell before Ja Hasell, CIC; books 12 & 13 p. 467.

3960. Sept. 9, 1765 William Burk (Craven Co) to Jeremiah Prichard, planter (same); for £7.3.8 proclamation money sold on both sides of Chinkapin Cr; border: begins at Lewis Conner's corner in James Stevenson's line and joins William Davis; includes George Morgan's improvements; granted Apr. 4, 1760 to Arthur Caraway who sold Oct. 14, 1765 to William Burk. (signed) William Burk's mark "+"; (witness) William Lavender & William Messer; [note at end indicates Prichard paid Burk £7.3.8 on Sept. 9, 1765]; wit. oath Jul. 1766 by William Messer; books 12 & 13 p. 471.

3961. May 10, 1765 John Robinson (Beaufort Co, NC) to John Burch (Craven Co); for £10 proclamation money sold 100 ac on E side of Swifts Cr; border: joins the swamp between "the" high bridge & place where Mathias Tolar lives [no more description]; being upper end of grant Jul. 13, 1736 to Jacob Robinson. (signed) John Robinson; (witness) Scarbrough "Tankark", Samuel Dunbare [or Dunvare], & David Dunn; wit. oath Jul. 1766 by David Dunn; books 12 & 13 p. 473.

3962. Feb. 11, 1765 Thomas Bartlet & wife Penelope (Pitt Co, NC) to James Barrenton [or Barenton], planter (Craven Co); for £15 proclamation money sold 50 ac on E side of Swifts Cr & N side of Permeto Swamp; border: begins at mouth of the branch above the bull going over & joins the swamp; being "plantation" where John Paget deceased dwelt and it "fell" to his daughter Penelope by heirship now wife of said Thomas Bartlet; part of 100 ac granted Apr. 13, 1743 to Richard Hart. (signed) Thomas Bartlet & Penelope Bartlet; (witness) Joseph Bryan, John Hall, & Joel King; wit. oath Jul. 1766 by Joseph Bryan; books 12 & 13 p. 475.

3963. Feb. 1, 1766 Thomas Gaskins, planter (Craven Co) to Peter Ipock [or Peter John Pock] (same); for £4.10 proclamation money sold 50 ac on N side of Nuce R; border: "next to" James Arthur [no more description]; part of survey by Farnifold Green for said Gaskins "according to patent" on Mar. 23, 1763. (signed) Thomas Gaskins' mark "X"; (witness) Scarbrough Tankard, Simon "Bexley", &

James Arthur; wit. oath Jul. 1766 by Simon Bexley; books 12 & 13 p. 477.

3964. Jul. 4, 1766 Samuel Griffis, taylor (Craven Co) to John Frank, planter (same); for £40 proclamation money sold 150 ac on N side of Trent R & W sie of Chinkapin Cr; border: begins at a red oak near mouth of a small branch that runs through said Frank's "plantation" and joins land where John Frank lives. (signed) Saml Griffis; (witness) John Carruthers & Jacob Rehm; Jul. 1766 acknowledged; books 12 & 13 p. 478.

3965. Sept. 27, 1765 James Stevenson & wife Mary (Craven Co) to John Mills (same); for £200 proclamation money sold 150 ac in fork of Smiths Cr; where Capt. John Mills formerly lived; granted in 1702 to John Howard; [reference to grant for metes & bounds]. (signed) James Stevenson & Mary Stevenson; (witness) Charles Rew, Thomas Pitman, William Wall, & William James; Jul. 1766 acknowledged by James & Mary Stevenson and Mary Stevenson renounced dower before Jas Davis esq; books 12 & 13 p. 480.

3966. Jul. 1, 1766 John "Councill" Bryan (Craven Co) to Abraham Beesley, planter (same); for £16 sold 100 ac on N side of Nuce R & main fork of Coor Cr; border: begins at Thomas Smith's corner white oak. (signed) Jno C Bryan; (witness) John Green & Will Green; wit. oath Jul. 1766 by John Green; books 12 & 13 p. 482.

3967. Oct. 30, 1761 Thomas Sitgraves & Ann Cady Bryan, executor & executrix of will of Ann Cady Bryan deceased (Craven Co) to William McCoy (same); for £20 proclamation money sold 100 ac on S side of Coor Cr & upper side of Green Pond Br; border: begins at white oak in said branch & joins mouth of Green Pond Br. (signed) Thomas Sitgraves & Ann Cady Bryan; (witness) John Green & William McCoy (sic); wit. oath Jul. 1765 by John Green; books 12 & 13 p. 483.

3968. Jun. 20, 1765 Martin Worsley, cooper (New Bern, NC) to John Smith, merchant (same); on Sept. 11, 1762 Worsley mortgaged lot #303 in New Bern to William Sitgraves, merchant (of Philadelphia, Pennsylvania) for £156 proclamation money; mortgage was to be void if Worsley paid Sitgraves £56 proclamation money with legal interest by Dec. 25, 1763; Worsley satisfied the mortgage by paying £156 with interest through power of attorney dated Jul. 27, 1765 by William Sitgraves to Richard Blackledge and Worsley received receipt from Blackledge Apr. 10, 1764 (sic) when Worsley agreed to sell lot to John Smith; SO for £140 (sic) proclamation money sold lot #303 in New Bern; border: begins at corner of New Street & Craven Street, runs 13 poles on Craven Street, & 6.5 poles on New Street; sold Feb. 30, 1749 by New Bern commissioners to Mathew Arthur who sold Feb. 23, 1754 to John Williams who sold Oct. 12, 1754 to Samuel Lawson who sold Oct. 29, 1755 to James Parkinson who sold Jul. 16, 1756 to John Isler but not registered & "by consent" of John Isler sold by James Parkinson to William Sitgraves & registered in Craven Co register's office and sold May 22, 1758 by William Sitgraves to Thomas Sitgraves who sold Aug. 31,

1762 to Martin Worsley. (signed) Martin Worsley; (witness) William Low & Susannah Mansfield; wit. oath Aug. 22, 1766 by William Low before Jas Hasell, CIC; books 12 & 13 p. 485.

3969. Jul. 3, 1766 James Cadwell, planter (Craven Co) to Absalom Taylor (same); for £140 proclamation money sold 162 ac on S side of Nuce R & E side of Southwest Cr; border: begins at a pine tree on said creek; sold Apr. 24, 1746 by John Taylor (of Craven Co) to Thomas Low "vide record Nov. 18, 1738". (signed) Jas Cadwell; (witness) Farnifold Green & John Green; Jul. 1766 acknowledged; books 12 & 13 p. 489.

3970. Oct. 8, 1765 Thomas Wharton, planter (Craven Co), heir of William Wharton (late of Craven Co), to John Gilliard (same); for £155 proclamation money sold 116 ac on Nine Swamp; border: begins at upper corner pine of the whole tract beside the swamp near "the plantation" fence; part of 580 ac known as St. James' Park which is part of 2,540 ac granted in 1727 to Thomas Jones who sold in Apr. 1731 to Walter Lane who sold in Oct. 1731 to William Hancock who sold in 1734 to William Tunnicliffe who died intestate and land descended to his only child Jane wife of John Carruthers jr who sold 116 ac on Jul. 9, 1750 to Thomas Wharton who "some time after" sold to John Starkey jr who sold to William Wharton since deceased. (signed) Thomas Wharton; (witness) Jesse Bryan, Frusau [or Freesaw] Becton, & Fred Becton; [note at end indicates Gilliard paid Wharton £55 on Oct. 8, 1765]; wit. oath Jul. 1766 by Frederick Becton; books 12 & 13 p. 491.

3971. Apr. 20, 1765 William Gibson, carpenter (Onslow Co, NC) to Peter Anders jr, planter (Craven Co); for £40 proclamation money sold 340 ac on S side of Trent R; border: begins at Hudler's former corner white oak on the river, joins James Lipsey, & a branch; part of 640 ac granted Mar. 27, 1754 to said William Gibson that began at Hudler's former corner white oak on "the" river, joins a marsh, James Lipsey, & a branch. (signed) William Gibson; (witness) Thomas Pollock, John Granade, & Robt Orme; wit. oath Jul. 1766 by Robt Orme; books 12 & 13 p. 494.

3972. Aug. 11, 1766 Thomas Smart, planter (Craven Co) to John Smith, merchant (New Bern, NC); for £5 proclamation money sold 300 ac on S side of Trent R; border: begins at John Perry's corner hickory & joins land where Robt Perry lived; being West half of grant [date blank] to [omitted] and sold Feb. 12, 1765 by Thomas Robinson to Thomas Smart. (signed) Thos Smart; (witness) John Smith, Rawlings Williams, & William Low; wit. oath Aug. 23, 1766 by Wm Low before Jas Hasell, JC; books 12 & 13 p. 497.

3973. Jun. 20, 1763 George Hays, carpenter (Newbern, Craven Co) to Philip Ambrose, merchant (same); for £21 proclamation money sold 0.5 ac in lot #102 on Broad Street in New Bern; sold Sept. 8, 1746 by New Bern commissioners to John Carruthers sr and by "several conveyances" became vested in George Hays.

(signed) George Hays; (witness) John Williams & Richd Cogdell; [note at end indicates Ambrose paid Hays £21 on Jun. 20, 1763]; Jun. 25, 1763 we certify lot #102 was built on by "John Carruthers" within time limit as per certified record recorded in Craven Co by James Davis, James Durham, & Richard Davis, New Bern commissioners (signed) John Clitherall jr, Joseph Green, Peter Conway, Jno(?) Rice, & R Cogdell clk; wit. oath Jul. 1763 (sic) by John Williams esq; books 12 & 13 p. 499.

3974. Oct. 31, 1765 David Fonvielle, planter (Craven Co) to John Clitherall, merchant (same); for £552.6.6 proclamation money sold (a) 500 ac where said David Fonvielle lives [no more description]; & (b) 11 Negroes: Senitoy(?), George, Abraham, Dick, Prince, Billey boy, Bett, Moses, Sett, Martin, & Patience; Negro Dick is now delivered to Clitherall in place of all the property (sic). (signed) David Fonvielle; (witness) James Coor & Peter Clitherall; wit. oath Jun. 9, 1766 by James Coor before Jas Hasell, CJ; books 12 & 13 p. 503.

3975. Feb. 9, 1765 John "Physiock", planter (Craven Co) to Peter Physiock (same); for regard, love, parental care, & affection gave (a) [omitted] ac on Slocumb [Cr] from Grave Neck to Spring Br; border: joins head of the spring branch, "the" back line; & (b) [omitted] ac on Hancocks [Cr] which I bought of Abraham Jones [no more description for either tract]; (c) Negro woman Juda; & (d) chest of drawers, a large chest, a case of bottles, 6 silver table spoons, 2 large pewter basons, a fourth of my moveable estate, a feather bed & furniture; except use & services of the premises reserved to John for his natural life. (signed) John Physioc; (witness) Roger Jones & Alexander Mahan; wit. oath Oct. 1766 by Alexander Mahan; books 12 & 13 p. 505.

3976. Jan. 9, 1764 John Physioc, planter (Craven Co) to Charles Physioc (same); for regard, love, & fatherly affection gave (a) [omitted] ac on S side of Nuce R being manor "plantation" where John Physioc lives; (b) 1,100 ac "adjoining" [no more description]; (c) Negro woman Squash; & (d) a large chest, a case, 6 silver table spoons, pair of silver salts, a feather bed & furniture, 2 large pewter basons, fourth of my moveable estate; except use & service of above premises reserved to John for his life. (signed) John Physioc; (witness) Roger Jones & Alexander Mahan; wit. oath Oct. 1766 by Alexander Mahan; books 12 & 13 p. 507.

3977. Jan. 9, 1764 John Physioc, planter (Craven Co) to Sidey [Sidney--lined out] Physioc (same); for regard, love, & fatherly affection gave (a) [omitted] ac on S side of Nuce R & W side of Slocombs Cr; border: begins at a spring branch and runs down the creek to the lower corner [no more description]; (b) Negro boy Jeffery; & (c) a small chest of drawers, a case of bottles, 6 silver table spoons, a feather [bed] & furniture, a silver pepper box, a fourth of my moveable estate; except use & service of the property reserved to John for life. (signed) John Physioc; (witness) Roger Jones & Alexander Mahan; wit. oath Oct. 1766 by Alexander Mahan; books 12 & 13 p. 509.

3978. Feb. 9, 1764 John Physioc, planter (Craven Co) to Rebeca Austin (same);

for regard, love, parental care, & affection gave (a) [omitted] ac on S side of Nuce R & W side of Slocombs Cr; known as Grave Neck [no more description]; (b) Negro woman Pindar; & (c) a small desk, 6 silver table spoons, 2 large pewter basons, & fourth of all my moveable estate; except use & service of premises reserved to John for his life. (signed) John Physioc; (witness) Roger Jones & Alexander Mahan; wit. oath Oct. 1766 by Alexander Mahan; books 12 & 13 p. 510.

3979. Dec. 20, 1755 tripartite at New Bern between Honorable James Hasell esq (NC) first part, Ann Nan Bade Durlace Baron Nome Rosentaine, widow second part, & David Dewar mariner (NC) third part; a marriage, by God's permission, is intended between James Hasell & Ann Nome Bade Durlace Baron Nom Rosentine; Hasell owns considerable estate in land, money, Negroes, & goods and Ann owns sundry money & goods; SO to provide for Ann, Hasell agrees to a bond to David Dewar for £2,000 sterling; bond void if Hasell wills Ann "so much" of his estate so she will be paid £1,000 sterling within 12 months after his death, if the marriage happens & if Ann survives him [or ?] Hasell to will Ann the amount of estate she has at time of the marriage; Hasell to "enjoy" all money & goods Ann has for his life. (signed) Jas Hasell, Ann Nom Bade Durlace Baron Nom Rosentaine, & David Dewar; (witness) Richd Spaight & Will Mouat [or Mowat]; wit. oath Oct. 21, 1766 by William Mouat before Thomas Lloyd, associate justice of Wilmington Dist court; books 12 & 13 p. 512.

3980. Feb. 1, 1765 Arthur Howe esq (Edenton, Chowan Co, NC) to Thomas Clifford Howe esq (Craven Co); for sold ; sold due to writ of fieri facias from Edendon Dist Superior Court due to suit by Thomas Iko [or Ho] Howe against Edward Mosely for £547.9.11 proclamation money returnable to court May 20 next and Joseph Blount esq (of Chowan Co, NC) had a suit & advanced Arthur Howe £704.7.9 proclamation money to pay execution and Arthur & Thomas Howe "by names of" William & Thomas Howe gentlemen signed a bond Jan. 15 last for £1,408.15.6 proclamation money conditioned on payment of £704.7.9 by Jan. 15 next; SO to secure payment & for £0.5 proclamation money sold in trust following Negroes: Sackey, Jack, Tom, Terry, Benny, Isaac, Molley, Katt, Willoughby, Daniel, Lucy, Nancy, Joan, Any, Palyra, Virgil, Ben, Celsy, & Doll; sale void if Arthur pays debt on time. (signed) Arthur Howe & Thos C Howe; (witness) Ann Fenner & Richd Fenner; possession of Negroes was made by delivery of Terry in name of other Negroes; wit. oath Dec. 10, 1766 by Ann Fenner before Jas Hasell, CJ; books 12 & 13 p. 517.

3981. Sept. 1, 1766 Richard Ellis, merchant (New Bern, NC) to Levi Gill; for rents mentioned leased for 18 years part of lot #13 in New Bern; where said Ellis lives; border: begins on side of the street about 4 feet N from said Ellis' stable & chair house and joins Capt. Rook's store house; land is 22 by 24 feet; lease begins May 1 last; yearly rent is £3.10 proclamation money to be paid in 2 equal installments on Nov. 1 and May 1. (signed) Richd Ellis & Levi Gill; (witness) Chrisr. Neale [only one witness]; wit. oath Oct. 1766 by Christopher Neale; books

12 & 13 p. 520.

3982. May 30, 1766 Benjamin Williams sr (Johnston Co, NC) to my loving nephew Benjamin Williams, son of James Williams; for love, good will, & affection gave 0.5 ac front lot #17 in New Bern; border: begins at Henry Bryan's corner on the front, runs 6.5 poles up the river, & 13 poles back from the river. (signed) Benja Williams; (witness) Thos Haslin & Richd Cogdell; wit. oath Oct. 1766 by Richard Cogdell; books 12 & 13 p. 522.

3983. Nov. 2, 1764 George Lane (Craven Co) to my well beloved grand children Mary Howard & Rachel Howard, daughter of John Howard by his wife Esther; for natural love & affection gave 3 cows & their increase marked with my own proepr mark a round crop in each ear & a slit in each; cattle to remain in management of John & Esther Howard for their life and cattle & increase to be equally divided between Mary & Rachel on death of their parents. (signed) George Lane; (witness) Thomas Hammond & John Lane; wit. oath Oct. 1766 by John Lane; books 12 & 13 p. 523.

3984. Oct. 8, 1766 Rocksolanah Martin, widow (Craven Co) to William Good (same); for £100 proclamation money sold 0.5 ac in lot #80 in New Bern on Pollock Street & Handcocks Street; sold Jun. 6, 1743 by Walter Lane & William Handcock, New Bern commissioners, to said Rocksolanah Martin acknowledged in court Jun. 19, 1744 & recorded in Craven Co register's office book 9 p. 30. (signed) Rocksolanah Martin; (witness) Rigdon Brice & Gabriell Pickren, & John Kennedy; [note at end indicates Good paid Rocksolanah "per" Joseph Martin £100 (witness) Bartho Howard & Will Green]; wit. oath Oct. 1766 by Rigdodn Brice; books 12 & 13 p. 525.

3985. Oct. 16, 1765 Joseph Leech esq (Craven Co) to Thomas Leech, gentleman (same); for £5 proclamation money sold 640 ac on N side of Nuce R & upper side of Duck Cr; border: begins at a pine near mouth of the creek [no more description]; sold at public vendue by, due to execution from suit by Ann Cary, Henry Stephens, & Edward Woodcock executrix & executors of Robert Cary deceased against Theophilus Pew deceased in hands of James Power administrator, Joseph Carruthers, late Craven Co sheritf, to Joseph Leech. (signed) Joseph Leech; (witness) William Bethell & Rigdon Brice; wit. oath Oct. 1766 by Rigdon Brice; books 12 & 13 p. 527.

3986. Oct. 8, 1766 James Carraway, planter (Craven Co) to William Carraway (same); for £10 proclamation money sold 175 ac on N side of Neuse R; border: begins at a hickory at upper side of mouth of a branch near the bluff land and joins a swamp; granted Sept. 24, 1754 to said James Carraway. (signed) James Carraway; (witness) Chrisr Dawson & Wm Bryan; wit. oath Oct. 1766 by William Bryan; books 12 & 13 p. 529.

3987. Oct. 20, 1764 Arthur Johnston (Craven Co) to Jacob Shepard (same); for

£262.10 proclamation money sold part of lot #15 in New Bern; now occupied by Nathaniel Richardson; border: joined on N by lot [number blank] of John Clitherall esq, on S by lot of Thomas McLin & others, Craven Street on E, & on W by lot [number blank] occupied by Richard Cogdell; lot is 174.5 feet long on Craven Street & 107 feet 3 inches wide "West"; sold Dec. 19, 1734 by the town commissioners to Nicholas Routledge and by "several" conveyances became property of Arthur Johnston. (signed) Arthur Johnston; (witness) Thomas Sitgreaves & Chrisr Neale; [note at end indicates Shepard paid Johnston £262.10 on Oct. 20, 1765 (sic)]; Oct. 20, 1765 Susannah Johnston, wife of Arthur, sold her dower right to Shepard in consideration of money paid to Arthur Johnston (signed) Susannah Johnston (witness) Thomas Sitgreaves & Chrisr Neale; Oct. 1766 deed & dower renouncement proved in court & James Davis appointed to obtain dower renouncement of Susannah Johnston which was done in court; books 12 & 13 p. 531.

3988. Oct. 11, 1765 Peter Conway, gentleman (Newbern, Craven Co) to Gabriel Cathcart esq & collector of port of Beaufort, NC; for £434.15 proclamation money leased for 3 years 2 lots: (a) house, kitchen, & other out houses & 0.5 ac where they stands in lot #258 on Broad Street in New Bern; where Conway lately dwelt & now in occupation of Honorable Charles Berry; & (b) lot #286 in New Bern; border: joining rear of lot #258 on N; except Conway leased land to Charles Berry on Aug. 16 last (sic); yearly rent is £50 proclamation money. (signed) Petr. Conway; (witness) Amb Cox Bayley & Richd Fenner; Oct. 11, 1765 acknowledged before Chas Berry; [note at end indicates Cathcart paid Conway £434.15 on Oct. 11, 1765]; books 12 & 13 p. 535.

3989. Mar. 16, 1762 Frederick Isler, merchant (Craven Co) to John Becton, son of Frederick Becton; for good will & natural affection gave Negro girl Nancy & her future increase. (signed) Frederick Isler's mark "F"; (witness) Adam More & Fred Becton; wit. oath Jan. 1767 by Frederick Becton; books 12 & 13 p. 539.

3990. Aug. 21, 1766 Willis McCoy, planter (Craven Co) to William Brice Fonvielle, planter (same); for £18.5 proclamation money sold 100 ac on S side of Coor Cr & upper side of Green pond Br; border: begins at a white oak on said branch & joins mouth of Green pond Br. (signed) Willis McCoy; (witness) "Whichcote" White & William Murfrey; wit. oath Oct. 1766 by Whichcote White; books 12 & 13 p. 540.

3991. Oct. 13, 1765 Stephen Glare, planter (Craven Co) to Amos Small, planter (same); for £50 proclamation money sold 60 ac near Cluls Run Marsh; border: begins at a white oak; part of land sold Dec. 28, 1764 by said Stephen Glare sold to said Amos Small but land is now resurveyed by Peter Sted, the first owner, "a part was left out". (signed) Stephen Glare's mark "+"; (witness) Jas Monald, Edmd Hatch jr, & Edmund Hatch; wit. oath Apr. 1766 by "Edmond" Hatch; books 12 & 13 p. 542.

Craven County, NC Deed Books 11-13

3992. Dec. 3, 1766 Robert Orme, gentleman & Thomas Webber, merchant (Craven Co) to Eleanor McDowell, widow (same); for £79.11 proclamation money sold 10 hair bottomed mahogany chairs, 1.5 (sic) rush bottomed chairs, 6 leather bottom mahogany chair, an elbow mahogany chair, a black walnut desk & book case, 3 large looking glasses, 4 small ones, 8 feather beds with bed cloathes bolsters & pillows, 4 pair of hand crons(?), 48 pewter plates, 4 mahogany tables, & sundry other household furniture; sold Apr. 8, 1766 by Peter Conway, gentleman (of Craven Co) to us for £79.11 proclamation money by conditional bill of sale to become our property Nov. 10, 1766 as by conditions in said sale and now sold by consent of Peter Conway. (signed) Robt Orme & Thos Webber; (witness) John Rees & Jane Powell; wit. oath Jan. 1767 by John Rees; books 12 & 13 p. 544.

3993. Nov. 14, 1766 Hon. Edward Brice Dobbs esq (Ireland) to George Ormsly, planter (Craven Co); for £30 proclamation money sold 640 ac about 10 miles above New Bern on both sides of the main road to Johnston County & a branch of Batchelor's Cr caled Jumping Run; border: begins at corner pine his "former" survey, joins Fonvielle, Richard Graves, & another survey. (signed) Edward Brice Dobbs, by attorney Fredk Gregg; (witness) John Spicer & Jane Powell; wit. oath Jan. 1767 by John Spicer; books 12 & 13 p. 545.

3994. Sept. 10, 1765 Peter Conway, gentleman (Craven Co) to Jane Powell (same); for £25 proclamation money sold 0.5 ac in lot #288 on Metcalf Street & New Street in New Bern; sold by New Bern commissioners to Joseph Hennis who sold to Patrick Kennedy who sold to Peter Conway. (signed) Pctr. Conway & Mary Conway (sic); (witness) Rd Cogdell & Robt Orme; [note at end indicates Jane paid Conway £25 on Sept. 10, 1765]; wit. oath Jan. 1767 by Robt Orme; books 12 & 13 p. 547.

3995. Aug. 16, 1765 Sarah Bryan, widow, to my well beloved children Hardy Bryan, Nathan Bryan, Isaac Bryan, Lewis Bryan, & Mary Bryan; for natural love & affection gave all my "sole" real & personal estate; except my riding "mair" called Blase which I reserve for myself; each child to have a feather bed & equal part of the furniture; my eldest son Hardy to have first choice and then the others to take theirs, with elder taking before the younger; Nathan Bryan gets my red chest, a large iron pot, & one of my largest pewter dishes; Isaac Bryan gets my case with 12 bottles; Mary Bryan gets my mare yearling called Jeny, 2 "water" plates, 6 silver tea spoons, pair of silver "shugar" tongs; remainder of my estate goes to son Hardy Bryan. (signed) Sarah Bryan; (witness) Fredk Becton, William Isler, & Jesse Bryan; wit. oath Oct. 1766 by Frederick Becton; books 12 & 13 p. 549.

3996. Oct. 6, 1766 Benjamin Fordham, planter (Craven Co) to James Coor, trader (Newbern, Craven Co); for £10 proclamation money sold 2 lots #371 & 372 in New Bern on Norwoods Street & Crooked Street; granted Oct. 2, 1750 to said Benjamin Fordham. (signed) Benjamin Fordham; (witness) John Hartley &

Joseph Hartley; Oct. 1766 acknowledged; books 12 & 13 p. 551.

3997. Jul. 12, 1763 Stephen Wilcocks, millwright (Craven Co) to Josaph Leech, merchant (Newbern, Craven Co); for £60 proclamation money sold [omitted] ac on Crooked Run [no more description]; sold Dec. 28, 1761 by my father John "Willcocks" deceased to I & within bounds of land I(?) bought of Stephen Swilly; includes a saw mill. (signed) Stephen Wilcocks; (witness) Thomas Wilcocks & Charles Hardison; wit. oath Nov. 10, 1764 by Charles Hardison before Frans Corbin, AJ; books 12 & 13 p. 552.

3998. Jul. 12, 1763 Thomas Wilcocks & Stephen Wilcocks, millwrights & sons of John Wilcocks deceased (Craven Co) to Joseph Leech (Newbern, Craven Co); for £66 proclamation money sold 160 ac on S side of Crooked Run; border: begins at Thomas Wilcocks' corner of said grant & joins Swilley; part of grant Jun. 30, 1758 to Samuel Hatch recorded in book 11 p. 309 in Secretary's office and sold by said Hatch to John Wilcocks who gave it to Thomas & Stephen Wilcocks. (signed) Thomas Wilcocks & Stephen Wilcocks; (witness) Joseph "Chilly" & Charles Hardison; wit. oath Nov. 10, 1764 by Charles Hardison before Frans Corbin, AJ; books 12 & 13 p. 554.

3999. May 27, 1765 Joseph Collins, planter (Carteret Co, NC) to Thomas Pollock, gentleman (Craven Co); for £65 proclamation money sold 80 ac on SW prong of Mill Cr; border: begins at William Wickliff's corner sweet gum & joins the creek swamp; granted Sept. 25, 1754 "to me" Joseph Causey. (signed) Joseph Collins; (witness) "Gordius Rickitson" & Edmund Hatch; wit. oath Oct. 1767 (sic by Edmund Hatch; books 12 & 13 p. 556.

4000. Jan. 1, 1766 Thomas Pollock esq (Craven Co) to William Shippard & Henry Shippard, planters (same); for rents mentioned leased for 70 years 200 ac on N side of Trent R; border: begins at a cypress on the river side; includes improvement of William & Henry Shippard; includes use of "timber & timber trees" for use of the "plantations" or repairing or building of houses thereon; yearly rent is £0.33.4 proclamation money with first payment on Jan. 1 next. (signed) Thos Pollock; (witness) Timo. Edwards & Jacob Mitchell; wit. oath Oct. 1766 by Jacob Mitchell; books 12 & 13 p. 558.

4001. Feb. 11, 1764 John Gates, planter (Craven Co) to William Smith, planter (same); for £10 proclamation money sold 100 ac on S side of Neuse R & W side of Handcocks Cr; border: begins at a pine in the fork of the creek, joins a gut, & a branch. (signed) John Gates' mark "Ӻ"; (witness) James Handcock & Sin Loftin; Oct. 1766 acknowledged; books 12 & 13 p. 561.

4002. Aug. 27, 1766 John Moore (New Bern, NC) to Thomas Delomar, planter (Craven Co); for £15 proclamation money sold 58 ac N side of Neuse R & S side of head of Lower Broad R; border: begins at mouth of Ash Br, joins Isaac Simmons, S prong of Ash Br, back line of the patent issued Apr. 11, 1745, said

Moore's last corner of "said" patent, head of his "other" patent, & edge of a swamp; part of 3 grants [no details] and 3 ac is "an old" patent. (signed) John Moore; (witness) John Carruthers & Benj Blackledge; wit. oath Oct. 1766 by John Carruthers; books 12 & 13 p. 563.

4003. Oct. 7, 1766 Thomas Prner [or Pmer], planter ("Cartwright" Co, NC) & Caleb Prner, planter (Craven Co) to William "Rumsey" & William Wilton, merchants (New Bern, NC); for £120 NC money sold 240 ac on S side of Nuse R; border: begins at a sweet gum on the river side, joined on W by Jacob Slobuck, & on E by William Pratt; sale void if Thomas & Caleb pay Rumsey & Wilton £120 NC money or £60 by Nov. 1, 1767 with lawful interest and £60 by Nov. 1, 1768 with lawful interest. (signed) Thomas Prner's mark "Y" & Caleb Prner's mark "C"; (witness) Susanna Meads & John Rumsey; wit. oath Oct. 1767 (sic) by John Rumsey; books 12 & 13 p. 565.

4004. Sept. 3, 1764 Thomas Stevens, planter (Craven Co) to Jeremiah Slade, planter (same); for £6 proclamation money sold 50 ac on S side of Cove Cr; border: begins at a white oak on the creek side; includes former plantation of Solomon Peters where John Wallen lives; sold Jul. 2, 1767 by Hanis Clark to Thomas Stevens. (signed) Joseph (sic) Stevens' mark "+"; (witness) Elihu Hall & Joseph Allen; wit. oath Oct. 1766 by Joseph Allen; books 12 & 13 p. 567.

4005. Jul. 11, 1766 William Spight [or Sprights], planter (Craven Co) to Samuel Norris, planter (same); for £20 proclamation money sold 150 ac on N side of Nuse R & near Wiggins' Landing; border: begins at a black jack on Wiggins' line by a glade, crosses a road, & joins a branch; includes William Handcock's survey; granted Apr. 21, 1764 to said William Spight. (signed) Wm Spight; (witness) Giles Clements & Sabra Clements; Oct. 1766 acknowledged; books 12 & 13 p. 569.

4006. Jul. 12, 1765 James Handcock (Craven Co) to Frederick Acreman, turpintine maker (same); for £30 proclamation money sold 250 ac on S side of Nuce R & E side of Slocumbs Cr; border: begins at a pine beside a pocosin & joins head of a branch; granted Sept. 1, 1759 to John Donelson. (signed) James Handcock; (witness) "Daniell" Steven & Tamar Handcock; Jan. 1767 acknowledged; books 12 & 13 p. 570.

4007. Oct. 30, 1765 Joseph Crispin, mariner (Craven Co) to James Hollis (same); for £23 proclamation money sold 150 ac on N side of "mane" branch of Dawsons Cr; granted Nov. 27, 1762 to Joseph Wright who sold to said Joseph Crispin [reference to grant for metes & bounds]. (signed) Joseph Crispin; (witness) Thomas Bedford & William Hollis; [note at end indicates Hollis paid Crispin £23 on Oct. 30, 1766]; wit. oath Jan. 1767 by William Hollis; books 12 & 13 p. 572.

4008. Sept. 27, 1765 Frederick Isler, planter (Craven Co) to John Gilliard (same); for "good causes" sold 275 ac on Nine Swamp; joins land where I lived [no more description]; sold Apr. [blank], 1760 by William Bryan to me. (signed) Frederick Isler's mark "F"; (witness) Henry Isler & Fredk. Becton; wit. oath Jan. 1767 by Frederick Becton; books 12 & 13 p. 574.

4009. Mar. 28, 1768 Abiah Bangs (Newbern, NC) to James Davis, printer (same); for £20 proclamation money sold 30 ac on E side of Green Spring Cr; border: begins at an oak in said James Davis' line near a branch that makes out of said creek; granted Sept. 27, 1754 to said Abiah Bangs. (signed) Abiah bangs; (witness) Jams. "Greeny" & William Bexley; wit. oath Jan. 1767 by James Greeny "jr"; books 12 & 13 p. 575.

4010. Aug. 16, 1766 Samuel Lamberth, planter (Craven Co) to William Rodgers, planter (same); for 150 proclamation money sold 200 ac; border: begins at John Gilstrap's corner hickory in Tracey's Neck; being all of a patent. (signed) Samuel Lamberth's mark "C" (sic); (witness) Fredk Becton & Michael Becton; wit. oath Jan. 1767 by Frederick Becton; books 12 & 13 p. 577.

4011. Oct. 6, 1766 John Parrey sr (Craven Co) to John Parrey jr (same); for £20 proclamation money sold 50 ac on S side of Trent R & on "loer" side of Island Br; border: begins at a gum on Half moon Br, joins Island Br, a dam, & the river; part of tract "taken up" by John Parrey jr. (signed) John Parrey; (witness) Michael Koonce & Robert Parrey; Jan. 1767 acknowledged; books 12 & 13 p. 579.

4012. Oct. 15, 1765 John Tutle (Craven Co) to Thomas Clifford Howe esq (same); for £80 proclamation money sold 640 ac; border: begins at a red oak on N side of Trent R below Joshua Cr otherwise called King fisher Cr, joins mouth of Bull Br, & "the" main branch; granted Apr. 17, 1729 to Thomas Jones who sold Apr. 15, 1730 by Walter Lane & "confirmed by deed" Apr. 17, 1730 by said Jones to said Lane who sold Jan. 2, 1756 to Sevier Lane who sold Dec. 14, 1765 to John Tutle. (signed) John Tutle; (witness) Absolem Keinsey, Phebe Tallman, & Elizabeth Holland; wit. oath Jan. 1767 by Phebe Tallman; books 12 & 13 p. 581.
4013. Oct. 4, 1766 Jacob Jones (Craven Co) to John Bryan (same); for £12 proclamation money sold 50 ac on N side of Nuse R & N side of Broad Cr; border: begins at mouth of a branch that [comes] out of Whiteons Cr below said land, joins head of a branch that parts said land from Jones Clive's [or Eive] land, & head line of "the" patent; part of grant Dec. 23, 1728 to Col. John Waley. (signed) Jacob Jones sr's mark "Ⅎ"; (witness) Jacob Jones jr & James Combs; wit. oath Jan. 1767 by Jacob Jones jr; books 12 & 13 p. 583.

4014. Jul. 10, 1766 Elihu Hall, gentleman (Craven Co) to Bazell Smith, planter (same); for £40 proclamation money sold 250 ac on S side of Nuse R & head of Otter Cr; border: begins at Geo Phy Lovick's back line formerly Jos Hall's line & joins Jacob Taylor; granted Dec. 21, 1763 to [Elihu Hall]. (signed) Elihu Hall; (witness) Rawlings Williams & Jacob Taylor; wit. oath Jan. 1767 by Rawlings Williams; books 12 & 13 p. 585.

Craven County, NC Deed Books 11-13

4015. Jan. 8, 1767 Bazell Smith, planter (Craven Co) to Littleton Davis, wheel wright (same); for £12 proclamation money sold 50 ac on head of Otter Cr & S side of Nuse R; border: begins at Geo Phy Lovick's upper corner on said creek, joins a branch, & "the" patent line; part of 250 ac granted Dec. 21, 1763 by Gov. Arthur Dobbs to Elihu Hall. (signed) Bazell Smith; (witness) Rawlings Williams, John Williams, & Arthur Williams; wit. oath Jan. 1767 by Rawlings Williams; books 12 & 13 p. 587.

4016. Nov. 10, 1766 John Oliver, planter (Craven Co) to Arthur Barono, planter (same); for £35 proclamation money sold 150 ac on S side of Trent R; border: begins at Marck Meves' corner white oak on upper prong of Popler Br in said John Owens' line and joins Flat Swamp; granted to William Wickliff. (signed) John Oliver's mark "Ŧ"; (witness) John Parrey jr & Robert Parrey; wit. oath Jan. 1767 by John Parrey; books 12 & 13 p. 589.

4017. Jul. 25, 1766 Charles Shanewoolf (Craven Co) to Joseph Hill (same); for £10 proclamation money sold 150 ac on N side of Nuse R & E side of "Goos" Cr; border: run "full courses" of said patent & joins Nathaniel Gabril's line that was sold out of the grant sold by Bryan to Joseph Right who sold to said Charles Shanewoolf; part of grant to John Bryan at upper end of 75 ac sold out of the grant to Cason Brinson; except for lightwood on the land. (signed) Charles Shanewoolf; (witness) Chrisr Dawson, William Shine, & Thomas Berry; wit. oath Jan. 1767 by Chrisr Dawson; books 12 & 13 p. 591.

4018. Sept. 20, 1766 Thomas Bracher (Craven Co) to Tobias Koonce, planter (same); for £7 sold 50 ac on N side of Trent R; known as Bracher's old field; border: joins Tobias Koonce; being all the land said Bracher holds on N side of Trent R by grant Apr. 8, 1752 to John Williams. (signed) Thomas Bracher's mark "B"; (witness) Benj Lavender & Reece [or Rice] Duling; Jan. 1767 acknowledged; books 12 & 13 p. 593.

4019. Sept. 19, 1766 Thomas Smart, merchant (Craven Co) to Henry Pibos, carpenter (same); for £30 proclamation money sold 100 ac on S side of Trent R & in Deep Neck; border: begins at a white oak on the river side & joins Michael Sheffor; being upper part of survey taken up by Matthew "Whilks". (signed) Thos Smart; (witness) John Parrey jr & John "Shelfer"; wit. oath Jan. 1767 by John Parrey jr; books 12 & 13 p. 595.

4020. Sept. 17, 1766 Isaac Barrenton (Craven Co) to John Barrenton (same); for £0.40 proclamation money sold 50 ac on N side of Nuce R & W side of Upper Broad Cr; border: begins at mouth of a small branch on upper side of "said" Isaac Cornfield, joins David Lewis, & a swamp; part of 300 ac granted Nov. 22, 1738 to [omitted] ac. (signed) Isaac Barrenton; (witness) David Lewis & Mary Todwin [or Todeven]; wit. oath Jan. 1767 by David Lewis; books 12 & 13 p. 597.

4021. Dec. 3, 1766 [7th year of reign of King George III] John Moore (Craven Co) to Thomas Delamar (same); for £18 proclamation money sold 100 ac on S side of head of main branch of Lower Broad Cr; border: begins at mouth of Deep Run Br, joins said Moore's back line, land said Delamar lately bought of said Moore, Ash Br, & the creek swamp; being 18 ac sold by Isaac Simmons & wife to said Moore and remainder is part of grant to said John Moore. (signed) John Moore's mark "I" & Thomas Delamar (sic); (witness) Chrisr "Neall" & Will Moore jr; wit. oath Apr. 1767 by Will Moore jr; books 12 & 13 p. 598.

4022. Dec. 30, 1766 John Mallard (Craven Co) to William Cockson (same); for £8 proclamation money sold 100 ac on W side of Jumping Run; border: begins at N corner of side of Jumping Run. (signed) John Mallard's mark "P" (sic); (witness) John Cummins & William Nelson; Jan. 1767 acknowledged; books 12 & 13 p. 600.

4023. Nov. 4, 1766 William Lipsey, planter (Craven Co) to Simon Foscue, planter (same); for £150 proclamation money sold 100 ac on N side of Trent R; border: begins at a black gum between said land & Casper Granade's. (signed) William Lipsey; (witness) Lemuel Hatch & Edmund Hatch; wit. oath Jan. 1767 by Lemuel Hatch; books 12 & 13 p. 601.

Index to Craven County, NC Deed Books 10-13

Index to Craven County, NC Deed Books 10-13

Index to Craven County, NC Deed Books 10-13

Index to Craven County, NC Deed Books 10-13

Green, Henry 3866
Green (Grun), James 3374, 3402, 3479, 3524, 3558, 3590, 3879, 3881
Green (Greeny), James jr 3380, 3776, 3794, 3848, 4009
Green, John 3398, 3563, 3622, 3790, 3816, 3817, 3860, 3861, 3948, 3959, 3966, 3967, 3969
Green, John C 3818
Green, Joseph 3973
Green, Robert 3776
Green, Robert jr 3778
Green, Thomas 3389, 3453, 3517, 3565, 3568
Green, Whitford 3646
Green, William 3743, 3895-3897, 3966, 3984
Green, William jr 3743, 3768, 3784, 3818, 3832
Gregg (Greg), Frederick 3762, 3889, 3993
Gregory, Mathew 3649
Griffin, 3731
Griffin, Barron D 3558
Griffin, Benjamin 3703, 3819, 3910, 3912, 3954
Griffin, Benjamin sr 3955
Griffin, Jacob 3456, 3495
Griffin, Jas 3531
Griffin, Jesse 3910, 3955
Griffin, Major 3392
Griffin, Solomon 3703, 3716, 3916
Griffis, Samuel 3453, 3496, 3498, 3693, 3964
Griffith, Ann 3684, 3699
Griffith, Edward 3623, 3684, 3702, 3849
Griffith, Rachael 3623
Grimes, Robert 3510, 3514, 3556, 3557
Grinder, Andrew 3518
Groenendeyke (Grunnindike), Cornelius 3826, 3827, 3917
Guerry, Andrew 3774

Guerry, Anne 3774
Guess (Guiss, Guss), John 3395, 3472, 3875
Gums, Robt 3601
Gurganus, David 3574
Guthery, Benjamin 3458
Guttery, Ebenezer 3399
Guttery, Esther 3399
Guttery, Mary 3399
Guttery, Wm 3803
Hackburn, John 3717
Hagin, Martin 3675
Hais, George 3322
Hall, Benjamin 3475, 3477, 3490, 3723, 3723
Hall, David 3701
Hall, Elihu (Elihue) 3573, 3679, 3719, 3739, 3779, 3791, 3915, 4004, 4014, 4015
Hall, Jas 3483, 3485
Hall, John 3962
Hall, Joseph 3634, 3634, 3636, 3686, 3692, 3701, 3719, 3742, 3791, 4014
Hall, Jude 3354
Hall, Nathaniel 3475
Hall, Robert 3748
Hall, Samuel R 3419
Hall, Sarah 3739
Hall, Thomas 3748
Halloway (Hollaway, Holloway), John 3712, 3731, 3911, 3912
Halloway (Holloway), William 3910, 3916
Hamilton, Richard 3533, 3536, 3538
Hammond, 3928
Hammond, Thomas 3983
Handcock, Evan 3638
Handcock (Hancock), James 3527, 3558, 3647, 3653-3655, 3750, 3781, 3782, 4001, 4006
Handcock, James jr 3654
Handcock, James sr 3638
Handcock, John 3638
Handcock, Roger 3618

Index to Craven County, NC Deed Books 10-13